ALSO BY ROBERT RUBY

Jericho

UNKNOWN
SHORE

UNKNOWN SHORE

The Lost History of England's Arctic Colony

———◆◆◆◆◆———

ROBERT RUBY

Henry Holt and Company • New York

Henry Holt and Company, LLC
Publishers since 1866
115 West 18th Street
New York, New York 10011

Henry Holt® is registered trademark of
Henry Holt and Company, LLC.

Published in Canada by Fitzhenry & Whiteside Ltd.,
195 Allstate Parkway, Markham, Ontario L3R 4T8.

Library of Congress Cataloging-in-Publication Data

Ruby, Robert (Robert Steven)
    Unknown shore : the lost history of England's arctic colony / Robert
Ruby.
        p.   cm.
    Includes bibliographical references and index.
    ISBN 0-8050-5215-1 (hb)
    1. Frobisher, Martin, Sir, ca. 1535–1594—Journeys.   2. Northwest
Passage—Discovery and exploration—English.   3. Canada, Northern—
Discovery and exploration—English.   4. Explorers—England—
Biography.   5. Hall, Charles Francis, 1821–1871—Journeys.   I. Title.

    G650 1576 .F58 2001
    971.9'501'092—dc21

                                                        00-063230

Henry Holt books are available for special
promotions and premiums. For details contact:
Director, Special Markets.

First Edition 2001

Designed by Paula Russell Szafranski

Printed in the United States of America

1   3   5   7   9   10   8   6   4   2

For Holly

and for Sam Ruby

The waters become hard like stone,
and the face of the deep is frozen.

JOB 38:30

Contents

UNKNOWN SHORE

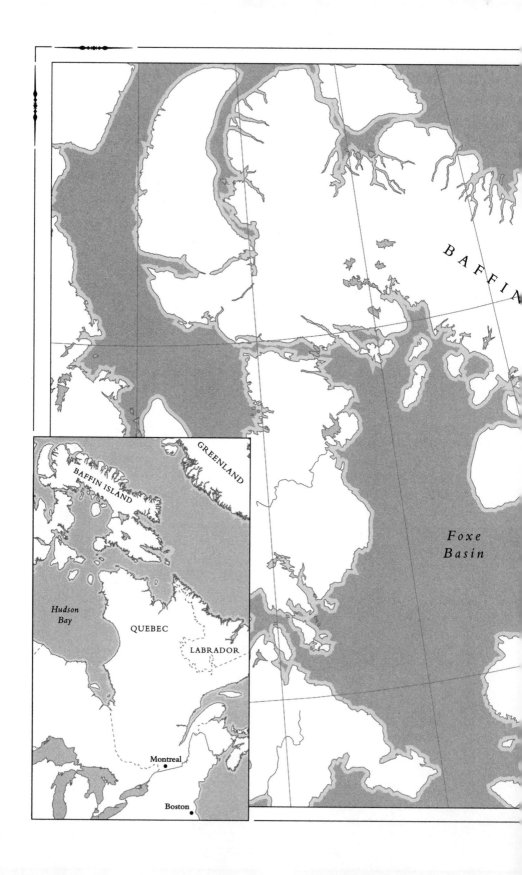

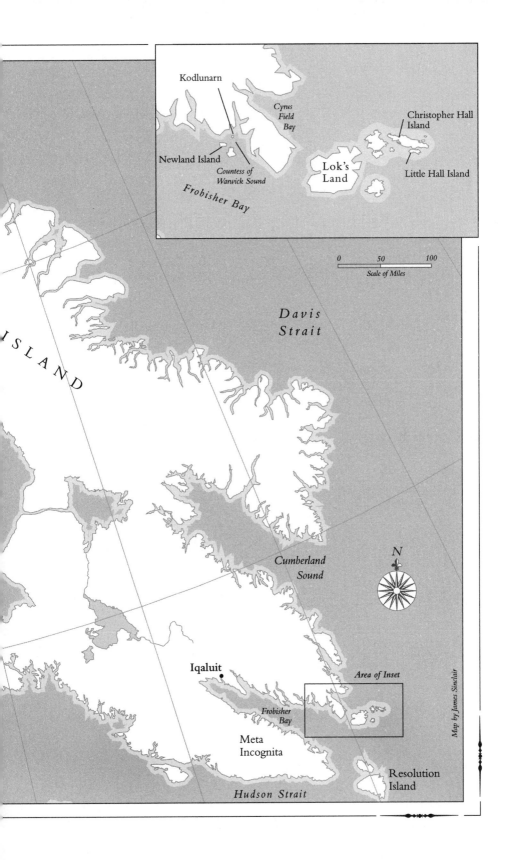

Kodlunarn

Cyrus Field Bay

Christopher Hall Island

Newland Island

Countess of Warwick Sound

Lok's Land

Little Hall Island

Frobisher Bay

0   50   100
Scale of Miles

Davis Strait

ISLAND

Cumberland Sound

N

Iqaluit

Area of Inset

Map by James Sinclair

Frobisher Bay

Meta Incognita

Resolution Island

Hudson Strait

Prologue: North

It was a campfire story, the fire fed by seal blubber. People sat around the fire as it burned in a soapstone lamp in an igloo lit a soft milky white. A long, long, long, long time ago—the gray-haired woman telling the story actually began with those words—a great many ships came with white men who built a house on a small island. They left behind wood and other rare, valuable things which were put to use by the Inuit, the people of this land. The storyteller's name was Petato, a one-word name.

Listening in 1861, Charles Francis Hall recorded her words on the linen pages of a notebook. He had traveled two days across ice to reach her, and Petato had already helped him strip off his several layers of frozen socks. In a further act of hospitality she lifted her caribou jacket and placed his cold bare feet against her warm bare torso. Hall was an entrepreneur turned small-time newspaper publisher recently turned Arctic explorer from Cincinnati, Ohio, and he resumed taking notes while enjoying her radiant heat. Petato lived along the coast of Frobisher Bay on Canada's Baffin Island, a landscape that in every sense lay profoundly north. It was north of trees and of ordinary comfort, and fifteen hundred miles north of New London, Connecticut, Hall's point of departure from the United States a year and a half before on a three-masted whaling ship. He had come in search of stories about lost explorers, but the tale offered by Petato and other Inuit was not the one he was expecting.

Everything about the north suited Hall well. Without having fully planned it, he was exploring the Arctic in a way few previous visitors had attempted—by living with the natives. Most outsiders called them "Eskimos," but Hall sometimes used the name they preferred for themselves, "Inuit." In 1861, he was thirty-eight years old, with a long matted beard framing a square face. As a young man in New Hampshire, he had learned blacksmithing, and in Ohio he had entered the dull, expert business of manufacturing metal seals for embossing court papers, before finding his way into newspaper publishing. Work always interested him more than pleasure, and he believed pleasure should be carefully metered. He considered alcohol to be deviltry. So was gambling, especially on the Sabbath. Swearing was not to be tolerated. Upon his arrival on Baffin Island, his luggage included a wooden sledge, thermometers, a library of closely read books about the Arctic, rifles, a tooth extractor, and his notebooks. Wanting a life lived in exclamation points, he was thrilled not to be in Cincinnati. "Everything relating to the arctic zone is deeply interesting to me," he confided in his journals. "I love the snows, the ices, icebergs, the fauna, and the flora of the North! I love the circling sun, the long day, *the arctic night, when the soul can commune with God in silent and reverential awe!*" Already one could hardly imagine him by any name other than *Mr. Hall;* certainly he was never *Charlie.* He was sufficiently earnest and thorough to want to know all the stories of the Inuit.

He dressed as his hosts did, in caribou fur and sealskin. Visiting their camps, he developed a taste for their diet. Chewing his first sample of uncooked whale meat, he tried to deceive his digestive system by pretending the food was turkey breast, before deciding the better strategy was to swallow the strip of whale meat whole: "Tougher than any bull beef of Christendom," he wrote of the meal. Offered seal blood as a drink, he took a long draft, then, as etiquette demanded, passed the bowl and waited for the next round. "Not only good but really excellent." You can sense him waving his arms for emphasis as he describes the experiences in his book *Life with the Esquimaux,* which was drawn from the notebooks. "My opinion is, that the Esquimaux practice of eating their food *raw* is a good one—at least for the preservation of *their* health," Hall advised. "To one *educated* otherwise, as we whites are, the Esquimaux custom of feasting on uncooked meats is highly repulsive, but *eating meats raw or cooked is entirely a matter of education.*"

He recorded in the journals all the stories the Inuit told him. A blind man, remembering from the years when he had sight, described trenches the white men had dug a long, long, long time ago, on the island where Petato said they had built a house. A grandmother said the whites had come three times: first in two ships, then in two or three ships, then in many, many ships. Several Inuit were taken away by the whites, it was said, and never returned. It was said some of the white men stayed behind and tried to sail home in a wooden ship built in the treeless landscape. Lacking a written language, the Inuit repeated the stories in lieu of consulting a history book. Petato heard them from her mother, who had heard them from her own grandmother, who learned them from a grandfather: stories about white people arriving by ship and taking an island as their own, only to abandon it.

In August 1576 the weather-torn English ship *Gabriel* came within sight of Baffin Island with, at most, eighteen sailors. Martin Frobisher, the captain, had only the *Gabriel*—two vessels fewer than when he had sailed from London in June. None of the sailors had expected so much ice, acres of it blanketing the ocean white, and the summer nights' endless glaucous light.

On deck his men stood at the base of a small temple of ropes. The rigging narrowed as it rose, like a cathedral's arch executed in hemp. Even by the standards of the 1570s, the *Gabriel* was a modest-sized vessel: the records say twenty or thirty tons. A naval ton measured volume, not weight: a "tun" began as a cask of Bordeaux wine—two hundred and fifty-two gallons of wine—and evolved into the sixteenth-century "ton." In no more than thirty tons, the *Gabriel* accommodated the eighteen men and their weapons, food, and water. You could pace the length of the deck—forecastle, waist, sterncastle—in perhaps twelve steps; the width, in four steps. Someone standing up in a rowboat alongside would reach the height of the deck. In truth, the ship was less a cathedral than a parish chapel. Nothing about it was sleek, or handsome, or grand.

Sailing northwest from England, Martin Frobisher came in search of a shortcut to Asia. During the previous fifteen years he had shown talent for seizing vessels regardless of whether they belonged to England's allies or to her enemies. Now he wanted to enrich himself and earn a reputation for something besides piracy. Pacing the *Gabriel*'s deck and stepping over frayed ropes, he could see respectability and fame five miles off the bow, in the form of a broad waterway leading west without visible end, behind a barrier of ice floes. As postulated by the most learned scholars of the day, China and the rest of Asia—Cathay, as people called the region—should lie a short distance beyond the western exit of the newly sighted waterway. An easy passage to Cathay should be right there, in the northwest. But the ship was blocked from entering the passage by ice.

London merchants envisioned a northwest route as a business opportunity. Compared with their Spanish and Portuguese counterparts, they were beginners in long-distance trade and seemed allergic to taking risks. Their England was a middling, unstable kingdom of modest reach, a weakling country quite different from the England of our later imaginations, where every man struts on muscular sea legs and is a playwright. In that imagined place, the countryside is untroubled and the kingdom is at peace. None of which was the case in Frobisher's era. Within living memory, English armies had battled Scots invading from the north, and the French had torched English coastal towns. For most of the sixteenth century, the Spanish and Portuguese had dominated the oceans, their naval power far superior to England's. English merchant vessels ingloriously hauled coal from Newcastle to London, crowded the rivers in order to keep the cities supplied with food, ventured south to Bordeaux to load casks of wine, or carried English cloth across the North Sea to Antwerp, the main business center of the Continent. Cloth was the coin of English trade. The cloth marketed in Antwerp paid for England's essential imports— Dutch grain, Baltic hemp, German mercenaries for the army— and silk and other luxuries from Cathay. All of this was ordinary business, and little was adventuresome.

If English mariners found a shortcut to Cathay—so the thinking went—the London merchants could trade English products without the need for foreign middlemen. Seeing a waterway beyond the ice floes, Martin Frobisher convinced himself it was the hoped-for northwest passage. Later he would persuade his queen, Elizabeth I, that he was right. In any case, no one aboard the *Gabriel* would have wanted to argue with him about the matter or about the ship's course. He possessed a vile temper, was slippery in money matters and immodest in a charmless way. So the crew searched on, as he instructed, for a path around the ice.

Frobisher began exploring a territory that still requires a difficult journey to reach. But he would reach Baffin Island three times. Inuit preserved a memory of the visits in tales describing whites arriving not once but several times, stories the elders told their children and their children's grandchildren and, eventually, Charles Francis Hall. Frobisher's venture would grow from the little *Gabriel* on the first voyage to a fleet of fifteen ships and nearly four hundred men on the last, the largest Arctic expedition in history.

His voyages across the North Atlantic began as success stories. The prospects of a new route to Asia and of correspondingly vast wealth made his supporters feel wise and deserving of their imminent good fortune. The letters investors in the expedition sent to Queen Elizabeth—found today in the British Library in London and the Public Record Office in Kew—glow with pride and self-regard, and they are matched by congratulatory letters written in return.

Frobisher's life is hinted at in a few scattered items: the letters he wrote, a set of ledgers maintained by one of his partners, ships' logs, journals kept by some of the mariners, and a flattering portrait or two. Eventually he joined Francis Drake, Walter Raleigh, and a handful of other explorers in the pantheon of Elizabethan heroes. But even in his lifetime Frobisher stood slightly apart from the others, his exploits always marked by scandal. From early on, people associated him with large gambles gone wrong, money squandered, and bad temper. His Arctic adventures became less a stirring legend than an embarrassment his countrymen wanted to forget—a pumpkin instead of a golden coach.

Inuit found their encounters with him worth remembering, however, and Charles Francis Hall—notebook in hand—listened carefully.

This is the story of two men's travels, Frobisher's and Hall's, and what they shared three centuries apart: heroism, desperation to make one's name, and an obstinacy that both propelled them forward and held them back. It is a story about the England of Elizabeth I, Inuit, and the hard labor of exploration. Frobisher explored the land, and Hall no less intrepidly investigated stories about the fate of white men who had come deep in the Inuit past. The Inuit learned, at some cost, about the strangers and their world.

I was drawn as much by the name as by the actual place. Queen Elizabeth, clever with her Latin, called the land Martin Frobisher explored Meta Incognita. For a long time no one was certain whether her "Unknown Shore"—or "Unknown Limit" or "Unknown Boundary"—was an island or a continent, and no one could place it with confidence on a map. The name still remains in use for part of the territory Frobisher saw: on a modern map Meta Incognita is the mountainous, southeastern spit of Baffin Island. It is just a cold sliver of the domain Elizabeth envisioned for herself.

In 1999, it became part of the new Canadian territory of Nunavut. With an area ten times the size of Great Britain, Nunavut has twenty-seven thousand people and twelve miles of road. The year-round population of Meta Incognita is zero.

From having lived in the Middle East, I knew about heat. Cold was something new. In my kind of desert, people would wake early in order to nap at midday, when the heat put all living things on trial, and then reconvene in the evening. To fix their routes, they had given names to dry riverbeds and cliffs that, to outsiders, were indistinguishable from a hundred other sandy places. The Arctic demanded an equally attentive, measured life, and favored the same husbanding of energy. I traveled in early spring to Iqaluit, the town at the head of Frobisher Bay, when the bay was still deeply frozen. I wanted to travel on the ice toward the land Frobisher had explored.

Residents of Iqaluit—"many fish" in Inuktitut, the language of the Inuit in Canada's eastern Arctic—divide the world into unequal halves. Where they lived was the north. The south, the other half, was a distant foreign place accommodating everyone else. You were "in the south" whether you lived in Toronto or Miami. Southerners could not read the sky; could not butcher a seal; constantly hurried; wrongly believed they and not the weather could control the course of a day. They didn't understand ice, the bringer of animals to the hunter, and knew dangerously little about how to dress or eat.

My guide on the trip was a woman named Meeka Mike. She was compact, watchful, her face an unlined oval fine enough to be a cameo. Some of Meeka's dogs, when they stood on their hind legs, could rest their muzzles atop her head. She was very strong—righting a three-hundred-pound snowmobile proved no problem—and had long fine hands with the slender fingers of a raptor. She helped me across every kind of thin ice.

She was always just "Meeka," because family names seemed less important in the north. In the 1940s the Canadian government labeled the area the "E" district—"E" for Eastern Arctic and for Eskimo. Every native was assigned an "E" number stamped onto a disc to be worn like a pendant, with the words ESKIMO IDENTIFICATION embossed on the other side. A man known to his friends as Nowdlaq might be registered by the government as E7-011. At the end of the 1960s, the E-numbers were replaced with names assigned during what authorities dubbed Project Surname.

If Nowdlaq's father was named Joe, Nowdlaq became Mr. Nowd-laq Joe.

Iqaluit climbs tundra and boulders on the northern shore of Frobisher Bay. Its houses are scattered like boulders on the hills, every building at a different angle to the unpaved roads. In spring the town is whitewashed by ice. In summer it turns a leathery brown, the color of tundra ground into fine powder. The winters have the variegated gray of an oyster shell on a dimly lit background of white. Most of the buildings stand on stilts intended to absorb the heavings of the permafrost. Because of the stilts, Iqaluit—with five thousand residents, a parliament building for the Nunavut government, a movie theater, an indoor swimming pool, and satellite TV—looks as if it were about to be trucked somewhere else.

Meeka grew up with nine older siblings and two younger ones on the land, not in a town. Her parents lived the traditional Inuit life—hunting and gathering—until the children were old enough for school. Then the family moved to Pangnirtung, overlooking the old whaling grounds of Cumberland Sound. "Pang" had a school, and Inuit were in the habit of visiting a few times a year to do business at an outpost of the Hudson's Bay Company. Her father became Pang's jack-of-all trades, and for extra cash worked as a hunting guide. As part of Meeka's education, he sometimes took her on the hunting trips.

We spent a day sorting winter camping gear. The household regarded an Eddie Bauer down parka as a sort of entertainment, or a prank, and loaned me a parka made of caribou fur, as well as fur trousers made from polar bear. With help from many hands the polar bear trousers could be pulled atop blue jeans worn atop long johns. Everyone dressed as animals do, fur side out.

Meeka drove one snowmobile and her friend Metuq took the other. Metuq, a lithe sixty-five-year-old with a young laugh, had recently traveled to the south for a pacemaker; her doctors had perhaps forgotten to counsel her against lifting twenty-gallon drums filled with gasoline. Hooked to the back of each snowmobile was a long wooden sledge carrying extra fuel and hampers of supplies, and Meeka added two rifles to the cargo.

I rode on one of the sledges when we started traveling on the ice of Frobisher Bay. Crests and troughs in the ice preserved the effects of the tides and wind. The tides in Frobisher Bay never stopped: in autumn they raised and lowered the early ice, fractured it repeatedly, folded it like a crusty dough. Where the bay was shallow, close to shore, the early ice touched bottom when the tides ebbed, then was lifted as a jumble of white blocks by the flood tide, only to touch bottom again at low tide. It was constantly rearranged until the shallows froze solid. After the uplifts and fracturings, the ice along the shore became an all-white boulder field. Every day, the tides reshaped the boulders and opened or closed fissures between the bay's plates of ice. A geologic age was compressed into a cold season.

Maybe for the sake of her own amusement, Meeka let me drive part of the way. Every wave of ice seemed part of a white-water rapids, the snowmobile falling away in the troughs. Where everything was a shadowless white you could never be certain of the first wave's height, and by then the next was lifting you in the air. The sudden drops felt as if a canoe in white water had broken at the center thwart. There was a correct instant to lean left or right, or to rise from the seat. Metuq described the sensation: "Bumpety-bump."

A dog team would have needed triple the amount of time to cover the same distance. I never heard anyone in the north say he wished the snowmobile had never been invented. Meeka kept nine boisterous dogs chained to the ice back in Iqaluit. But two snowmobiles could haul more weight than Tuttu, Sukku, Shadow, Mo, Taqulik, Kajuq, Qujjulik, Kuanni, and Ittuq could, even when they were smartly pulling together.

Dogs have to be harnessed and fitted into traces, which become tangled once the pack is under way. In order to move a heavy load from rest, dogs have to be trained to pull as a team. They are harder to start than a snowmobile and can be harder to stop. Dogs need to be fed every other day when they are pulling, and a strong healthy dog eats a half ton of meat in a year—half a walrus, it turns out. There is no reverse gear, and discipline problems never end. In Iqaluit we saw one of Meeka's dogs escape from his chain and attack an adolescent brother, the two leaning on each other as they stood, gnawing at each other's throat. It was the fourth fight of the day.

Dogs, however, had worked well with a certain way of living. Ownership of a snowmobile presumed a different kind of life, one predicated on having money and a tie to the culture money entails. To acquire a vehicle and the gasoline for it, you needed a wage-producing job or some product you could dependably sell, such as furs. Or assistance from a government. Dogs, however, remained safely outside the cash economy. Traditionally, sledges were made from driftwood and antlers, and harnesses from sealskin and sinew. No dog ever broke a camshaft, and their fuel injectors never froze. And dogs were smart. They would change course—usually—approaching thin ice, when their paws felt the wetness leaking through a surface about to give way. In the direst emergency, they could be eaten.

We drove the snowmobiles on the frozen bay toward a rising yellow moon. Later that night, we stopped to make tea, and looked back and saw the bright curtain of the northern lights. A wavering blue veil of lights lit one quadrant of the sky. In a deeply pleasing illusion, the lights seemed nearly within reach. In Inuit tradition the northern lights are spirits enjoying themselves in the heavens by kicking a ball back and forth, or holding torches to show new arrivals from earth the route through the sky. The curtain of lights billowed toward us as if caught by the wind.

We kneeled in the lee of the sledges as we drank the tea. The moon, floating higher, illuminated the frozen whitecaps of the bay. No geometry could be more handsome than a yellow-white sphere drawing an arc across a blue silk sky, over an infinite white ground.

If you weren't of that place, the north was also barrenness without end. The expanse of ice might as well be a small locked room with every surface painted white. To feel at home and unafraid there, you needed to have an eye for subtle variation. Every day, the wind rearranged the dusting of snow, letting a different backdrop of rocks poke through the white. Every day, landmarks disappeared or took new shapes.

Meeka conferred with Metuq about our progress. Even a frozen bay has a "right" trail, and the north favored efficiency of movement. A smooth path required less energy than the ups and downs of elevation. In a setting where calories were hard to obtain and necessary for survival in the most literal way, Meeka preferred the smoothest route over the shortest. Route chosen, we resumed our trip, bumpety-bump, toward the mouth of Frobisher Bay.

CHAPTER ONE

Different Directions

The one portrait that is unquestionably Martin Frobisher painted from life hangs quite high above the porter's desk at the Bodleian Library at Oxford. You have to step back all the way to the opposite wall to pick out the figure from the gloom.

Frobisher almost storms off the canvas. I did not expect a contemplative figure by Titian or a sweet smile, but nor did I expect this hard stare. He grips a pistol in his right hand, index finger at the trigger, but looks far deadlier himself, cocked with temperament. Your eyes travel first to that pistol. Here is force and aggression, the painting says; here is someone who will fire the gun or bludgeon you, even at the cost of breaking the bones in his hands, rather than give way. His left hand hovers near the hilt of a sword in a golden scabbard. This is not the look of a listener. You marvel at his not striking the painter. Standing so imperiously, he dwarfs anyone seeking to walk past the porter.

The portrait dates to 1577—in retrospect, the best of times for Frobisher. The painter is Cornelis Ketel, a prestigious name of the time. Born in the Netherlands, Ketel became a favorite of wealthy London merchants with connections to the royal court. He was commissioned to paint Frobisher and the thirty-ton *Gabriel,* among others. His patrons were evidently quite satisfied, because he came to the attention of Queen Elizabeth: Ketel is probably the artist responsible for a portrait of the queen dated to about 1580. That portrait is unsigned, but the pose—a mirror image of the posture Frobisher adopts—and the queen's slender, long-fingered hands are Ketel's mark. The royal hands that in her portrait grip a sieve—a symbol of virginity, borrowed from Roman mythology—are the same strikingly feminine hands with which Frobisher wields his pistol and sword.

In Frobisher's portrait, a globe stands on a table behind him, to signal his knowledge of distant places. A similar prop was used to the same effect in later portraits of Francis Drake and Walter Raleigh. The table and the wall behind it appear to be draped with velvet, and Frobisher stands on a stone floor as fine as that at the Bodleian.

You look for a beautiful face or the suggestion of a muscled body, but Martin Frobisher broods. His face seems small above a high ruff, a new fashion permitted by the court's recent discovery of starch. His brown beard is roughly trimmed. Unlike most subjects of Elizabethan portraits, he looks uncomfortable in his fashionable gold-colored doublet and puffy trousers, which reach just below the knee to the requisite tight hose. He is a ruffian in courtier's clothes, ill at ease in an outfit for fawning at court.

The portrait brings a little irony to the Bodleian. Frobisher was not illiterate, but it is a close call. His correspondence in the British Library and the Public Record Office shows an airy, irregular scrawl, the handwriting of an unpracticed hand moving across smooth vellum the color of fresh cream. The spelling of English words was still in flux in the 1500s, but this too Frobisher took quite far. He was breathtakingly inventive in his writings; an otherwise admiring biographer called his spellings "terrifying." They preserve the voice of a person from the north of England, far from London, guessing his way through the written language.

He was born in the Yorkshire village called Altofts. In Yorkshire, every vowel and every *r* is pliable and stretched to its ultimate limit.

Through his correspondence, Martin Frobisher can still be heard to speak a few words. *Service,* in his handwriting, becomes *sarves* (SAAR-vez). *Towards* is *touards* (toe-ORDS). He writes in one of his letters, "Since my comynge fourthe I hayd butt 3 dayyes liberty." *Aye hed buht 3 dahys.*

The flux and inventiveness extended to his name. In letters written on consecutive days to Elizabeth's Lord Treasurer, the person we call Frobisher signed himself *Frobiser* at the end of one page, but *Furbissher* on the outer leaf. In the next day's letter he was *Frobissher.*

One of his descendants is the keeper of a lovingly researched family tree. It records a total of twenty-four generations, beginning with John Frobysler, who was of Scottish extraction and came to Wales about 1255. By the end of the 1300s one of John Frobysler's great-great-grandchildren, named Frobyser, was in Altofts in Yorkshire. Every entry on the tree is neatly written in black India ink, and the inky branches cover a living room wall. Martin's father, Barnard, rests on a branch called Frobysher. One of Martin's older brothers is Ffrubisher. The flux was in the era and not just the untutored man.

He was probably forty-two in the portrait. His descendants' best reckoning for his year of birth is 1535. The date fits with what little is known of him as a child in Altofts with two older brothers and two sisters. His reputation would radically change more than once, which in a sense is reflected by the portrait by Cornelis Ketel. Sometime after Ketel completed the painting, the canvas was trimmed. The right side of the canvas betrays the cutting. One of Frobisher's shoes walks off the right edge of the painting. It was not what the painter intended; given the styles of the time, the image was awkward. And though this is to make almost too much of it, the trimming mirrors the changes Frobisher suffered in his own standing.

People knew even then, in 1535, that Altofts would never boom. Wakefield, three miles to the south, was the market town with the

Martin Frobisher, by Cornelius Ketel, 1577. "The best seaman and bravest in the country," a Spanish agent reported. (The Bodleian Library, Oxford University)

cloth mills, while a mile to the east, Normanton had the church. Altofts, then as now, was a kink in a narrow road where a few cows grazed.

Today, Altofts' High Green Street passes, in four blocks, the butcher shop, the post office, the traffic light, the gas station, and the pub before terminating at Church Street. The houses, all in the same dark red brick, stand in rows as orderly as sailors aboard a ship awaiting inspection by an admiral. On Church Street is the cemetery and the elementary school—Martin Frobisher First School, 187 pupils. Every block has a large crop of For Sale signs and posters objecting to plans for using an old quarry as a toxic-waste dump. From certain angles, the town looks intensely urban; the houses crowd the edge of the road. Nevertheless, it remains just a detour from Wakefield and Normanton. Holsteins stand in a pasture between the cemetery and the brown trickle of the River Calder. If they raise their heads they can see the roaring river of traffic on the M62 near the big junction that swings the cars north to Leeds.

In Frobisher's day, Yorkshire farmers planted corn. When rain threatened to turn all of Yorkshire's West Riding into marsh, or when corn prices dropped, they kept more of the land in pasture for the cows. A big farm would have ten acres and five cows. A successful yeoman might add chickens, bees, and a dozen sheep. The women of the household knitted rough wool stockings for extra income, or took wool cloth to the mills at Wakefield for more expert weaving.

Barnard Frobisher was several classes above having to worry about making ends meet. As one of the major landowners, he held the post of bailiff and was churchwarden in Normanton. He would have been knowledgeable about finance. Margaret Frobisher, his wife, was the sister (or perhaps cousin) of Sir John Yorke, the master of the Royal Mint at the Tower of London. Martin was the Frobishers' fourth child, and he lived amid the commotion of his older brothers, John and Davey, and Jane and Margaret, his sisters. He was schooled enough to acquire his imperfect scrawl. But the most important event of his childhood was the death of his father when Martin was seven. His mother died seven years later. As the orphaned third son, he went to live in the household of Uncle John Yorke: of those years, nothing is known.

It is not until 1553 that Frobisher reemerges, walking onto the docks at Portsmouth, on the English Channel, at age eighteen. Whether by his own choice or that of John Yorke, he was about to go to sea.

Young men became sailors because they planned on joining their family's trading business, or because they wished to escape farming, or because they lacked an inheritance. In general, they went to sea to improve their station. Change of that kind was harder to accomplish in a village or in guild-regulated crafts. Farmers remained farmers; craftsmen—bakers, brewers, carpenters, coopers, grocers, haberdashers—likewise expected to stay in place. Ideally, a young would-be mariner would acquire the necessary sailing skills aboard a vessel owned by relatives. As a second choice he could be apprenticed at age eleven or twelve as a ship's "boy." In either situation, the young man could reasonably hope to rise through the ranks aboard merchant ships.

John Yorke had invested money in three ships at the Portsmouth dock. The term for him was *adventurer*, which had a different meaning than it does today. Adventurers invested their capital—ventured it—in outfitting vessels. These entrepreneurs either owned the ships outright, supplied the merchandise for trading, provided the rigging and weapons, or played all those roles. In return, they received a share of the profits from the voyage. As investors, they regularly mixed private and public roles. Adventurers might simultaneously own ships and serve as commanders in the Royal Navy. If blessed with the right connections at court, adventurers would borrow vessels from the navy for modest sums and reduce their costs further by "borrowing" the navy's munitions and victuals.

In that way, John Yorke and adventurers like him could enrich themselves. A senior government minister could own a vessel, lease it to the Royal Navy, then persuade the navy to provision the ship for double the number of sailors actually on board. The owner would profit from the lease and pocket an additional sum from selling the extra supplies that the navy had provided at no charge. Such practices were regarded as proof of a man's energy and cleverness.

For a young man on the Portsmouth docks, though, merchant ships held more promise than did the Royal Navy. In 1553 the

Royal Navy consisted of mostly worn-out hulls from the wars against France and the Scots. King Henry VIII had borrowed money at 14 percent interest to pay for the fighting, and his nine-year-old son, Edward VI, had inherited the debts along with the ships. For lack of money for repairs, most of the ships were rotting in the Thames. They were used for the dull work of transporting soldiers north to fight the Scots or the Irish, or to the Continent to fight the French, or for endlessly patrolling the English Channel. The navy was regarded as a conveyance system without much intrinsic value—a dead end except for officers at the top. Sailors in the navy earned about six pounds a year, while on an adventurer's ship they could pocket more in a voyage lasting just a few months. On an adventurer's ship they had their monthly wage, the additional income earned from trading goods of their own at the ports of call, and prize money from captured vessels. If their captain captured a foreign ship, the sailors were entitled to a third of the seized cargo and had the right to pillage whatever was on deck or belonged to the prisoners.

The biggest risk takers were fishermen sailing from Bristol for cod. Bristol ships had reached Iceland by 1410, and some Bristol captains had at least heard talk of Greenland. Searching for fish, a few Bristol ships probably reached the Norse settlements on Greenland's western coast. Even with the expense of the voyage, fish were cheaper and more plentiful than poultry or meat. From Greenland, a big summer storm could blow a ship west across the Davis Strait, through the fields of icebergs that glow a soft blue-green. One big blow, and a ship could reach North America: the Norse had already made that crossing. From Greenland, they had reached a rocky landscape they named Helluland, which is probably modern-day Baffin Island. Farther south was a forested territory they called Markland—probably Labrador. South of Markland, in about A.D. 1000, they came to Vineland, which is Newfoundland. They judged this island inviting enough to establish a settlement there.

Giovanni Caboto, of Genoa and Venice, had sailed west from Bristol in 1497. After a month at sea aboard the caravel *Mathew,* he reached a rocky coast whose waters teemed with cod. John Cabot, as he is better remembered, saw unmistakable signs of habitation on the one occasion he went ashore: trees had been felled, and his men found snares for catching game. He concluded that his "New Found Land" was near Cathay, and claimed it for England. He returned to Bristol a hero. "He is called Great Admiral," a Venetian living in London wrote home, "and vast honor is paid to him and he goes dressed in silk, and these English run after him like mad."

Bristol fishermen had probably come to those waters even before Cabot did. They may have reached the New World in advance of Christopher Columbus. After Cabot's return, a Bristol merchant reminded Columbus in a letter that, "as your Lordship knows," Bristol men had long ago reached those northern waters. Being fishermen, the Bristol men had apparently been reluctant to publicize the location of their find. They caught and gutted the cod, salted them, and dried the fish in the open air until sufficiently cured for the monthlong trip to England. It seemed wise to keep detailed descriptions of the fishing grounds to themselves.

Cabot's crew apparently had great tolerance for roll and pitch. In the 1990s, to mark the five hundredth anniversary of his voyage, British shipwrights worked for two years building an approximate replica of the *Mathew*. Their new *Mathew* was equipped with a satellite navigation system, an array of radios, electronic chart plotters, and an engine driving twin bronze propellers. Polyester sails eliminated the problems of rot and stretch. Bronze bolts along with marine glue served as the fasteners, in place of wooden pegs. Instead of a shifting cargo of rocks as ballast, the hold of the new *Mathew* contained twenty-nine tons of lead ingots secured into form-fitting place. Yet all those improvements produced a ship that still frightened its modern-day crew. The vessel's trim in normal seas was deemed "barely adequate" but probably authentic. After encountering a gale, the new *Mathew* entered port at the end of a towrope. Shipwrights rewhittled the masts, rethought the rudder, and modified the propulsion system; the bunks were rejigged because the sixteen-member crew had found its quarters unendurably cramped. The ballast was moved into a new, external keel intended, as were the other changes, to improve the ship's stability.

These problems hint at the awfulness of Cabot's voyage—how much the original *Mathew* must have alarmed everyone aboard.

John Cabot sailed west again in 1498 with five ships, carrying enough provisions for a year. One of the vessels, badly damaged by a storm, came ashore in Ireland several months later. Cabot was not on it, and neither he nor any of the other four ships were seen again. Within a few years Bristol merchants made the Newfoundland fishery a stable, profitable business. But protein, in the form of cod, interested them more than exploring the territory.

John Yorke had invested in at least one other voyage before Martin Frobisher arrived in Portsmouth. Backed by Yorke and others, Captain Thomas Wyndham in 1552 had led three ships to North Africa and profitably returned home with almonds, sugar, and dates.

In 1553, Yorke and his fellow adventurers raised their ambitions: the investors hired Wyndham to sail to the Guinea Coast, the underside of Africa's bulge into the Atlantic. Eighteen-year-old Frobisher planned to sail with him. Wyndham contributed a ship of his own, the *Lion,* to the expedition and became a full partner. The most serious drawback to the plan was that Portugal claimed a monopoly on trade in West Africa, including along the Guinea Coast. But the investors viewed that as just another risk of business.

Since the 1470s, Portuguese traders had profitably exchanged glass beads and colored cloth with African natives for slaves, who then were sent to Portugal's sugar plantations on the stifling, disease-ridden islands in the Gulf of Guinea. The mortality rate was 80 percent a year. Yellow fever and malaria killed the Portuguese, while the slaves died from overwork. In Lisbon this was deemed an acceptable expense. A loose string of trading posts along the coast obtained ivory and malagueta pepper, a hot spice that smelled like cardamom. Merchants in Antwerp called malagueta pepper "grains of paradise," or "Guinea grains." In the 1480s, stonemasons from Portugal built the fortified city of São Jorge da Mina, which became better known as just el Mina, "the Mine." In an average year the garrison at Mina sent home 750 pounds of gold from the African interior. To increase the harvest of metal, the Portuguese sold slaves captured elsewhere along the coast to the native traders who came to Mina, creating a gruesome sort of synergy. The slaves were forced to carry the other trade goods into the interior, then were sent farther inland to work the gold mines.

Sailing along that coast, Europeans saw a numbingly flat, almost featureless landscape. A few high stands of palm trees were the only landmarks the pilots could find. Few ships traveled farther east beyond Mina, into the Bight of Benin with its endless reeking swamps.

Thomas Wyndham possessed a character thought fitting for such a place. In the sketchy records he is full of choleric energy— "a most expert pirate," the French said of him. As a commander during the wars against the Scots, he threatened to burn every village on the Scottish coast. As a sea captain, he seized foreign ships whether they were enemies or allies. This enthusiasm impressed his superiors, who promoted him to vice admiral and then nearly to the top of the heap, as master of ordnance. But he continued his piracies.

In its mildest form, piracy was breaking and entering. At its harshest, it was armed robbery, kidnapping, and murder. Depending on the circumstances, it was also considered proper behavior.

The Admiralty court in London issued letters of reprisal— essentially, licenses for piracy. A letter of reprisal conveyed official permission to hijack ships belonging to England's enemies. The word coined later for the practice was *privateering:* private plundering with the blessing of one's government. English captains attacked French and Scottish ships. With the potential profit being so large, they also seized vessels belonging to England's allies: Dutch, Portuguese, and Danish ships.

Piracy served the state more cheaply than a navy did. When a privateer reached port with a prize in tow, an Admiralty official inventoried the cargo. The captain paid custom duties to the crown and gave another share to the Lord High Admiral, from whom the money filtered down to many vice admirals and deputies. Other shares found their way to outfitters who had supplied the vessel on credit, merchants who specialized in the sale of prize goods, shipbuilders, the vessel's owners, and the ship's captain and crew. The adventurers stood to make even more if part of the cargo could be spirited away before the official inventory was made, or if the goods were intentionally undervalued or were smuggled ashore at any of a hundred coves where no one from the Admiralty could perform an inspection. Depending on the politics of the day, the Admiralty might levy fines against privateers seizing ships belonging to friendly states. Captains could also be jailed, but the Admiralty, sotto voce, might congratulate them for their fine haul and quickly free them. Walter Raleigh called these vastly enriching trips "journeys of pickery." Francis Drake termed them "a little dew from heaven."

The privateers were subversives in ways that went beyond their pillaging. They made risk taking respectable, launching a way of creating wealth independent of land or a title bestowed by a king. In the 1550s the cloth trade in Antwerp was beginning to fray, which expanded their opportunities. Out of necessity, London merchants began to see the advantage of trading goods in ports beyond Antwerp. In searching for the new markets, merchant ships explored new waters—as did the privateers. When the opportunities became unmistakable, powerful figures at court became investors in the voyages. John Yorke was willing to risk his capital if the sailors would risk their lives. Who had more experience with danger than the privateers? What better man to storm ashore in West Africa under the eyes of the Portuguese than a captain willing to burn half of Scotland? On a small scale, and without having really intended it, the privateers created opportunities for wealth and advancement. They liberalized cautious, fractious, conservative England.

John Yorke may have forcibly sent Martin Frobisher on the voyage, or Frobisher may have tired of the household, or perhaps he wanted adventure. At the Portsmouth dock he met Thomas Wyndham's three ships: the *Lion,* the *Moon,* and the *Primrose,* the flagship. Frobisher was too old to be joining as a ship's boy, and he does not seem to have been one of the "factors"—the merchants' appointed agents, who took charge of the merchandise and conducted the bartering. Below Wyndham, in rank, were the ship's master, or pilot, in charge of the charts, navigation instruments, and the trim of the sails; the boatswain, who was responsible for the anchors and cables; and the quartermaster, who took charge of the rudder. There might have been a purser, cook, carpenter, and master gunner. Frobisher, as the nephew of an important investor, stood somewhere comfortably above the rank of ordinary seaman.

A contemporary described Wyndham's sailors as "men of the lustiest sort." They were the illiterate young men outside any of the alehouses near the waterfront, surrounded by a strong perfume of beer. Wyndham's agents promised the sailors high wages—twelve shillings a month for a common seaman, instead of the customary eight. If a sailor needed clothes, the agent could supply them as an advance on wages. Depending on their means, sailors came aboard with a waistcoat to wear over a shirt, a doublet that went atop the waistcoat, a jerkin worn over the doublet, and a cloaklike gown, which served as their only protection against rain. William Brown, impressed into service as the *Primrose* quartermaster, carried aboard a sea chest containing long woolen hose, his red breeches, a flannel petticoat, and his gun. Captain Wyndham hired Antonio Pinteado, recently of Portugal, as chief pilot, since Pinteado had already sailed in the Gulf of Guinea.

On August 12, 1553, their anchor raised, sails unfurled, the sailors watched Portsmouth recede into a thin brown line. Wyndham reached Madeira in mid-September. Resuming his old habits, he plundered two vessels there. After another month the *Primrose,* the *Lion,* and the *Moon* made the West African coast. They loaded malagueta pepper at the mouth of the Sess River (now in Liberia), plundered another ship, and traded some of their merchandise for gold near Mina (on the coast of Ghana). They saw an endless green swamp, and elephants there waded into freshwater lagoons near the shore. Slathered with palm oil against the mosquitoes, the natives were as black as Yorkshire coal, and as naked as the animals; their boats were hollowed-out logs, reminiscent of the troughs from which London hogs ate their slop.

Wyndham and Antonio Pinteado, the pilot, argued in the heat. Pinteado advised that they stay near Mina, but to Wyndham every mile of that dull, humid coast looked the same. He favored sailing farther east, for more pepper. Pinteado said the climate was even worse in the east, especially in the rainy season. Their food would turn rancid, he said, and when the rains started, the sailors' clothes would rot off their backs. Wyndham settled the argument by threatening to cut off the pilot's ears—that, or he could lead the way east.

The *Primrose,* the *Lion,* and the *Moon* sailed another 450 miles east, to the mouth of the Benin River.

Wyndham stayed aboard the *Primrose,* while Pinteado traveled upriver with the factors. They negotiated with the local king for peppers. As far as we can deduce from later events, Martin Frobisher probably remained on the *Primrose.* Over the next month, the natives harvested eighty tons of peppers, enough to guarantee the factors a comfortable retirement. But Pinteado was right about the climate. As the weather turned hotter, Wyndham's men began dying. In a single day, five men died, probably the first English sailors to fall victim to yellow fever. The illness began with a rush of fever, followed by a terrible exhaustion accompanying a strange restlessness—a fever of body and mind—before the final delirium.

Wyndham sent a message upriver ordering Pinteado to return. Pinteado sent a message back describing the amazing wealth of pepper, the glory right there at his feet. Wyndham responded by smashing everything in the pilot's cabin, including the navigation instruments. His actions are described in an account written some months later in England by Richard Eden, a Cambridge-educated scholar fascinated by exotic travels whose writings emphasized the rewards of exploration. Eden evidently talked to some of Wyndham's sailors about their experience: they were frightened by seeing shipmates die without a single shot being fired and terrified of disappearing in that hot stink, all for the temptation of twelve shillings a month and that damnable pepper.

By the time Pinteado reached the *Primrose*, Wyndham was dead. Some of the officers spat in the pilot's face—"some calling him Jew, saying that he had brought them thither to kill them," Eden reported. They demanded that he immediately lead them home, refusing to wait for the factors still upriver. For lack of able-bodied sailors, the *Lion* and the *Moon* were abandoned, as were the factors and most of the pepper. Pinteado was among those who died during the voyage home. Of the 160 men who had sailed from Portsmouth, 40 returned to England, including Frobisher. At home, the investors tried to cheat them out of their wages.

Thus did Martin Frobisher complete his early education in seamanship, trade, and avarice.

Frobisher collected his pay and may have visited Altofts. Three months later, he was ready to sail again. West Africa still tempted the adventurers. True, some of them had lost business partners or relatives in Wyndham's misadventures—the men left behind were never again heard from—but now the adventurers knew for a fact that the region had both gold and Guinea grains for the taking.

This time John Yorke and his partners chose a Mr. John Lok as commander. John Lok possessed an impeccable lineage in mercantile affairs, being a son of the mercer (a dealer in fine textiles) who had clothed Henry VIII's court in silk and cloth of gold. The elder Lok had spent part of every year in Antwerp, overseeing the family's business interests. His sons inherited his many London properties along with valuable connections at court. One of John Lok's brothers, young Michael, helped look after affairs in Antwerp and, when Antwerp soured, performed the same service in Spain and Portugal.

In these months, Frobisher evidently chose sailing as his profession. By the end of 1554 he was aboard one of John Lok's ships, enveloped again in West Africa's swampy heat. "Some of our men of good credit, that were in this last voyage to Guinea, affirm earnestly that in the night season they felt a sensible heat to come from the beams of the moon," Richard Eden reported later. "They say furthermore that in certain places of the sea they saw certain streams of water, which they call spouts, falling out of the air into the sea, & that some of these are as big as the great pillars of churches." At the mouth of the Sess River, the Englishmen obtained malagueta pepper. Lok then bartered for gold at Samma, a village with a small Portuguese garrison. As a guarantee of their peaceful intentions, the native chief at Samma demanded that the Englishmen send him a hostage.

Martin Frobisher volunteered. Until that moment, he is invisible on this voyage, and why he chose to step forward is known only to him. In the two accounts of the event—one by Richard Eden, the other by Frobisher himself—there is no hint that he was forced into it, nor is there evidence of anyone trying to hold him back. This is another risk he is willing to take. He headed toward the beach in a pinnace, a glorified rowboat ideal for navigating coastal waters, accompanied by some of the factors. "Martin, by his own desire and assent of some of the commissioners that were in the pinnace, went ashore to the town," Eden wrote. When the pinnace left, he was in Samma on his own.

Samma's chief turned his hostage over to Portuguese soldiers, who fired at the English ships. Lok weighed the potential profits against the dangers of a clash, then sailed away from Samma. Business mattered more than a crew member, and casualties were only to be expected. Twenty-four sailors would die of one or another ailment by the time Lok returned to England; losing one more as a hostage hardly mattered. Lok arrived home with malagueta peppers, 250 elephant tusks, and 400 pounds of gold—that's what mattered to the investors. His cargo also included black slaves, Eden reported, "whereof some were tall and strong men and could well agree with our meats and drinks." Some of these blacks would return to West Africa as the adventurers' agents.

Frobisher later said the Portuguese held him in rather privileged captivity at Mina for nine months. By his account, the garrison there refused to travel even a mile beyond the fort out of fear for its safety. Soldiers instead relied on him to find poultry and goats during his own excursions. His route home from Mina can be guessed at, since Portugal and England were allies. Either he was released into the custody of the next trading fleet from England, or the Portuguese transferred him to Lisbon and freed him there.

A small circle of intellectuals advocated undertaking riskier, more ambitious voyages. Sebastian Cabot, the son of the lost John Cabot, proposed sending mariners to search for a northeast route to Cathay. Cathay and the islands of the Pacific were rich in gold and had porcelain, enormous quantities of silk and satin, and the spices Europe desired, as first described two and a half centuries before by Marco Polo. These lands remained unseen by English mariners. Cathay seemed to promise limitless wealth to whoever found the most direct route there.

Sebastian Cabot advocated organizing an expedition that would sail east toward Scandinavia, skirt around Scandinavia's northern edge, then travel east along the northern edge of Russia. He had spent years in Spain as a navigational adviser, before returning to England. Since Cabot possessed a famous name, people listened to him. He told of breathtaking voyages to North America he may or may not have actually made. According to his stories, he had sailed north of the Arctic Circle and almost as far south as the tip of Florida. A chronicler remembered his saying that if not for the threat of a mutiny, he would have found a passage to Cathay himself, in the northwest. You could pick an argument over how many trips he made to North America: three, two, or one. But he was more experienced than anyone else in England in the theory and practice of navigation.

The English adventurers knew they would have to go north; the choice that remained to them was between northeast and northwest. In 1493 a papal bull had awarded all discoveries in the south to Portugal and Spain. The Portuguese reached Asia by the southeast—the hot glide down the African coast and around the Cape of Good Hope, then the leg across the Indian Ocean. Ferdinand

Magellan, on behalf of Spain, pioneered the southwestern route, sailing through the long strait at the bottom of South America and across the Pacific. Of the 265 men who left Spain with him, only 18 completed the three-year voyage. They had survived the fifteen-week crossing of the Pacific by eating leather stripped from the rigging, rats, and sawdust. But however difficult their discovery, the southeast and southwest routes were already taken.

Sebastian Cabot gained support from a man named Dr. John Dee, a sort of wizard lacking only a conical hat displaying stars and crescent moons. In all England, no one else was of quite the same stamp. Courtiers gossiped that he was a sorcerer; children avoided him out of fear that he would cast a spell. He even looked the part of dour wizard. In his portrait Dee wears a voluminous black gown that highlights his white mustache and long beard. He possessed an altogether gloomy handsomeness, his mustache drooping like a thirsty plant, rooted in a milky beard. One can almost hear the silky rustle of the gown and see him sweep past the incubations and boilings in the alchemical laboratory attached to his house.

Dee was alchemist, mathematician, astrologer, a polymath of numbers and of the occult. He interested himself in navigation and exploration, as well as in medicine, metallurgy, mining, the charters and seals of ancient estates, and the Cabala. He believed that if he studied widely enough he would be rewarded by divine revelation of some higher knowledge. He devoted a large part of his career to searching for a set of general laws—his own unified field theory—in hope of explaining the hidden powers assumed to lie behind the visible world.

He had attended St. John's College at Cambridge, where an odd matter permanently colored his reputation. As a student he had helped stage a performance there of *Pax,* a comedy by Aristophanes. In the play's first minutes, a giant dung beetle flies with a man on its back in search of the gods. Young John Dee obligingly made a giant make-believe beetle "fly" to the ceiling with an actor riding as a passenger. Not everyone in the Cambridge audience saw the ropes attached to the beetle, or saw the pulleys above the stage, or understood their workings. So gossip spread about the stage assistant's eerie talents.

After Cambridge he studied mathematics on the Continent under the guidance of Gerhard Mercator, the greatest cartographer of the day, and Gemma Frisius, Mercator's teacher. Dee said he also found time to obtain a law degree (thus *Dr.* Dee). His Cambridge connections served as a calling card when he returned to England. They gained him an introduction to William Cecil, a rising official in the royal court. Through Cecil, he entered service as a tutor for eminent young men, the most important of whom were the sons of John Dudley, Duke of Northumberland. Dee's lessons ranged from mathematics to alchemy to the tracking of a ship's course by the sun and stars.

He possessed two large globes made by Mercator—one depicting terrestrial geography, the other the skies—and a fleet's worth of compasses and geographical manuscripts. Reading explorers' accounts, he made notes about what records mariners should keep (wind directions, currents, the distance run by the ship) and how best to establish friendly relations with natives in new lands. He searched too for flaws in Spain's territorial claims, the better to look for opportunities for England.

Dee kept a diary that contributed to his strangeness, jottings made in the margins of his growing collection of books and manuscripts. Equal weight was given—one sentence for each—to his second marriage and his cat's capturing a wounded sparrow. In the written entries servants come and go; his son Arthur injures an eye in a make-believe sword fight; the household has the honor of a visit from the royal dwarf, Mrs. Tomasin. The diarist hears unsettling noises ("all the night very strange knocking and rapping"). March is wet but not windy. In a nightmare he observes his own death ("I dreamed that I was dead, and afterward my bowels were taken out"). Worse, in the nightmare someone comes to burn his library.

His library was the largest scholarly collection in England—three thousand printed volumes, plus a thousand manuscripts. They were a tangible manifestation of his hope to gain knowledge of all the

John Dee, by an unknown painter, ca. 1574–1586. Dee was a mathematician, alchemist, scholar of the occult, and adviser to navigators. (Ashmolean Museum, Oxford)

cosmos. He would eventually install the library at a grand-sounding estate inherited from his mother in the village of Mortlake, on the south bank of the Thames near London. Mortlake was convenient to the royal palace at Richmond and within a day's ride of the palace at Greenwich. The books were scattered among four or five rooms furnished with Mercator's globes, a clock precise enough to count off seconds (rare for that era), a large magnet that he greatly prized, and the many compasses. Pilots and his other students were tutored in the library, as well as in the alchemical laboratories spilling from the main house into the side buildings.

His laboratory apparatus included crystal balls and a mirror for communicating with spirits. The mirror, now in the British Museum, is a seamless disk of obsidian, a smooth black circle about seven inches in diameter with a small square tab as a handle. Its surface is always alive with reflections. Look into the dark circle, and the circle stares back with a distorted face. One of his crystal balls—an entire genus of objects that seems not quite real—is a smoky globe small enough to enfold in one's hand or conceal in the pocket of a doublet.

He believed in the existence of northern passages to Cathay, as surely as he believed in the worth of alchemy. The scholarly consensus was that the Earth was a finely balanced mechanism. Its waters were assumed to be arranged symmetrically, at the risk of the planet's otherwise tumbling uncontrollably through the heavens. Since vessels had navigated around the southern tip of Africa, a similar waterway surely existed, *had* to exist, above Russia, for reasons of balance. For the same reason, great scholars assumed that a waterway awaited discovery north of the New World, as a counterweight for the Strait of Magellan in the hemisphere's extreme south.

Sebastian Cabot was waiting, in a sense, for a man like John Dee. They shared the same faith in the existence of northern passages to Cathay. Cabot received the royal court's approval for organizing a venture to explore waters to the northeast. There was little difficulty in attracting investors: two hundred adventurers, including John Yorke, joined him. John Dee provided lessons in celestial navigation for the man appointed chief pilot, Richard Chancellor. Their discussions touched on the expedition's route, a line drawn across mostly blank parchment to some "there." Hugh Willoughby, an army man without much maritime experience, was chosen as commander of the expedition.

On May 10, 1553, Willoughby's three ships slid into the current of the Thames at Ratcliff, a densely populated community of shipwrights, sailors, and outfitters east of London. Some weeks later, a storm separated the ships. Richard Chancellor piloted the *Edward Bonaventure* to the fleet's agreed-upon meeting place on the Scandinavian coast. After waiting a week without sighting the other vessels, he cleared the top of the Scandinavian peninsula alone, then sailed east another five hundred miles into the White Sea. The *Bonaventure* then turned south. It anchored, in late summer or early autumn, at the future port of Archangel on Russia's northern coast. The crew aboard the *Bonaventure* were the first Englishmen to see those waters and visit that shore.

Willoughby led the two other ships on the same slow turn above Scandinavia. They traveled farther north and farther east than did Chancellor, until ice forced them to find an anchorage. It was mid-September. Willoughby noted in his journal that the season seemed much later—"very evil weather . . . as though it had been the deep of winter." His men watched everything turn hard and white. At least some of them survived into January, as evidenced by entries in the ships' logs; Willoughby and the last of the sailors then starved, or died from scurvy or from the cold. In the spring Russian fishermen would find the ships manned by frozen corpses.

At Archangel, word had spread of Chancellor's arrival. Authorities sent word to Moscow about the *Bonaventure*'s cargo of fine cloth. Without waiting for a response, they then led the Englishmen the thousand miles to Moscow by sled, encountering along the way a messenger from Moscow carrying letters of welcome. If Chancellor could not reach the Great Khan in Cathay, he would settle for an audience with the Duke of Moscow. Duke Ivan Vasilevich—Ivan the Terrible, Great Lord and Emperor of all Russia, Great Duke of Vladimir and Novgorod, King of Kazan, King of Astrakhan, Lord of Pskov, Great Duke of Perm, Commander of all Siberia—kept him waiting in Moscow twelve days before issuing an invitation. After presenting a letter of introduction, Chancellor drank from Ivan's gold tankards and ate from golden plates. Ivan was no less impressed by his guest.

Chancellor sailed home carrying a letter from Ivan Vasilevich warmly inviting English merchants to Russia. In London, Sebastian Cabot's pool of investors organized themselves into a formal partnership: the Merchant Adventurers of England for the Discovery of Lands, Territories, Isles, Dominions and Seignories Unknown, better known as the Muscovy Company. The royal court granted the company a charter guaranteeing it a monopoly on all exploration "northwards, northeastwards, or northwestwards." Whether by land or sea, explorers heading in those directions—the only directions left—would have to be company men. The Muscovy Company was also promised a monopoly on trade with all the territories it managed to discover.

For the company's first venture, Chancellor in 1555 sailed the *Bonaventure* back to Archangel. His first priority was trade: English cloth for Russian tallow, flax, hides, and rope. His second was to resume the investigation of how one might reach Cathay. In 1556, he headed home. His passengers included Russia's first ambassador to England. After four months' sailing, the *Bonaventure* reached the east coast of Scotland. A gale there broke the anchor cables. When the storm threatened to drive the *Bonaventure* onto rocks, Chancellor urged the Russian ambassador into the ship's boat.

The local inhabitants stripped the wreckage of the *Bonaventure* of its guns once the storm passed, took the cargo of Russian wax and tallow, found sables Ivan had sent as a gift to the royal court, and stole furnishings from Chancellor's cabin. Every movable object was pillaged. The ambassador, miraculously, survived. Richard Chancellor—the best-trained navigator in England—drowned with most of his crew.

There were, of course, other preoccupations in England besides a route to Cathay. Whether the monarch was Protestant or Catholic, the 1550s were an insecure time.

Three years in a row, during King Edward VI's reign, the harvest failed. Great landowners compounded the problems in agriculture by closing off fields to create private pastures for their sheep, reducing the acreage available for farmers. The land produced more wool but less food, and more people went hungry. Farmers in the southwest protested by blockading the city of Exeter, and in the east they demonstrated against the land rents. An army of mercenaries originally hired to battle the Scots subdued the protests by killing six thousand people. Given the weapons of the day, the killings occurred one by one: the farmers were run through by the sword or hanged, one at a time.

Protestant Edward remained more boy than king. He was physically frail and suffered from a debilitating cough. His strength usually returned if he rested for a long period, only for the coughing to resume. It was the normal course for the wasting disease his physicians called consumption, a disease for which they offered no cure. Pulmonary tuberculosis travels a course of remissions followed by relapses of coughing and a sense of slow strangulation deep within one's body. "The sputum which he brings up," a witness to the young king's sufferings reported, "is livid, black, fetid, and full of carbon; it smells beyond measure." Edward, age fifteen, died July 10, 1553.

Queen Mary, his half sister, was devoutly Catholic. Her determination to lead the country back to the Church of Rome helped spark an armed rebellion; the uprising led to another long season of executions. Mary's half sister, Elizabeth, was among those imprisoned in the Tower of London on suspicion of treason. Failing to find evidence for any wrongdoing by Elizabeth, the queen's counselors considered executing her for her Protestantism or, less drastically, removing her from the scene by marrying her off to a foreign prince. But she went free after two months. At about that same time, John Dee was imprisoned on suspicion of "calculating and conjuring." He had apparently studied the queen's horoscope—dangerously akin to casting a spell—and a courtier accused him and several associates of bewitching the courtier's children. Dee laconically noted that his dungeon mate in the Tower was one Barthlet Grene, "who was burnt." After three months, Dee was freed on the condition that he submit to questioning by Edmund Bonner, the much-feared Catholic bishop of London. Bonner demonstrated unseemly pleasure in interrogating Protestants before condemning them to death by burning. Dee, always willing to accommodate authority, whatever its face, got along with him famously. My "*singularis amicus,*" he said of the bishop—my friend in a million.

Conditions failed to improve in the countryside under the new queen. The harvest failed twice more, and epidemics of influenza killed perhaps five percent of the country's population. When Mary married Prince Philip of Spain, unrest boiled over, out of fear that the country would become just another outpost of the Spanish empire. In 1558 England lost the city of Calais, its last toehold on the Continent, to the French. An official of the royal court cataloged the wreckage: "The realm exhausted. The nobility poor and decayed. Want of good captains and soldiers. The people out of order. Justice not executed. All things dear."

Queen Mary died on November 17, 1558, after a five-year reign.

Elizabeth, the new queen, had her mother Anne Boleyn's high forehead and the long Boleyn nose. Beginning in childhood, she was aware of being brighter than most of the people around her. At age thirteen, in a letter to her half brother Edward, she announced that while her face might be imperfect, she would never be embarrassed by her mind.

The day Mary died, Elizabeth asked the long-serving court official William Cecil for help. She and Cecil that day were seen sitting side by side, the posture that in a sense they maintained for the next four decades: Her Majesty in close company with the counselor she usually trusted most. As her first appointment Elizabeth named Cecil principal secretary of state. Later, he would become Lord Treasurer. From that first day forward, except when the queen was preoccupied by romance, he rarely left her inner circle.

On the second day of her reign, Elizabeth chose Robert Dudley as Master of the Horse. Tall, exceedingly handsome with reddish hair, gifted in conversation, Dudley was a son of the Duke of Northumberland, and had been tutored by John Dee. In state processions, the Master of the Horse always rode immediately behind the queen. It privileged him with nearness. Elizabeth enjoyed riding as much as Dudley did, and they indulged in this pleasure together almost every morning. In the evenings, he danced as energetically as the queen. Courtiers saw that they were already smitten with one another. William Cecil was one center of power; Robert Dudley became another.

An "age" began as unremarkably as that: Elizabeth, twenty-five years old, choosing two confidants. In the eyes of other monarchs, she was a heretic and a bastard; her unmarried state was another disability, since she lacked a child of her own as an heir. She was appallingly vain, removing her doeskin gloves to allow the court to admire her slender hands. But Elizabethan England would be trans-muted into a place where everything appeared to shine. She became akin to a state religion, the focus of her subjects' faith that all would go well. That bright image emerged during Elizabeth's lifetime, helped bolster the country's confidence, and was transformed into a symbol of the kingdom for later generations. In the Elizabethan England we imagine today, her courtiers have only their country's interests at heart, and Elizabeth herself displays a grandmother's generosity and warmth—an image that is not entirely accurate.

In a first encounter, the Spanish ambassador sensed her tough-ness: "She is a woman of extreme vanity, but acute." An envoy from Venice contented himself with surfaces: "Her face is comely rather than handsome, but she is tall and well-formed, with a good skin; although swarthy, she has fine eyes." Depending on the wit-ness, her hair was yellow or reddish. The color and everything else about her appearance mattered greatly to her, as noted by Mary, Queen of Scots' minister to England after an audience with the English queen.

> She desired to know of me, what color of hair was reputed best, and whether my Queen's hair or hers was best; and which of them two was fairest. I answered, the fairness of them both was not their worst faults. But she was earnest with me to declare which of them I judged fairest. I said, she was the fairest Queen in England, and mine the fairest Queen of Scotland. Yet she appeared earnest. I answered, they were both the fairest ladies of their countries; that her Majesty was whiter, but my

Queen was very lovely. She enquired which of them was the highest stature: I said, my Queen. Then, saith she, she is too high; for I myself am neither too high nor too low.

She believed in omens, and sought advice for choosing a coronation date. Robert Dudley recommended John Dee, his former tutor, as a scholar of portents.

In one of his recent works, Dee had explained the use of geometry to track the paths of stars and the planets, which, in turn, might aid the prediction of terrestrial events. The zodiac's influence on the Earth was accepted as fact. Learned men studied the zodiac, diagnosed causes of witchcraft, read portents in children's fingernails, consulted magic mirrors. Elizabeth accepted his recommendation of January 15, 1559, as an astrologically favorable date for her coronation. This consultation was to be Dee's entrée into Elizabeth's court. Her Privy Council—the queen's cabinet— would later seek his advice about the possible dangers posed by a comet. On other occasions, he was consulted about the queen's toothaches. The Privy Council urgently sought his help after finding a wax image of the queen with a pin stuck in its breast. In the minds of her counselors, the image constituted evidence of a plot against her. "My careful and faithful endeavors was with great speed required," Dee wrote of the event, ". . . wherein I did satisfy Her Majesty's desire, and the Lords of the Honorable Privy Council within a few hours." (He did not disclose how he exorcised the danger.) These consultations established Dee's preeminence at court as a scholar and interpreter of mysteries.

To remain in Elizabeth's good graces, even the greatest men had to spend time at the royal court. She demanded wooing. One was expected to behave like a devoted lover pursuing a flawless mistress, while a hundred other men pursued the same strategy. Her courtiers sought in every sense to move *inward,* to a more intimate place. The sexual imagery was well understood in her own day. At each of the queen's palaces, courtiers vied to penetrate from the Great Hall into the more exclusive Presence Chamber, and then from the Presence Chamber into the Privy Chamber, where her counselors conducted the formal business of government. Beyond the Privy Chamber lay the apartments of the Royal Bedchamber.

Courtiers idled away weeks in those gilded, crowded rooms waiting for a glance. While waiting, they lost money they didn't have at dice and cards, and then borrowed money from the queen to support their extravagant lifestyle. Because of their precarious finances, the courtiers became her most beholden subjects. In return for a glance of royal favor, Elizabeth wanted to be pleasured in some way—impressed by wittiness, tantalized by the cut of silk breeches. "To fawn, to crouch, to wait, to ride, to run," Edmund Spenser tartly wrote of the courtier's life. "To spend, to give, to want, to be undone." A gift of pearls, presented through Robert Dudley or some other great lord, served equally well. So did gold. Everyone jostled in the same plush hell for her attention.

Robert Dudley was her true favorite. They had met as teenagers, each apparently giddy about the other. As queen she nicknamed him Eyes; one can speculate that he helped her see pleasure. They unsettled the Privy Council with their publicness—they rode together, danced at royal balls, and were playful in the same ways of any amorous couple. He was already married. She made him a member of the Privy Council, awarded him lands in Yorkshire, granted him properties in eight other counties, and appointed him high steward of Cambridge and chancellor of Oxford. Englishmen were imprisoned in the Tower of London for gossiping that the Virgin Queen was pregnant with his child. When Dudley's wife was discovered dead of a broken neck, ambassadors discreetly inquired whether Dudley had arranged for her to be murdered. (The answer is, probably not.) In 1564, the queen made him Earl of Leicester, the name he was known by thereafter. Marriage did not seem out of the question, but it was also impossible. Though he was a widower, his political rivals were too numerous, the gossip about the murky circumstances of his wife's death too corrosive for a royal marriage to be within reach. Flirting with marriage, the queen understood that her powers were greater in her unmarried state than if she were anyone's wife. The more noble the suitor, the

Queen Elizabeth, attributed to Nicolas Hilliard, ca. 1575. Diamonds, pearls, a large ruff, and a display of the hands of which she was so vain were the trademarks of her portraits. (Courtesy of the National Portrait Gallery, London)

more power he would expect to take as her husband. This was not the only reason she never married Leicester, nor any of the foreign princes presenting themselves as suitors; but it was one of them.

William Cecil, her confidant from that first day and the kingdom's treasurer, was made Lord Burghley. Her nickname for him was Sir Spirit. Burghley oversaw the queen's finances and distributed royal favors, and for a time his authority made him nearly a second in command. When Elizabeth was absent, he took charge of the Privy Council meetings. In the portraits he commissioned, he quietly gazes through untroubled gray eyes. Everything about him is understated: his ruff modest, the sword at his hip a minor element in the scene. His most powerful weapon was his intellect. Burghley settles for posing in a black coat with a quiet parade of silver buttons down the front. One such painting hangs high on a wall at the Bodleian Library next to the stormy portrait of Martin Frobisher. Lord Burghley rides a donkey in the scene. There he is, the second most powerful person in the kingdom, riding a painterly show of humility.

Elizabeth ushered in a profitable era for Martin Frobisher. He thrived by becoming a pirate. Due to the nature of the work, the record of his doings has many gaps. Except in the proceedings of the Admiralty Court, privateers rarely left a trail of documents. His route can be traced only when authorities cite him for some illegal act, or congratulate him for carrying out a mission of their own devising. The court records themselves can be misleading, since arrests were sometimes mere show for the consumption of diplomats sending reports back home to ministers incensed by the privateers' depredations. Likewise with imprisonments: even in jail, a mariner could have his interests protected by supporters well connected to the Admiralty. In the 1560s, Elizabeth's Privy Council quietly backed privateers who attacked ships belonging to Catholic factions in France. A few years later, the council turned a similarly blind eye on attacks against Spanish vessels, especially ships supplying Spain's army in the Netherlands. In this way, the privateers emerged as a distinctly Protestant force. Privateering became the weapon of choice for Protestant adventurers wanting to break the Spanish stranglehold on profitable commodities such as gold, sugar, and slaves. The privateers helped too in securing the Channel as an *English* waterway.

Frobisher tried every kind of scheme for getting rich. In 1559, witnesses testifying at the Admiralty Court mentioned his name in connection with a plan for capturing the Portuguese fort at Mina, in West Africa. The plotters had apparently hoped to seize not just an occasional ship but the headquarters of the West African trade. Considering his time spent as a prisoner at Mina, Frobisher would have been a good source of information about its defenses. But nothing came of the plan.

In 1563 he participated in a series of raids that captured Spanish and French ships carrying wine. His partners in the venture included his brothers, John and Davey. John Frobisher was the captain and co-owner of a ship, and Davey apparently specialized in disposing of stolen cargoes. The brothers seemed practiced at playing shell games with pillaged goods. While authorities searched for the wine, the brothers moved it from one sympathetic keeper to another. Martin went to prison for some unknown period of time for this crime; the authorities never recovered the wine. In 1565 or '66, after a murkier offense, Martin was imprisoned again.

He married a Yorkshire woman at about this time, Isabel Riggart, the widow of "a very wealthy man," by her account. Her late husband had provided handsomely for her and their grown children. Whatever Isabel's other qualities, her inheritance would have made her an attractive wife. But like Frobisher's brothers and sisters, she is mostly lost except for her name.

English mariners profited from unrest on the Continent. In 1568, French Protestants battling the country's Catholics began relying on English privateers to harass enemy shipping. Queen Elizabeth loaned the French Protestants money, and they freely enlisted English captains, including Martin Frobisher; he captured vessels on their behalf without much troubling himself about the nationality of the ships. The pirated cargoes were then profitably sold in England. In 1569, Dutch Protestants issued him a second foreign commission, allowing him to extend his takings. In this rough violent profession he was a democrat. He interested himself more in cargoes than flags. Wine owned by English merchants tasted no less fine than wine belonging to Spaniards; he took both.

But his brazenness created enemies at home. Merchants in the seaport of Rye asked the Privy Council for protection against his theft of English cargoes. Citing "diverse and sundry piracies," the council ordered his arrest. With the burden of a heavy fine, he went to prison a third time.

His situation was less dire than it seemed, however. Well-placed friends looked after his interests while he remained in custody. A ship of his own passed from new owner to new owner until it was acquired by the wife of the Lord High Admiral, the Lord High Admiral being the person best placed to speak favorably about his abilities to the queen.

Frobisher's imprisonment was part of an elaborate show. Queen Elizabeth, for as long as seemed decent, pretended to be unaware that privateers were bringing pirated cargoes into English ports. The Admiralty meanwhile enjoyed a share of the profits. Knowing the weakness of the navy, Elizabeth depended on the privateers to assert the country's interests at sea. She worried that the privateers might go too far in antagonizing other powers, especially Spain, yet appreciated the damage they inflicted.

Frobisher won his release with his reputation enhanced. Lord Burghley spoke well of him in correspondence with other men. The Privy Council awarded him command of four ships newly outfitted at navy expense and formally thanked him for his "true and faithful service heretofore done"—the service of privateering.

He was assigned the task of leading the new squadron in search of privateers. The Privy Council pretended to see no irony in the orders. No other captain was better qualified to know the privateers' habits. Some of his supporters posted a bond as a guarantee against his seizing friendly vessels. The bond, however, was not so large as to make piracy unprofitable if it were forfeited.

Receiving the commission, seeing the four ships, smelling the ocean rather than a prison cell, Frobisher had reason to feel satisfied. Ten years earlier, he and his brothers were trying to hide stolen cargoes; now the queen's counselors honored him. Before, the authorities pursued him; now he was invested with authority himself. Before, no opportunity could be passed over, even if it was for a foreigner's cause; now he could search for opportunities that served only himself.

The Admiralty sent Frobisher's new squadron to Ireland. Not for the first time, Irish lords were revolting against English rule. In English eyes, Ireland was as uncivilized as West Africa, the Irish as barbarous as animals but dirtier and less endearing. While transporting supplies or perhaps reinforcements, Frobisher took the opportunity to seize several foreign ships. At around this time he most likely came to the attention of Humphrey Gilbert, commander of the English forces there.

Gilbert served as one of the great dashing men at Elizabeth's court. He was brave, vain, horribly ill-tempered, and possessed the same great intellectual curiosity as his young half brother, Walter Raleigh. Before coming to fight the rebels, Gilbert was already looking far beyond Ireland. In an audience with Elizabeth, in 1565, he asked for a royal patent—a license—to search for a northern passage to Cathay.

He presented his case to her in friendly competition with Anthony Jenkinson of the Muscovy Company. Jenkinson had already attempted to reach Cathay by land. From Moscow, he had traveled by horseback, then by boat down the Volga and across the Caspian Sea, then by camel until, after eight months, his party reached Bukhara (in today's Uzbekistan), where unrest in the lands to the east prevented his traveling farther. Seventeen months passed by the time he returned to Moscow. Next, at the company's behest, he tried opening trade with Persia; three more years of travel failed to generate much success. The Muscovy Company thus concluded that any land route to Cathay would be too difficult.

Now, during his audience with the queen, Jenkinson proposed reaching Cathay by sailing northeast, as previously attempted by Hugh Willoughby and Richard Chancellor. Humphrey Gilbert at first had no preference about the route, then proposed sailing north*west*. In marshaling his arguments, he prepared a treatise citing every rumor, from the time of the ancient Greeks forward, favoring the existence of a passage there. He did not claim that the

idea of a northwest passage was original to him, only that the
waterway seemed to be waiting to be found by an Englishman.

In 1497 John Cabot had believed himself near Cathay when he
reached Newfoundland. Sebastian Cabot, his son, claimed he would
have found the northwest passage himself if his crew had not
insisted on turning back. Sailing in the service of France, in 1523,
Giovanni da Verrazzano believed he glimpsed the Pacific after
making landfall at the Outer Banks of North Carolina: from across
the dunes and scrub, the calm open waters of Pamlico Sound displayed all the qualities he expected of the Pacific. On land he
encountered dark-eyed natives who proved "sharp-witted" and
"nimble and great runners," qualities that other travelers had
attributed to the inhabitants of Cathay. But his examination of the
coast from North Carolina to Nova Scotia failed to find a suitable
passage by water.

Every few years cartographers refashioned their maps. The geography, like a distant lover, changed according to expectations and
desires. In 1537 Gemma Frisius, one of John Dee's eminent teachers in Europe, had produced a globe showing most of the Arctic
covered by an imagined arm of Asia. Between that hypothetical
Arctic land and the guessed-at northern edge of North America
lay a narrow channel of water. Sailing west through that channel,
mariners would see Asia on the right, America on the left. In 1564
Abraham Ortelius, another of Dee's scholarly friends, rendered the
passage on his own map as a wide, nearly straight boulevard.
Humphrey Gilbert, borrowing their ideas for a map of his own,
enlarged the boulevard above North America into a broad open
sea, a passage even a novice could navigate.

His treatise listed the benefits of finding the waterway: England
would have its own trade route to Cathay; profitable trade of some
kind could be conducted along the route with the natives of
America; and expeditions could establish a colony or a resupply
station somewhere on the American coast. "We might inhabit
some part of those countries," Gilbert wrote, "and settle there such
needy people of our country, which now trouble the common

wealth." He had never seen America but regarded it as a promising dumping ground for thieves and paupers.

The proposal was the first serious overture to Elizabeth for building a North American colony. Gilbert intended it as a business proposition: he wanted title to one-tenth of whatever territory his expedition found, exemptions from customs duties, and a lifetime appointment as governor of new lands.

In the jockeying at court, his petition was one of many requests for favors. Elizabeth may have had doubts about the cost. Like her father, Henry VIII, she worried about subversion from abroad, the drain of soldiers in Ireland, and the empty treasury. In any case, Gilbert's proposal needed an endorsement from the Muscovy Company; the company's charter guaranteed it a monopoly on northern exploration. But the company had no use for an interloper like Gilbert.

His proposal, neither rejected nor approved, died from inattention.

Frobisher credited himself for the idea of a northwest passage. His supporters told the story for him in later years, none more persuasively than a professional mariner named George Best. Apparently well educated and belonging to the retinue of one of Elizabeth's courtiers, Best himself would sail twice with Frobisher, once with the rank of "gentleman," and the second time as captain of a ship in Frobisher's fleet. Readers could learn the broad outlines of the story from the title of his pamphlet: *A True Discourse of the late voyages of discoverie, for the finding of a passage to Cathaya, by the Northwest, under the conduct of Martin Frobisher Generall.*

Frobisher labored fifteen years organizing the expeditions, said Best. The many years of preparation were Best's invention, or he was repeating what Frobisher wished people to believe. But Frobisher's interest was genuine by 1574. "He began first with himself to devise, and then with his friends to confer, and laid a plain plat unto them," Best said. Frobisher's "plat"—his map—showed that a voyage to Cathay "was not only possible by the north-west but also, as he could prove, easy to be performed." He also possessed "secret intelligence" supporting his theories; Best cautioned that the matter could not be discussed in the pamphlet: these were state secrets. Frobisher wanted to sail northwest for straightforward reasons: "to accomplish or bring true certificate of the truth, or else never to return again, knowing this to be the only thing of the world that was left yet undone, whereby a notable mind might be made famous and fortunate."

So the chance for fame and wealth, the prevailing force among all Elizabeth's mariners, was the wind behind him. Frobisher aspired to be something other than a make-believe admiral piloting a scow hauling dung. He would seek a shortcut to Cathay and to a fortune.

He learned the workings of the court. The competing centers of power—Lord Burghley, who controlled the purse strings, and the Earl of Leicester, who commanded the queen's heart—debated his ideas until they understood the important point. They could support an expedition that, if it indeed found a route to Cathay, could make them vastly richer. On one side of the debate lay the valuable products of Cathay and the Pacific Islands. On the other side was the danger that Frobisher would die at sea or lose a ship stuffed with merchandise. This seemed an acceptable risk: great lords had lost explorers in the past, much as they lost sheep on their estates when the animals drowned crossing rivers in flood. In December 1574, Burghley wrote the Muscovy Company endorsing Frobisher's plan to reach Cathay by sailing northwest.

In the view of the company, however, Frobisher was just another interloper. First Humphrey Gilbert and now this Yorkshireman wanted the Cathay trade for his own benefit. But what had Martin Frobisher ever done for the company? The company directors duly noted Burghley's letter and granted Frobisher an audience. He was invited for a second quizzing, and a committee was appointed to study the matter. Through maneuver and delay, the company tried to protect its own interests. The directors had risked their own money in establishing trade with Russia; allowing an outsider to search for a northern route to Cathay was akin to giving away money. A delegation informed Burghley of the company's decision to reject Frobisher's proposal.

Frobisher despised the merchants and criticized them for being more interested in profits for themselves than in advancing geographic knowledge. He chose to ignore that his motivations were identical to theirs. The Muscovy Company thought only of lucre, he explained through his friend George Best, while the great lords were a source of wisdom. He was counting on support from Burghley and Leicester, as well as from Leicester's brother the Earl of Warwick.

Warwick was another favorite of the queen. He had bravely led an English army under terrible conditions in France, and for that and other loyal service Elizabeth had appointed him to the Privy Council. The northwest project became one of his pets. In the first weeks of 1575 Warwick, along with other members of the Privy Council, sent the Muscovy Company another letter. Organize an expedition for finding a northwest passage, the letter ordered, or grant Frobisher permission to do so.

Permission was duly granted.

One of the Muscovy Company directors who questioned Frobisher more closely was Michael Lok. He was a brother of John Lok, who had captained Frobisher's second voyage to West Africa. Michael Lok had made a considerable fortune in (probably) the cloth trade, and belonged to the small class of businessmen well above the level of shopkeeper. He had interested himself in the New World, collected maps and treatises on navigation, and fancied himself something of an expert on geography. What today is called emerging markets—then Russia, the New World, and Cathay—intrigued him. In the early 1570s, he became London agent for the Muscovy Company. Every shipment arriving from Russia, and all the cargo headed there from England, required his approval.

Lok told associates that he, not the Earl of Warwick, labored during those months as Frobisher's "chief friend." Sensing an opportunity for greater profits, Lok resigned his position at the Muscovy Company in favor of working with Frobisher. That was the story Lok repeated years later, even as others tried to shift responsibility to avoid blame for things that had gone wrong. Eventually Lok fell so far into disgrace, was *pushed* so far down, that his competence is difficult to judge. What he presciently understood was that money could make money. Instead of being hoarded, it could be invested: you had to take risks, as he did in the cloth trade. Later, some investors in Frobisher's adventure resented learning that capital could also evaporate, but the problems that lay ahead were not any one person's fault.

On February 9, 1575, six days after the Muscovy Company granted Frobisher a license, Lok wrote a letter ("I made a writing") inviting adventurers to sign a parchment on which they could indicate the amount they wished to invest. Lok himself, "for the better encouraging of others," pledged one hundred pounds.

The ledgers he maintained are mostly in his own hand, a consistent painterly script in browning ink. Every capital letter is, by modern standards, something of an event, an occasion for swirls and languorous indirection, each line with its own heraldry. The *E* in *Earl* has a spine curved like a crescent moon, festooned with flagpoles and pennants. Each *f,* even in a mundane *of,* is a full inch high with antenna and a flagellate tail. The pounds, shillings, and pence are written in lines as straight as if done by an engraver. Lok's occasional doodles of addition and subtraction reside in the margins. His hand at the beginning is unhurried and august, as fluid as the ink on the nib of his quill, everything writ large, as if to reflect his confidence. When the amounts at risk begin to rise, he switches to a sharper nib to squeeze more money onto each page. A visible disorderliness creeps into the later entries, as if to reflect the doubts crowding the investors' minds. But in 1575 Michael Lok and Martin Frobisher are full, trusting partners.

They conferred almost every day. Lok shared his books and maps with Frobisher, who changed lodgings to be closer to his new mentor. They rehearsed the presentation designed to lure investors. "Herewithall Mr. Frobisher was a glad man," wrote Lok, "and hoped of great good fortune toward him, and told me great matters of venturers that he would procure." In a burst of optimism,

Lok commissioned construction of a ship and hired a master, who would navigate. If a reasonable number of gentlemen would sign the parchment, he expected Frobisher to go to sea that summer.

Frobisher encountered a cool reception when lobbying at court. Courtiers worried about his ways with money and his willfulness. Even if you believed in the existence of a northwest passage to Cathay and trusted Frobisher's ability to find it, you had reason to wonder if he would divert the expedition to privateering. He claimed to be a changed man, but at just this time the clerk of the Privy Council received a new complaint about his piracies.

Worse, plots swirled around him. An Irish earl being held in England tried to recruit him for an escape attempt, until someone betrayed the plan. Then Spain tried to enlist him for its navy or perhaps as a spy; the details were never clear. "He is the best seaman and the bravest in the country," a Spanish agent wrote home. "I have promised him a safe conduct to go and come free from debt and the consequences of past events." There is the hint that Frobisher needed money—if he defects he can be "free from debt." His interest in allying himself with Spain was just a feint, however, part of an underworld of Elizabethan spycraft and double-crosses. Someone at the Privy Council probably knew of the Spanish proposal, and would have known Frobisher's responses.

The "someone" in charge of secrets was Francis Walsingham. His intelligence networks helped make him another center of power on the Privy Council. He advised Elizabeth on foreign affairs, as her principal secretary of state when Lord Burghley became Lord Treasurer. Walsingham's specialty was espionage. He was the master of coded writings and invisible inks; acted as the final interpreter of conversations overheard by a network of informers; served as paymaster for agents on the Continent; and ran couriers who managed to open letters without breaking their wax seals. In his portrait he is all darkness. Elizabeth nicknamed him her "Moor." His agents ruthlessly searched for Catholics secretly practicing the church rites, or who were hostile to the queen. The stool pigeons in the Tower of London were Walsingham's men. So were the interrogators and torturers who strapped prisoners to the rack.

One of his specialties was "projection," the putting into play of conspiracies of his own design against the government, as a way of seeing who would support them. Between them, he and Lord Burghley ran Elizabeth's government.

Lok and Frobisher failed to raise enough money for the voyage during the winter and spring. The expedition would not, after all, be leaving in 1575. Lok cancelled construction of the ship and dismissed the shipwright and master. "And now Mr. Frobisher was become a sad man," Lok said, "for that by this means his credit grew daily in question, and more & more disliking grew of his dealings; yet he continued still about London and the court, hoping and soliciting what he could against the next year."

In 1576, they again tried to raise money. Again, potential investors asked whether Frobisher could be trusted to act responsibly. This time, Lok better understood the problem.

> Mr. Frobisher had very little credit at home and much less to be credited with the ships abroad; this matter was cause of the overthrow of the voyage in the year before, and this matter also now was like to overthrow it this year, and did cause most of the venturers to keep back their money in the end. . . . I did help this matter the best I could, and I stepped in with my credit for his credit, to satisfy all the venturers that he should deal honestly and like a true man with the ships in the voyage.

Lok hired a purser, who would take charge of the moneys and cargo, and drafted two masters to be responsible for navigation. They were especially trustworthy, said Lok, as if to contrast them with the captain. "This did satisfy most of the venturers."

Lord Burghley, after some reflection, invested £50 in the expedition. His name went into the account book. The Earl of Leicester, the queen's favorite, promised another £50, as did his brother the Earl of Warwick, Frobisher's chief supporter on the Privy Council. Francis Walsingham sensed that the expedition could needle Spain, and invested £25. The queen's favorite courtier-poet, Philip Sidney,

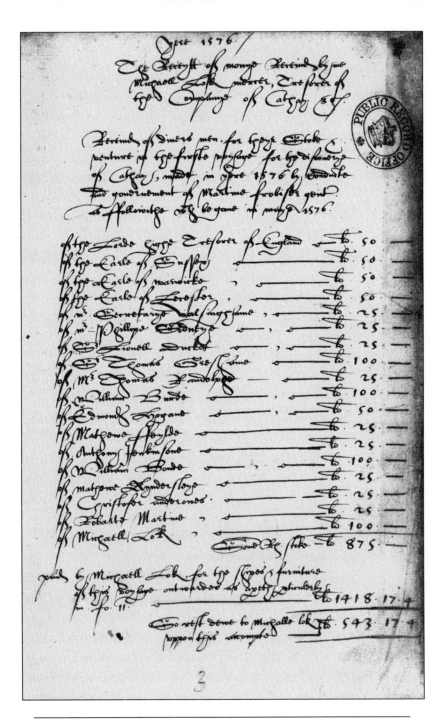

"Yere 1576. The Receytt of monye Receiud by me Michaell Lok mercer, Tresorer of the Companye of Cathay, &c." Lok's list of investors begins with "the Lorde high Tresorer of England" and ends with Lok himself. (Public Record Office E164/35 f.2)

did likewise. A dozen businessmen joined, most of them long-time associates of Lok's. Three of them matched him by investing £100 each.

Those are large sums, though they are hard to translate into precise modern values. There are price indices to consider, wholesale prices versus retail, differences in wages between London and the countryside. Farm laborers in the mid-sixteenth century earned eight or nine pence a day—about £10 a year if they managed to find work, and they paid rent and bought food out of that. Sailors in the navy earned £6 a year. John Dee lived comfortably at Mortlake with a large retinue of servants on an annual stipend of £80 from the court, income that also financed purchases for his library. The sum was enough to allow him to live as a gentleman and clothe himself sufficiently well to be received by Queen Elizabeth. On that £80 a year, he also entertained the queen as a guest at Mortlake. For an approximation of modern value, those sums should be multiplied by a factor of four hundred. So £1 in the 1570s becomes £400 (which is about $680). Michael Lok's £100 investment becomes £40,000.

Including Lok, there were eighteen investors. He collected a total of £875, significantly less than he had planned for. "Whereupon the shipping was diminished," he said. The intended fleet would have consisted of three ships of a hundred tons each. Frobisher would instead have just two ships of about thirty tons each, plus a pinnace—a "little boat."

Two of the ships—the *Gabriel* and the pinnace—were built from scratch. Lok purchased the third, the *Michael,* from fellow investors. The *Gabriel* and the *Michael,* in the shipwright's language, were barks, with fore-, main-, and mizzenmasts and a bowsprit, and probably carried six sails. In architecture the ships were interchangeable with any of a hundred other vessels crowding the Thames: about fifty feet long and perhaps fifteen feet in beam. A sailor of average height could probably stand in the empty hold, but just barely. From bow to stern he would see forecastle, waist, and sterncastle, which accommodated the captain's cabin. He would smell fresh tar on the rigging and the anchor cables.

Sailors caulked the hull and the deck with shredded hemp—oakum—and then sealed them with more tar.

Michael Lok recorded every expense in his ledger, including six shillings for the paper on which he wrote. Five pounds and change bought nine barrels of pitch and tar. Food and drink for the carpenters, "to hasten their work," cost two pounds. The sails, bought from Adrian Prussom, were two pounds five shillings. Lok purchased Russian iron as ballast for the *Gabriel*. Officers needed rapiers; crossbows and pikes went to the other men. A falconet—a weapon about six feet long with an inch-and-a-half muzzle—was the largest artillery piece the *Gabriel* or the *Michael* could carry. The falconets were priced by weight—so many shillings for every hundred pounds of cast iron—and the investors bought five. Hugh Morgan, an apothecary, supplied a medicine chest expensively stocked with thirty-odd drugs. Rhubarb was included for choler of the stomach, camphor to soothe itching. All these records of the purchases were later preserved rather than discarded, as a result of the finger-pointing that ensued. It is why more is known about the outfitting of Frobisher's expeditions than any other sixteenth-century voyage of discovery.

The ledger lists the ingredients for the sailors' meals. A food was suitable for purchase if it could be preserved in barrels for a period of months. Forty bushels of dried peas went into the hold, along with oatmeal, rice, and salt. Eleven live oxen came to the dock and were rendered into 5,300 pounds of beef, preserved by some of the salt. Hogs went into the hold as bacon. The ships took on nearly four tons of biscuits, the staple of every voyage. Sailors would soak biscuits in water to make them soft enough to eat, but after some weeks the bread would soften on its own and give birth to weevils. Barrels of flour, vinegar, and oil as a seasoning were carried aboard, along with five barrels of butter. When butter went rancid it could be used for greasing lines and pulleys. Cheese gone bad could be shaped into buttons for the sailors' coats. There were frying pans and iron pots for the galley, which probably was a small brick hearth in the hold, where any sparks could be caught by the slop of water and urine. The crew loaded eight tons of beer and hoped the casks were tightly hooped. As a luxury Lok also bought five tons of wine plus a quantity of aquavit—enough strong drink to reward everyone several times over for reaching Cathay.

For navigational advice, the learned John Dee offered tutorials for Frobisher and the pilots. Lok was "a virtuous Gentleman and Merchant," said Dee. Lok expressed no less pleasure at meeting that "learned man" Dr. Dee, for whom he had "a great good opinion." Their mutual regard, however, did not prevent a disagreement. Dee said the investors had sought his help. Michael Lok, however, said Dee had invited himself. Their dispute was part of a squabble for credit.

It must have been a fine season to be a wise man. Dee had recently written a much admired essay describing the usefulness of applied mathematics. The "Mathematicall Praeface," as he called it, displayed the range of his mathematical interests: heliosophie (a presumed science of spiral lines), horometrie (his study of clocks), hypogeiode (the science of digging tunnels straight), pneumatithmie (in which he described the workings, more or less, of a submarine or a diving bell), architecture, music, and navigation. He argued for mathematics' usefulness whether one were a scholar or a carpenter, saying that arithmetic and geometry were eminently practical tools for solving problems, that they were intellectually pleasing yet accessible. Mathematics could aid craftsmen as well as wizards. If properly educated in arithmetic and geometry, English mariners would be second to none in exploring the oceans, said Dee.

Dee visited Michael Lok's house, and Martin Frobisher joined the sessions. Teacher and students together examined maps, agreed on conjectures about the existence of a northwest passage, and then considered them certainties. The passage was there for everyone to see on the map of the world already published by Gerhard Mercator: his map showed a northwest passage—the Strait of Anian, he called it—between the northern edge of America and a long arm of Asia. Everyone at the tutorials believed in its reality as strongly as if it were a rendering of the Thames.

Then Dee moved the sessions to the headquarters of the Muscovy Company. Muscovy House, as the building was known, stood on Seething Lane, just north of the Tower. Walking on Seething Lane, Dee and Frobisher would have passed the diminutive St. Olave's Church, whose parishioners included a woman recorded in the burial registry as Mother Goose. London was a city of one hundred thousand people, just beginning to expand beyond the municipal walls built by the Romans. You could look south on Seething Lane and see the Thames, just beyond the Tower.

The books Frobisher was supposed to read include rather dry treatises on cosmography, tides, and the magnetic variation of the compass. More entertaining was a chronicle by the Frenchman André Thevet, who had reached Brazil in 1555. Thevet claimed to have traveled far enough north to see natives using snowshoes. He favorably compared maple syrup to good red wine. In each successive edition of his chronicle, his purported adventures extended farther north.

For a description of Cathay, Frobisher had *The Travels of Sir John Mandeville*. Its eponymous author was said to be a fourteenth-century English knight who had made a pilgrimage to the Holy Land and visited lands farther east. His descriptions of improbably exotic places had made the book a best-seller. In Mandeville's account, the gold and jewels possessed by the Great Khan of Cathay far outstripped the wealth of the royal courts in Europe. The Great Khan walked on silver floors and dined at a table made of jewels set in gold. Mandeville's Cathay was "a great country, beautiful, rich, fertile, full of good merchandise."

Gold was no less plentiful in the nearby land called Lamory, he reported. Everyone went naked there and women freely gave themselves to men—an Englishman's paradise. But the adults ate children: an Englishman would not be allowed pleasure without some terrible sin. Other territories, he reported, were inhabited by people with heads like dogs, people with eight-toed feet who walked on their knees, and giant Cyclopes who ate uncooked meat and raw fish.

The lessons on Seething Lane went quite well, Dee reported. He took pleasure in his erudition, and may have worn his black gown during the lectures at Muscovy House. Frobisher was more comfortable with a dagger than with books. But each man could see in the other the same hunger for fame, and each regarded himself the greater cosmographer, one by books and one by sea. Lessons not yet done, Dee followed Frobisher and the chief pilot onto the *Gabriel*. His students enjoyed every lecture and found their devoted teacher wonderfully skilled—at least, according to Dee. Their chief regret, he said, was their having met him too late for a fuller course of instruction.

By the beginning of June, Frobisher was living aboard the *Gabriel*. His little fleet was docked at Ratcliff, from where poor Hugh Willoughby had sailed into the Russian winter. Ratcliff was the last tying-up point before the Thames turned south toward Deptford, home of the royal shipyards. East of Deptford was Greenwich and Queen Elizabeth's favorite palace. As the weather turned warmer, the smell in Ratcliff grew stronger—from the London dung carts unloading their cargo, the dead animals floating in the shallows, and the dumped ballast. At low tide, said Dee, the banks of the Thames were "deep to the knees" in sewage. "Very stinking."

Muscovy House disappeared long ago. Seething Lane is now the address for Nieman's Pharmacy, Longman's Florist, and several insurance companies. The Prudential Assurance Company Ltd. has headquarters called Walsingham House, at the address where Francis Walsingham resided. There is a pub, a post office, a photo kiosk, and St. Olave's Church. Seething Lane intersects with a bland one-block street housing the regional headquarters of the Allied Bank of Pakistan. This is Muscovy Street. Products from islands near Cathay are parked along the curb—scooters by Honda, motorcycles by Kawasaki.

London's real estate boom has swallowed Ratcliff. Wharves have been succeeded by high-rise apartment buildings advertising a view of the Thames. The name *Ratcliff* survives, but just barely. Ratcliff, Frobisher's dock, a long time ago became a chandler's warehouse, and the warehouse has been handsomely transformed into apartments. Ratcliff is a single brick building with six apartments commanding just enough of aptly named Narrow Street to accommodate four cars parked nose to tail. The view takes in the pigeon-gray shore, the Thames's brown water, and dung-colored apartments on the opposite bank. A sign posted on the nearest jetty says, NO SHIPS OVER 200 TONS—about seven times larger than the *Gabriel*.

In 1576, the *Gabriel*, the *Michael*, and the pinnace prepared to sail to the northwest.

CHAPTER TWO

"A Land of Ice"

They left with the tide from Ratcliff on June 7, 1576, a Thursday. But did any expedition suffer less auspicious beginnings? That first day, the pinnace collided with another ship in the Thames and lost her bowsprit. Mariners were prey to omens—a rooster crowing at noon in port, black cats, a rose-colored moon the night before a ship sailed—and the collision did not bode well. Having sailed all of three miles, the ships anchored at Deptford for repairs.

Martin Frobisher chose the *Gabriel,* navigated by Christopher Hall, as his flagship. As pilot—"master," in the language of the day—Hall had responsibility for the charts and instruments. The investors were hoping he would also serve as a brake against the captain's impetuousness. Hall would sail on all of Frobisher's voyages across the North Atlantic and demonstrate remarkable skill as a navigator. On this first voyage he kept a log that doubled as a journal, in which he wrote in a calm, steadying voice. He recorded compass readings, water depths, and changes in the wind without much hint of emotion. He confined himself to facts. His word can be trusted. For lack of even one word of self-description in the log, his appearance, unfortunately, remains a mystery. He is a gossamer figure but the best navigator aboard.

On Friday, June 8, the three ships left Deptford. At Greenwich, coming into sight of the royal palace, they fired their guns and "made the best show we could," Hall said. Elizabeth waved from a window, and a palace secretary was rowed out to the *Gabriel* to convey her good wishes.

The ships reached the mouth of the Thames on June 12. They turned north. Frobisher and Hall planned to sail north along England's east coast and the coast of Scotland until they cleared land, then turn west. They intended to bear west across the Atlantic at latitude 60 or 61 degrees north, until the ships encountered land and a passage leading through it, all the way west to Cathay. Their plan was that simple: go north, then steady-as-she-goes west, with frequent checks of latitude.

Including the purser, surgeon, trumpeter, cook, and Frobisher and Hall, the *Gabriel* carried probably eighteen men. Seventeen were aboard the *Michael,* under Owen Gryffen as the ship's pilot. Their wages were more than double the standard navy pay. Some of the mariners had lobbied for a place. "Worshipful Sir," James Alday had written Michael Lok, the treasurer of the enterprise,

> having lately been acquainted with your intent to prosecute the old intermitted discovery for Cathay, if therein with my knowledge, travel or industry I may do you service, I am ready to do it, and therein to adventure my life to the uttermost point.

Alday was hired. Four men sailed in the pinnace. But after their collision during the first day, they may have already thought themselves unlucky.

By the time the ships cleared England, gales had forced them into port five times. By the time they cleared Scotland, the *Michael* had developed a worrisome leak. Two and a half weeks after leaving Ratcliff, Christopher Hall steered the fleet into calm waters at the southern edge of the Shetland Islands, where the crew made repairs. The Shetlands were the last certain landfall before the ships turned west, so the sailors also refilled the water barrels. As determined by Hall, squinting down the length of a cross-staff aimed at the sun, the ships were at 59° 46' north latitude. Pilots took readings with the cross-staff every day as near as possible to noon, at the risk of eventually blinding themselves from staring into the sun. Since the vessel was in motion, the deck rolling and pitching, a pilot would make more than one measurement, in order to bracket the precise hour of noon or to make up for the passage of a cloud or for his arm's unsteadiness. Frobisher wanted to reach as near as possible to 60 degrees north before turning west.

Before leaving the Shetlands, Frobisher and Christopher Hall wrote a letter to the learned John Dee, their tutor in advanced navigation. In the letter, which a fishing boat delivered to England, the officers wrote that they thought of him whenever they tried to apply his lessons. If the teachings made more sense in the classroom on Seething Lane in London than at sea—well, the officers' lack of scholarship accounted for the problems. The captain and pilot were merely "poor disciples"—that was the generous message they sent. The wording must have been Hall's, since Frobisher was not one for politesse, though Frobisher must have agreed to the contents. The message hints that the lessons with Dee had proved nearly worthless. Two and a half weeks at sea were more instructive than a lifetime in a classroom, or in Dee's library at Mortlake. Mariners had to struggle to read the ship's compass at night, were never certain of their longitude, and could make only a rough guess at the distance traveled in a day. At 59° 46' north, Frobisher signed the letter as "Your loving friend to use and command."

The ships entered a storm after making their turn west. They reduced sails. ("The first of July, from 4 to 8 a clock . . . we had so much wind that we spooned 'fore the sea," Hall wrote.) Then the North Atlantic gale took full charge, and masts were stripped naked. Sailors found it safer vomiting into the hold than over the side, where the risk of being swept overboard was great. Their only gauge for the situation was their experience of other storms.

Mariners spent every voyage waiting for some great test, while dreading that it would actually occur.

The storm blew for a week. During the last night, the *Gabriel* and the *Michael* lost sight of the pinnace. A wave may have swamped it or flipped it end over end, or perhaps the sailors were unable to bail water fast enough. Or the rudder post broke. In a seven-ton pinnace in an Atlantic storm, any of those situations would produce the same result. The *Gabriel* and the *Michael* never found the sailors or even a stick of wood. The pinnace simply disappeared. Everyone aboard the barks would have thanked God in their prayers for not having been aboard that toy ship.

On July 11, five weeks out from Ratcliff, the *Gabriel* sighted land bordered by ice. Frobisher was seeing, for the first time, the southern cape of Greenland. He steered the ship's boat toward shore until icebergs blocked the way forward, the coast itself being "like pinnacles of steeples, and all covered with snow." The ice formations dwarfed the waterspouts he remembered from the Gulf of Guinea. Some of the bergs disappeared into clouds like icy columns reaching to heaven; birds suddenly emerged from the fog, then disappeared again.

A combination of high wind and offshore rocks make the fjords of southern Greenland a dreadful place for ships. The latest edition of *Sailing Directions,* published by the U.S. Defense Mapping Agency, describes the dangers for vessels in the waters the *Gabriel* had just entered:

"Notorious for foul weather and heavy seas . . ."

"Winds from the southeast very strong gale strength . . ."

"Dangerous rocks up to four leagues . . ."

"Only ice-strengthened vessels may enter the port from January to early August . . ."

"Very strong mountain squalls."

Modern navigation guides presume that any vessel coasting Greenland has a steel hull. Its propellers should be steel or manganese-bronze, which best resist pounding from the ice. It is assumed the vessel carries a spare rudder assembly; that all the bulkheads have passed pressure tests for leaks; that the freshwater tanks have heating coils, to prevent the tanks from freezing and bursting. The Canadian Department of Fisheries and Oceans, in its edition of *Sailing Directions,* publishes a checklist of basic safety equipment for ships in the north: telephone poles (for use as fenders against ice floes), large hardwood mallets (as de-icing equipment), and wedges, clamps, jacks, sand, and quick-setting cement (to plug leaks). For cutting trenches in the ice when mooring the ship, the crew is advised to use chain saws. Of that equipment, none was aboard the *Gabriel,* and, in fact, little of it existed in 1576.

Taking a reading after seeing land, Christopher Hall recorded the ship's latitude as 61 degrees north. The charts prepared for him, however, placed Greenland elsewhere. The best maps from that era, including those prepared by Gerhard Mercator, wrongly located it farther north and far to the west. In its place, the maps imagined an island called Frisland.

Frisland was brought into existence, so to speak, by the Zeno brothers of Venice. In 1558 a member of the family published a book whose title summarized their presumed exploits: *The Discovery of the Isles of Frisland, Estland, Engroenland, Estotiland, and Icaria: Made by Two Brothers of the Zeno Family, Nicolo the Chevalier, and Antonio.* In 1380, the book recounted, Nicolo Zeno of Venice was sailing toward England when a storm blew his ship far off course, finally casting him and all the crew onto the shores of Frisland. A nobleman there took Nicolo Zeno under his wing, and together they conquered other lands to the west. Nicolo sent a letter to his brother, Antonio, in Venice, inviting him to the island. Reaching Frisland after a perilous journey of his own, Antonio used the island as his base for exploring even more distant territories. He told of cannibals and great conquests in letters to still another brother back home. The correspondence became the basis of the book, written by one of the brothers' descendants. The author said that he remembered the letters from when he was a child. But now they couldn't be found. His book included a remarkably detailed map showing Frisland with a crenellated shore in the North Atlantic. On the Zeno map, Frisland boasted seven towns and lay between imaginary Icaria and imaginary Estland.

As determined much later, not all of the Zeno brothers' story was fantasy. Their Frisland and some of the lesser territories matched the geography of the Faroe Islands, between the Shetlands and Iceland. By the time of the brothers' travels, the Faroes served as a regular port of call for ships from the Continent. Nicolo and Antonio were, after all, able to send letters from "Frisland" to Venice. Some of the brothers' military exploits can plausibly be placed in the Shetlands. One of the brothers may also have traveled as far west as Iceland. Their Frisland was a real, civilized land misplaced on a convincingly drawn map.

So Frisland appeared on a vellum sailing chart prepared for Frobisher and Hall before they left England. The land they supposed to be Frisland, covered by ice, lay within sight of everyone aboard the *Gabriel.* Hall had equipped himself with twenty compasses for the voyage, as well as a metal sphere on which one could plot alternative courses. He had a little solar system of metal rings, known as an armillary sphere, for plotting constellations, and a calibrated dial with which he could estimate the time of day from the position of the sun—when the sun emerged from the fog. For charting coastlines, he had the sixteenth-century ancestor of the theodolite. It was a flat stand of some kind fitted with an eyepiece for measuring angles and elevations. All his instruments, as well as the vellum chart, indicated that the *Gabriel* was coasting Frisland and that Greenland lay elsewhere.

Then the *Gabriel* lost contact with the *Michael.* It is not clear exactly when each pilot realized the other ship had disappeared for good, rather just sailed into a fog bank. But it happened somewhere near Greenland, and the *Michael* reversed course. Other than fright from the ice, the officers aboard the *Michael* had suffered no particular problem. But they preferred to return home rather than navigate the maze of floes. When the ship reached London, in September, the officers claimed that after losing contact with the *Gabriel* they had sailed west for another four days and only then turned back because of "monstrous high islands of ice."

The *Michael,* they said, had fulfilled its mission by determining the northwest route to Cathay to be impassable. They reported the *Gabriel* lost with all hands.

On its own, the *Gabriel* threaded through the ice and reached open water. What is striking is Frobisher's decision to continue sailing west, in the face of every reason to sail home. The pinnace had vanished in a storm, and he could assume the *Michael* was a victim of the ice—its hull ripped open by a berg, the crew long since dead. Yet he maintained course.

A few days after the *Michael's* disappearance, another storm slammed into the *Gabriel.* The wind churned the waves into dark high walls. It toyed with the ship by turning her sideways in a deep trough, leaving her on her beam-ends. The breaking waves poured over the waist. In the wind, sailors would have had trouble hearing their own shouts. Spars broke, barrels careened in the hold. As water poured in, merchandise intended for trade with the Great Khan floated away—pocketknives, cowbells, brass buttons, mirrors, straw hats. No one wanted to die rescuing a straw hat.

The *Gabriel* stayed broadside to the waves. Even the most hardened sailor might foul his clothes, shout a prayer, beg God to save him. One, two more waves sweeping the deck, and she would be on her side. She would founder hull up.

Frobisher himself grabbed the foresail and held on until the wind tore it away, along with the spar. Somehow he kept his footing. Crawling aft, he cut down the mizzenmast with an axe to reduce the storm's pressure on the ship—in those conditions, the less canvas, the better. He took charge, and imperiousness was his best quality. On the next wave the *Gabriel* began to right herself. As she rolled, water poured out of the hold and carried away more of the cargo, like coins dropped into a deep well. Everyone had already prepared to die, but everyone was alive. Frobisher had to stop the sailors from cutting down the mainmast; if they survived the storm, they would still need at least that for sailing home. When the wind finally dropped, they were no less alone yet were still afloat. It was July 13, and the captain had saved them.

Hall resumed his laconic reports: elevation of the sun, compass variation, wind. On July 21 ("the 21. day") he noted a course change for avoiding an especially large floe.

"The 26. we had sight of a land of ice: the latitude was 62. degrees, and two minutes."

Christopher Hall wrote just the one phrase the first day: "a land of ice." Not an ice floe but land. He refused to say more than he knew.

We never venture off a map in our own travels, and so never experience the wonder and terror of seeing territory for which the maps lack even a shape. We can, with effort, visit peoples who know nothing of our own territory, and can reach settlements whose inhabitants have never seen anyone of a different race. But we arrive with a sense of *their* place. Their clearing in the forest always fits onto a map showing what lies beyond the next bend in the trail. In 1576, Frobisher and Hall consulted charts that combined the guessed at with the hoped for. At best, the Englishmen knew their direction of travel, but almost never the extent of the lands they saw. When the weather allowed, Hall could stare down the length of his cross-staff into the sun to estimate how far the *Gabriel* had strayed from 60 degrees north, but some of the readings were off by a full degree. He roughly sketched a coastline, and either he or Frobisher marked the magnetic variation of the compass by drawing short arrows on the vellum sailing chart. But everything in sight was wholly new.

The *Gabriel* had entered another maze of bergs and floes. Hall was navigating the Davis Strait, between Greenland and Baffin Island. In that seascape of white forms, you can mistake a floe that is larger than a castle for something small, until you notice, having sailed toward it for half an hour, that it occupies the same place on the horizon. Floes take the shape of pianofortes and giant birds of prey, are bluish-white cubes larger than a queen's palace, and stand higher than the masts. The northern air—lambent, sharp-edged— is a distorting lens. You can see all-white mountain ranges that don't exist, like shimmering lakes glimpsed in a desert. Sailors today, even with sonar and a stream of satellite weather reports, exercise extreme caution in these waters.

On July 28, after morning fog burned off, Hall sighted land again. A wide skirt of ice prevented the ship's boat from reaching the shore, and the sailors played out a hundred fathoms of line—six hundred feet—without finding sea bottom. On the 30th, the *Gabriel* came within a mile of this land, but ice stopped the ship's boat again. On the 31st, at 4:00 A.M., Frobisher saw the land clearly enough to bestow a name on it: Queen Elizabeth's Foreland. Modern maps call it Resolution Island but Frobisher did not yet know it was indeed an island. Resolution Island was steep, barren rock that even without the problem of the ice, lacked an easy anchorage. It had thirty-three-foot tides and little maneuvering room for ships.

On August 1, the seas became calm enough for Hall to take soundings near an iceberg. "Sixteen fathoms," he recorded, "and little stones." Pilots "sounded" with a measured line weighted by a hollowed-out slug of lead filled with tallow, which, hauled up, brought back a sample of the sea bottom. An experienced pilot could learn the bottoms of a given coastline well enough to navigate a ship in dense fog; he would know his place on a coast by what the tallow brought up. On August 2, the iceberg toppled like a falling steeple, "making a great noise as if a great cliff had fallen." It could have swamped the ship's boat, yet Hall took more soundings near a scattering of islands: "Had ground at a hundred fathom, and fair sand . . . had 90 fathom, and small black stones, and little white stones, like pearls."

For ten days, the *Gabriel* tacked along the edge of the ice pack. Frobisher and Hall continued to try to reach shore, anywhere. Frobisher could see Resolution Island in the mostly frozen sea and, to the north, a second arm of land. A passage tending northwest lay in clear sight between them. Cathay, the officer believed, would be at the far end of the passage. On August 10, the wind shifted and, like a broom, swept away most of the ice from the entrance to the waterway. Hall and four sailors took this opportunity to row the skiff to one of the islands.

The Englishmen had a hard cold pull in a fast-running current. They heard the plash of their oars, then felt the heave, the waves outracing the boat. Hall had to assume this might be his only chance to reach land before winds brought back the ice. Frobisher himself had had no success, and this time he apparently remained aboard the *Gabriel*. The landscape was gray, white, and damp. Hall was the first to step onto the island, an outcropping of mostly rock a few hundred feet wide and about a mile long. After nine weeks at sea, everyone would have swayed walking the first few feet, as if still aboard ship and, after days of seeing just white, taken pleasure from the greenness of moss and patches of grass. Though it goes unmentioned in Christopher Hall's log, he named the land Hall's Island.

The sailors randomly picked up a few objects as proof of having indeed reached land. Most of their tokens were just grass with balls of dirt still clinging to the roots, as if that might impress the investors in London. Robert Garrard, one of the sailors, found a stone as black as coal and the size of a half-penny loaf of bread—maybe the size of a large brick. The tide already rising, Hall and his men then rowed back to the *Gabriel* with their finds. Everyone assumed Garrard's rock was indeed coal, and the cook as it happened needed fuel for the galley. So here was fuel. But the rock was the only token of the island that wasn't going to wilt or be just dirt. Perhaps the sailors simply liked its heft; maybe its blackness was appealing. For whatever reason, Martin Frobisher kept the stone.

On August 11, the *Gabriel* sailed into the newfound passage: "The 11. we found our latitude to be 63. degr. and eight minutes," Hall wrote, "and this day we entered the strait." He had miscalculated the latitude, could only guess the longitude, and rendered the event with no more drama than if the ship were venturing into the Thames. But here was a new waterway, and it lacked a name. Philip II of Spain had named the Strait of Magellan, at the bottom of the New World, after the European who first saw it. Frobisher considered himself Magellan's peer and christened the waterway Frobisher Strait.

Did Frobisher already consider the venture a success? He surely felt elated seeing the waterway. His anxiety focused probably on the danger that the ice would close behind the ship, trapping it. He knew little of ice and nothing of the new land; every mile sailed west would be riskier, the chance of returning home smaller.

On August 12, the Englishmen sailed thirty miles west in the waterway to a dagger-shaped island, which Frobisher named Gabriel Island. On the 13th they traveled thirty miles more, and a day later the *Gabriel* anchored in a sound where the sailors refilled the water barrels. The men also recaulked the ship. On the 16th ("very fair and calm"), ice formed around the ship. When ice attaches itself to a wooden hull, it pulls out the oakum and reopens every seam. So the sailors either resigned themselves to constant leaks or resumed caulking.

A captain in familiar waters could see a coastline in his mind's eye. He would depend for navigation on a store of familiar scents and colors and on his rutter. The rutter was the dog-eared book containing his notes about sailing times between ports, compass readings one should expect, and his own sketches of headlands. It served as his autobiography as a sailor on a given route. His soundings were recorded there, reminding him of the water depths and the nature of the sea bottom. Sand of this color, pebbles of that size. But Frobisher and Hall had none of that in Frobisher Strait.

They climbed the hills for a better view of what lay ahead. What seemed to be great continents lay on each side of the waterway. Frobisher presumed America was the vertiginous, snow-covered southern shore, as his maps forecast. So the northern shore must be Asia.

These first English visitors utter barely a word about the landscape. Most of the icebergs swept in from the Davis Strait melt into bergy bits by August; a bergy bit might still dwarf a thirty-ton ship. Bergy bits become growlers—slabs rising no more than a meter above the water. A growler melts into slush. The modern, scientific vocabulary for Arctic ice takes into account the ice's size, density, age, and salinity. Frazil ice consists of fine, flexible plates suspended in the water. When temperatures drop, frazil ice becomes the soupy layer called grease ice; the temperature still dropping, grease ice becomes ice rind, thin sheets that bend with waves. Ice rind, in still colder conditions, evolves into pancake ice.

The colors are especially beautiful in summer, for dusk never turns to darkness. The light show begins every evening at about ten o'clock, when the sky turns fluorescent green, then silky pink. Some of the ice turns green, like a pale lime sherbet, due to thriving colonies of diatoms. You can find in the menagerie of ice shapes the Winged Victory of Samothrace, the Colossi of Memnon in Luxor, and a perfect fifty-foot-high scallop shell. The islands in the waterway retain just a frosting of ice at their edges, each island looking as if it were assembled from small gray fragments, so many are the fissures in the rock. The floes float on dark water as if on a moving canvas. Because of the summer light, the hour never seems late.

But one strains to hear even one word from Martin Frobisher and Christopher Hall about *northernness*. Did they notice the burst of summer flowers on the islands? The scattering of bones left by polar bears? At first Elizabethan explorers paid little attention to a new landscape except when it seemed threatening. They took little interest in aesthetics. Frobisher wanted only to pass through. In 1576 he neither planted a flag nor read a proclamation claiming the territory for Queen Elizabeth. Like the investors back in England, he wanted commerce, not territory.

On August 19, in company with some of the sailors, Frobisher and Hall rowed the skiff to another island. They observed a school of porpoises, or perhaps seals, swimming in the water. The dark compact shapes, now approaching them, slowly took on the form of men in small boats. Frobisher's men quickly rowed back to the safety of the *Gabriel*. Hall then steered the skiff toward the strangers. Englishmen in a skiff and Inuit paddling kayaks thereby discovered one another.

Christopher Columbus in 1492 had rowed ashore in the West Indies to a welcoming party of natives as naked as the grasses. He gave them red caps and glass beads. "By the signs they made," Columbus wrote after this first encounter, "I think they were asking if we came from Heaven." The Tainos, as they were known, seemed as guileless as newborns. "Of anything they have, if you ask them for it, they never say no; rather they invite the person to share it, and show as much love as if they were giving their hearts; and whether the thing be of value or of small price, at once they are content with whatever little of whatever kind may be given to them." Columbus forcibly took several Tainos to Spain; a Spanish garrison he left behind meanwhile pillaged their settlements. When Columbus returned, the Tainos destroyed their own crops rather than feed the Europeans. The Spanish garrison had already died. That became the pattern for European encounters with new peoples: an idealized first impression, succeeded by a feeling of betrayal, and then violence. To justify their brutality, explorers wrote about their adventures as dangerous encounters with ravenous cannibals and insatiably lustful women, the chronicles doubling as sermons about the threat of godlessness. Amerigo Vespucci, the Florentine who explored parts of South America, wrote at curiously great length about the natives' lust and bodily functions. A Spanish official, after more than thirty years in the New World, insisted that the natives' heads were in fact not heads at all but thick helmets. The stories rendered natives as monsters in human form, and their reported depravity was cited to justify all the Europeans' cruelties. In the Caribbean, Spanish soldiers took bets as to whether a single thrust of a pike could decapitate a native. It sometimes couldn't. Would-be colonists from France sliced off natives' arms and legs, André Thevet reported, "to see if their swords were cutting well."

The natives paddling kayaks came ashore wearing sealskins. Christopher Hall rowed the skiff closer. He gave each man and woman a button hook, the instrument a properly dressed Englishman used for lacing his clothes. Through sign language, he agreed to allow one of the Inuit to visit the *Gabriel*. The native who clambered aboard did not much like the wine and meat Martin Frobisher offered him but seemed pleased by buttons and other trifles. What he made of the ship itself went unrecorded. But all seemed to go well. "Whereupon all the rest came aboard with their boats, being nineteen persons," Hall wrote, "and they spoke, but we understood them not."

The Inuit carried with them fish and meat, which, to the horror of the sailors, they proceeded to eat raw. Every sailor knew the stories of cannibals, so nothing could disturb Frobisher's men more than this—a people enjoying uncooked flesh. No one knew where such an appetite might lead. But looking at these people, Frobisher felt more certain that the waterway he called Frobisher Strait indeed led to Cathay. The natives had the broad faces and straight black hair of people said to be from the East. Their complexions were dark, their noses flat.

Hall studied their kayaks closely enough to see that they were made of sealskins stitched with sinew, stretched over a frame of bone. Meanwhile, the Inuit climbed the rigging as if they had practiced for this encounter. Scaling the masts, they studied their new, privileged view of the landscape. The meeting aboard the *Gabriel* was when each people could examine a different civilization, the moment when the world was reshaped for both Inuit and Englishmen.

They enjoyed each other's company. By the end of that first day, the Inuit had traded some sealskin clothes for cowbells and mirrors. The Inuit readily accepted the presence of visitors who, from the natives' point of view, had arrived on a strange, floating platform made of wood, its sails like animal skins from some monstrous, unknown creature. In the treeless landscape, wood was a great rarity, and metal was even rarer, so the Inuit prized the cowbells. But the ship's presence and the sudden material wealth caused no evident consternation; the Inuit exploring the *Gabriel* did not behave as if a god had arrived.

Long ago, Inuit had encountered other strangers. The Norse, by the 1200s, had probably engaged in trading metal for walrus tusks collected by Inuit, ivory the Norse then traded for grain from Europe. The archaeological record of Inuit-Norse contacts would barely fill a sailor's sea chest—it consists of a few iron knife blades, bits of woolen cloth, pieces of chain-mail armor—and hints at infrequent meetings at scattered sites. For Inuit, a wooden ship was akin to a rare species of migratory animal, arriving only in summer and wintering in some unknown place.

On August 20, a day after meeting the natives, Frobisher and Hall explored more of the land. They examined an Inuit camp, where the houses had stone walls, probably roofed with skins and moss, but which seemed coarser than the lowliest Yorkshire cottage. The camp included a lively population of dogs, and tents made of skins. Hall noticed several Inuit watching them, but he thought little of it.

Frobisher offered a different account of the excursion, one true to his own nature. It was a story of suspiciousness, betrayal, and bad temper. He spied several Inuit hiding behind a boulder and feared the worst of them. Hall kept everyone calm by negotiating an agreement by which one of the natives could come aboard the Englishmen's skiff in return for Hall himself remaining on land. He always showed greater interest in the Inuit than did Frobisher, and tried to learn their language. He touched or pointed to parts of his body and listened to what the Inuit said. One can follow the vocabulary lesson through his list of words transliterated from Inuktitut as it proceeds head to toe. "Hair," the natives said in their language. "Eye." He wrote seventeen of their words in the log, translating *eye*, *ear*, *tooth*, *thumb*, and so on, down to *boots*.

As agreed, one of the natives climbed into the skiff while Hall stayed on shore. Frobisher feared that the Inuit were secretly preparing to attack. Believing danger was in the air, he drew a knife against the native in the boat. But no attack occurred. Hall rejoined the skiff, and the sailors let the native go. Frobisher was then confident enough to invite another of the natives to revisit the *Gabriel*. The man who came aboard agreed to guide the ship the rest of the way through the strait into the sea leading to Cathay, or so Frobisher believed. The native would lead with his kayak, and the *Gabriel* would follow. Through sign language Frobisher came to believe that the trip would require two days' paddling; he energetically discussed the details and believed the native understood him. As advance payment for the man's services, the crew gave him a bell and a knife. But the agreement existed only in Frobisher's mind. Inuit knew nothing of an open sea at the western end of the waterway the Englishmen called Frobisher Strait: that sea did not exist.

Five sailors took the new guide into the skiff to bring him

ashore. Robert Garrard, who had found the heavy black stone on Hall's Island, is the only one of the five known by name. Frobisher instructed them to stay in sight of the *Gabriel,* to release the man at a well-defined point of land, and then immediately to return.

The Englishmen in the skiff may have been chafing to conduct trade of their own, since there were furs to be had for a trinket, not to mention the temptation of Inuit women. Sailors on long voyages always looked forward to some private trading, and this would be their first opportunity. Whatever their motivation, the five sailors ignored Frobisher's orders. Robert Garrard and his companions kept rowing after delivering the native to the appointed place. Maybe their new guide waved them on, or maybe they simply wanted to be on their own. Three of them went ashore, and Frobisher could see the two who stayed in the skiff, but they either didn't hear his shouts or chose to ignore them. They rowed out of sight. None of the five returned.

Frobisher's first encounter with the Inuit had occurred on August 19, a Sunday—a lifetime ago. The five sailors went missing on the 20th. Now it was the 21st. Including Frobisher and Hall, thirteen men remained aboard the *Gabriel.* They fired one of the falconets and the trumpeter sounded his horn, but the five missing sailors made no response. On the morning of the 22nd, a foot of snow covered the deck. For lack of the skiff, no one could go ashore unless he chose to swim. Then the crew saw Inuit paddling toward the *Gabriel* in at least a dozen kayaks. Frobisher moved a falconet into the waist and, to prevent anyone from boarding, ordered the men to cover the gunwales with sailcloth. He was back in his element—ready to fire at an enemy.

The Inuit, as if they understood the threat, stopped their kayaks.

Frobisher stepped away from the gun to try to tempt them closer. The native who had been the first to accept Hall's invitation to board the *Gabriel* and sample English food was the one person who paddled forward. Frobisher tossed a shirt into the water, but the kayaker let the current carry it to him. They seemed evenly matched in tactics, each man seeking to be the hunter, not the prey. Frobisher held out a bell, and the man came closer but not too close. Frobisher dropped it into the water and let it sink. Then he displayed a larger bell. When the man tried to grab it, Frobisher seized that outstretched hand, gripped the man's wrist, and had enough leverage—standing above him—to lift the native even though he remained in the kayak, and swing him and the kayak onto the deck. Frobisher's gentlemen friends told the story later in London, a story presumably heard from the captain himself: here was an Englishman strong enough literally to pick up an enemy right out of the water, like so much dross.

It doesn't quite ring true. Lean forward, bend down toward water several feet below, and lift an unwilling adult plus his kayak. It was possible, but could Frobisher alone have swung the man onto the ship? Could the captain have kept his footing on the deck? Some of the sailors must have extended a boat hook, or rushed to help when the man was nearly aboard. There would have been shouts from the crew and from Inuit watching from the water. In sign language and probably more shouts, Frobisher promised to free his new captive in exchange for the five missing sailors—Frobisher assumed the Inuit had kidnapped them no less than he had kidnapped the native. The Englishmen never learned the man's name: he was "this strange man" or "a man of the country." In the shouting and commotion and fright, the native bit through his tongue. His countrymen paddled away making a sound like the howling of wolves.

The only choice was to sail home. With barely enough able sailors to manage the *Gabriel,* Frobisher and Hall doubted if they had the strength to continue toward Cathay but feared remaining where they were. Lacking a guide, they knew only one course.

They cleared the headlands of Frobisher Strait on August 27. Hall, or perhaps Frobisher, sketched the waterway on the vellum sailing chart, showing it as a wide passage trending southeast to northwest sprinkled with islands, and drew the shore in green. After five days' sailing the crew sighted southern Greenland— "Frisland," Hall wrote in the log—but kept the ship well away because of "monstrous ice." When a "very terrible storm" blew a sailor overboard, the man miraculously caught hold of a foresail until Frobisher "pluckt him again into the ship." Hall wrote nothing about the native who traveled as an unwilling passenger. In October, the *Gabriel* reached English waters.

On October 9, 1576, the day the ship arrived in London, civilization was the smell of wood smoke rising from alehouses, the greenness of the land, even the sweet smell of dung along the banks of the Thames. Coal smoke seemed glorious compared to endless whiteness. Frobisher knew he had explored farther west than any other Englishman, but his countrymen knew nothing of his exploits. Hadn't the *Michael* returned weeks ago declaring him lost at sea? Did the sailors' relatives expect to see them outside of heaven? Here they were, all but five of them, back from the dead. Never mind the lice or the stink from the ballast. These men, and especially their captain, returned as heroes.

Courtiers believed that Martin Frobisher had found a passage to Cathay, indeed did not dare to doubt him, because Her Majesty Queen Elizabeth believed him. When she invited Frobisher to court, the great lords fawned over him. Within two weeks of the *Gabriel*'s return, courtiers were writing about "one Captayne Furbusher," who with great cunning had captured a dark-skinned stranger dressed in furs, in lands near Cathay. Of the native, it was said "he eateth raw flesh." So the native was a sensation.

Other than a letter from the Great Khan himself, Michael Lok—the venture's financier and chief promoter—could not have expected a bigger dividend. He and his partners had invested £875; the expenses, by the time the sailors collected their pay, totaled more than £1,400. For an ordinary venture, this would be a disaster. Already, though, Lok was planning a second expedition; he trusted his captain. While the sailors brought back nothing but balls of dirt, along with one black stone, the captain had delivered the marvelously unusual stranger—living proof that the *Gabriel* had nearly reached Cathay. In Lok's account book, he was "the strange man of Cathay or new land India."

In the 1560s, French sailors who had probably reached Labrador had captured a woman dressed in sealskin clothes. She was put on display with her young daughter in Antwerp and other cities, where promoters charged people admission for the chance to gawk at the strangers. The mother and child were probably Inuit. Handbills announced that the woman had been married to a man twelve feet tall whose appetite for human flesh was so great, he had killed twelve Europeans. But that was years ago in Antwerp. Englishmen had never seen for themselves anyone like the stranger who arrived with Frobisher.

In the ledger, Lok recorded the expenditure of one pound, ten shillings for proper English clothes for the stranger. His fellow investors commissioned Cornelis Ketel, the Dutch artist favored by the court, to paint a full-length portrait of the stranger wearing his furs, plus the portrait of Frobisher that now hangs at the Bodleian Library in Oxford. Ketel was asked to paint, in all, at least eight portraits of the native, but none survives. A small watercolor that may have been based on one of Ketel's paintings shows a bearded, dark-complexioned man wearing a hooded parka that has a tail reaching to the ground. He has patched trousers and high boots and grips a bow and arrow and a double-bladed paddle, which stands a third again taller than the man.

Michael Lok sought to correct the many false tales about the stranger. "I have thought good therefore to declare the very truth thereof to satisfy the world," he said, "& also to express his picture as well as may be done with ink & paper." Unfortunately, that sketch too has disappeared, but Lok went on to describe him in a report for investors already wanting to discuss preparations for a second voyage. His report was later damaged by fire, but he can still be heard tantalizing his audience about the stranger.

> He was very good shape . . . very broad face, & very fat
> & full his body. But his legs shorter & smaller [than the
> pr]oportion of his body required. And his hands . . . his
> hair coal black, & long hanging & tied [up a]bout his
> forehead. His eyes little and a . . . black beard. His color

of skin all over his bo[dy & fa]ce, was of a dark sallow,
much like to the tawny Moors; [or ra]ther to the Tartar
nation, whereof I think he was. Countenance sullen or
churlish and sharp withall.

In London the stranger could have taught his captors a new language or advanced their knowledge of the Arctic, but they apparently ignored the opportunity. The account book tells the rest of
the man's story. Lok paid an apothecary £1 and change when the
stranger fell ill. The crowding and the humid air could have done
him no good. For bedding, "spoiled in his sickness," 16 shillings.
Mr. Crowe, the surgeon, collected a handsome £5 for the autopsy
("opening of the Indian man") and the embalming of the corpse.
Lok paid for the coffin and the fee for the stranger's burial in the
cemetery at St. Olave's Church on Seething Lane.

Michael Lok wanted a grand name for his venture. Writing to the
queen, he proposed the name "Company of Cathay," with himself
as its governor and his friend Martin Frobisher as high admiral. His
fellow investors would be the founding stockholders. The Cathay
Company and no one else, he suggested, would search for new seas,
islands, continents "and other places whatsoever," whether inhabited
by Christians or heathens, in the north, the west, and the south.
The company, he went on, would control trade with the new territories. Without a company license, you would be prohibited
from sailing in any new waters or trading with new peoples.
Because so many courtiers wanted to become part of the venture,
he favored limiting the number of additional investors. He gave
thought to the share price, proposed a ceiling on the number of
shares any one investor could buy, and outlined a schedule for div-
idends—his confidence was that high. This seemed the rare sure
thing in which a lord could risk his estate. In recognition of his
own role, Lok suggested the future company pay him 1 percent
commission on its imports, plus another 1 percent to Frobisher.
Frobisher secretly proposed a different scheme. His petition to

the queen contained only four paragraphs, but it was deeply subversive, showing consideration only for himself. He wished to be named both high admiral and governor. As governor, he wanted 5 percent of the profits from trade with any newfound lands; as admiral, he wanted an additional 1 percent commission on the cargoes shipped from England. The petition made no mention of a new company or of Michael Lok. Since in his own estimation he had taken all the risks, Frobisher wanted the endeavor to be strictly between himself and the queen.

Elizabeth found the competing proposals brilliant. Simply brilliant. In their separate pleadings Lok and Frobisher convinced her that the new wealth was a sure thing, that all she need do to profit was again wave her hand from Greenwich Palace when the fleet left for the new territories and Cathay. She calculated the prospects as carefully as she would study a potential romance, wanting always to know the potential profit before taking the next step. She was breathtakingly tightfisted, even with her sailors; pennypinching was a Tudor family trait. Henry VII, her grandfather, had recorded the expenditure of every pence, as if he were a shopkeeper in Cheapside, and wasted nothing. Except for her loops of pearls, Elizabeth demonstrated the same miserliness, and she was as earthy as father, Henry VIII. She liked watching monkeys fight horses, and rather than attend a stage play the queen sometimes rode to the royal bear pits to see mastiffs tear at the throat of a chained bear. But she preferred wealth over almost anything.

That was why in January 1577 Elizabeth told her advisers she was investing £500 in Michael Lok's venture, and informed the Royal Navy that it was loaning Martin Frobisher the *Ayde* (*Aid*, in modern spelling) for a second northwest voyage. She was one of the adventurers now and more or less took over the business as her own because Lok and Frobisher had said it was worth pursuing. She appointed Lok and five other men as her commissioners to supervise preparations for the new expedition. Lok retained the title of treasurer, but he was now more akin to her employee than an independent investor. The court saw no need to issue a charter for the Company of Cathay, though the investors were welcome to use the name. She found no reason to promote Lok to "governor," since without a charter the company lacked legal standing, and she need not give Frobisher the title of high admiral or the outlandish privileges he wanted. The queen never owed her subjects an apology for taking control of what she believed should be hers.

But she couldn't resist fudging the numbers in her favor. The ship she proffered, the *Ayde,* had been built in 1561 or '62. The *Ayde* displaced about two hundred tons and, as the queen said, was only a loan. She set its value, though, at a very rich level: £750. A year before, Lok had bought the little *Gabriel* and the pinnace together, built to order, for one-fifth that amount. Of course, Elizabeth could assign the *Ayde* any figure she desired. Lok dutifully recorded the *Ayde* as a £750 investment.

Courtiers gossiped that the venture was the opportunity of a lifetime. Interviewed by the new commissioners, Martin Frobisher tried to erase every doubt and, as Lok remembered it, "vouched to them absolutely with vehement words, speeches and oaths, that he had found and discovered the Straits, and open passage into the South Sea called Mar de Sur which goes to Cathay." As part of the publicity machine, the Countess of Warwick commissioned the scholar Richard Willes to publish the first English translation of recent works describing Japan, China, and India. In the process, Willes conscientiously reviewed the arguments for and against the existence of a navigable passage in the northwest, and cautioned readers that even the best captain could find himself trapped by ice in the north, as poor Hugh Willoughby of the Muscovy Company had suffered above Russia. More encouraging, he said, was Frobisher's description of exceptionally strong tides in Frobisher Strait, as if the waterway were a constricted pipe carrying the back and forth of tides from two oceans, and that Christopher Hall had sounded depths worthy of an ocean. Willes cited those factors as evidence that Frobisher Strait could indeed lead to Cathay.

> M. Furbishers prosperous voyage, and happy return, will absolutely decide these controversies, and certainly determine where the whole passage lieth, how long it is,

what breadth it carrieth, how perilous, how prosperous the journey is, and what commodities the painful traveler can reap thereby, what gain the venturous merchant may look for, what wealth, what honour, what fame will to our English nation thereof ensue.

This enthusiasm existed even before gossip spread that Frobisher had found gold.

Michael Lok claimed credit for the discovery of gold. Before sailing from Ratcliff, Frobisher had promised that if he managed to return, he would give Lok the first thing found in whatever territories the expedition discovered. A few days after the *Gabriel* reached London, Frobisher handed him the heavy stone that was as black as coal, the rock found on Hall's Island by poor Robert Garrard before he and four other sailors disappeared among the natives.

Anyone in Lok's position, as treasurer of a venture deeply in the red, would have taken the same first step. Lok broke off several pieces from the black rock and gave some of the fragments to three assayers, including the chief assayer of the royal mint at the Tower of London. Separately, the three assayers melted the bits of stone in brick-lined furnaces as a first step toward separating and refining the stone's constituents. None of the assayers found anything of value. It was just rock.

The mother stone went onto a table or somewhere else in Michael Lok's house, and he was apparently tortured by the sight of it. In January 1577 he took another fragment to a fourth assayer. Why Lok chose Giovanni Battista Agnello—a native of Venice and the author of a book extolling alchemy—rather than some other man skillful in refining ores, and how the financier even knew of him, he never explained. But foreigners were considered more learned in metallurgy than Englishmen. The royal court showed a preference for foreign mining engineers; Lok did likewise.

Lok told Agnello nothing about the origins of the rock, nor

anything about the results of the earlier assays. Three days later Agnello notified the financier of the results of the latest assay. "He showed me a very little powder of gold, saying it came thereout," Lok said, "and willed me to give him a better piece to make a better proof." After Agnello produced gold from the "better piece," Lok told him about the experts who had found nothing of value, and demanded a third test. Lok wanted to be sure he would not make a fool of himself if he informed the court of the findings. Agnello reported the third results in a brief letter, a grain of gold enclosed therein.

This was the explanation Agnello gave for his success: *"Bisogna sapare adulare la natura."* "One must know how to enhance nature." He did not describe his enhancements, nor did he say how much was nature's work and how much his own. The one sentence— *"Bisogna sapare . . ."*—that was all.

In some of the English documents Agnello (*lamb,* in Italian) rather charmingly becomes Mr. John B. Lamb. Francis Walsingham, Elizabeth's secretary of state and master of secrets, learned through his network of informants that Agnello had little money. He seemed to have no special standing within the community of assayers and alchemists; the Venetian was mostly a cipher. But he believed in his findings strongly enough to ask Lok for the chance to buy, at his own expense, a hundred tons of similar black rock. "Then I dealt with him somewhat plain," Lok said, "and told him, that it would be a hard matter for us to have it, for that in truth it was had in the new land discovered by Mr. Frobisher, whereof there is a privilege granted to a company." Talking, they began referring to the rock as "ore." Agnello proposed schemes for Frobisher's returning to the new territory, where he might load more rock as if it were just ballast without anyone else being let in on the secret. For every plan that Lok rejected, Agnello had another; he offered to make the voyage himself with Frobisher.

Frobisher still knew nothing about the gold. The keeping of secrets was a dangerous game that Lok played. He admitted that withholding the news from Frobisher was "double dealing," and Lok also needed to inform the court; gold was as much within the queen's purview as war. Sounding overwrought, he sent Francis Walsingham a letter saying he had information of such great importance that it could be discussed only in person. After hearing him out, Walsingham agreed that Lok should submit a report to Elizabeth. The financier sent her Agnello's grain of gold and delivered to Walsingham fragments of the black rock so the secretary of state could judge the matter for himself.

It was ordinary rock—it was a deceit, Walsingham said. He broke the fragments into still smaller pieces, belittled everything about them, damned them as "an alchemist matter"—smoke and fumes. Agnello, just a trickster. It seemed to Walsingham just one more attempted extortion, but he was willing to ask assayers of his own choosing to conduct more tests. He took the matter seriously enough to watch one of the meltings. It found a hint of silver but no gold. Another man's results were the same—traces of silver, not a sliver of gold. "I found nothing," said a third man, who was told his sample came from Ireland, "or almost nothing." Lok kept returning to Agnello to hear him swear his certainty about the presence of gold and to Walsingham, who cautioned him about promises made by alchemists.

Sometime later in January 1577, Martin Frobisher came to dine at Lok's house. It would have been an unavoidably stressful meeting. Did the host betray his "double dealing" by appearing anxious? Was it loud good cheer that made the captain suspicious? All that Lok reports is that Frobisher arrived "very desirous" of news about the black stone.

It's not difficult to imagine a loud argument behind the bland phrase. Neither man, perhaps, took much interest in the food after Frobisher inquired about the stone. Their stone. *His* stone. Lok said he had distributed fragments to reputable assayers. Then, as if he saw shoals ahead, he changed course and lied. The assayers had found nothing of value, he told Frobisher, except for one man, who had detected "tin and a little silver." The good news, said Lok, was that the stone contained enough of those metals to make rock of that type worth gathering on a second voyage: the black rock "was worthy of the fetching away." He made it sound as if the

Francis Walsingham, by John De Critz the Elder, ca. 1585. Elizabeth's principal secretary of state, master of secrets, and supporter of John Lok and the Company of Cathay. (Courtesy of the National Portrait Gallery, London)

fetching were of no greater importance than the fetching of another half-penny loaf from a baker. "Whereat," Lok said of his guest, "he was very glad."

That was when the poison began seeping in. Frobisher was already hearing rumors from friends at court about the black stone. By February, Lok had still made no mention of gold to him. Frobisher had ample time to reflect on the deceit. Meanwhile, Lok was conferring at least once a week with Francis Walsingham about precious metals in the new, northern lands.

On March 11 Lok formally asked Walsingham for a patent—a license—to organize another voyage. Instead of promising to reach Cathay, he proposed an expedition to mine three hundred tons of gold-bearing ore. The sums extrapolated from Agnello's assays showed that the undertaking would be enormously profitable. Lok was confident of the figures. They showed that the stone would yield £30 a ton in gold. The three hundred tons he proposed mining would be worth £9,000 (roughly £3.6 million today, or $6.1 million). One-third of that amount would both cover the cost of the voyage and pay the expense of Agnello's melting and refining the ore in furnaces. Lok proposed paying the queen another third—an amount worthy of a knighthood—and the investors would have the remaining £3,000 as profit.

Walsingham chewed on the numbers. He was forever besieged by intelligent men with false hopes or treachery in their hearts. His way of teasing out more information was to express doubts about a venture's chances of success, and he cautioned Lok about the risk of losing every pence. Lok remembered the question Walsingham posed near the end: "He asked me if Mr. Frobisher knew of this matter, I said no, nor none other person by me, but only Your Majesty, and he and Battista [Agnello], which is the very truth." Elizabeth, Walsingham, the assayer, and Lok—that was the full circle of confidants.

By the end of March, Walsingham had finished weighing the matter. Without announcing any formal decision, he made his drift clear enough by telling Lok to bring Frobisher into the circle. They would need him to find the territories and the ore. "He [Walsingham] asked again if Mr. Frobisher knew of the matter, I said no. He willed me to impart it to him. I said I would, and so I did."

Lok keeps us almost wholly in the dark about the subsequent conversation with Frobisher. *"I said I would, and so I did."* We hear not a word about the atmosphere of the meeting or whether Lok apologized for his earlier lies or if the good news helped Frobisher forget his anger. Nothing could do more for a captain's standing than finding gold.

What a shock, then, when a man outside the circle asked Lok about the stone. William Winter, master of ordnance for the Royal Navy, was one of the commissioners whom Elizabeth had appointed to oversee preparations for the second voyage. The commissioners were meeting almost daily at either Lok's house or Winter's, cajoling investors together, commandeering supplies for the new voyage, fending off the meddlesome Privy Council. The gold, though, was supposed to remain a secret.

Winter knew about the gold, and he also mentioned the name *Agnello*. Agnello was a proud man who, it seemed, couldn't resist talking about his recent accomplishment. Winter's own circle of confidants had obtained pieces of the black stone and undertaken more assays. One Jonas Shutz had performed the work. He was German, seemed to know a great deal about smelters and every kind of metal, and had worked as Agnello's assistant—thus another leak of information. Shutz found the black stone oddly resistant to melting, but if other assayers had failed to find gold in it, he supposed their furnaces had been insufficiently hot. Or those men simply lacked the talent for working with difficult ore.

William Winter told Lok the stone was far more valuable than previously thought. Shutz calculated that a ton of the black rock would be worth £240, not Agnello's £30. An assay Shutz conducted while Lok watched found one part gold for every four hundred parts of ore. The people watching extrapolated the results: every hundred pounds of ore would produce four ounces of gold.

Gold is, in a sense, everywhere, but the quantities are very small. Given the right tools, it can be extracted from Scotch pines or Siberian reindeer moss. It is present in human hair. Soil contains (on average) five one-thousandths of one part gold for every million parts soil. Every million parts of freshwater contain three one-hundred-thousandths of one part gold. Roughly one-third that amount is in seawater, which has not stopped people from trying to mine it from the oceans.

Philosophers since the time of Aristotle had assumed gold was created by the sun's rays. Rays from stars, it was said, produced the lesser, dull-colored metals, such as lead; and sunlight over a long period of time could ripen and ferment those inferior metals into gold. Those beliefs made alchemy seem a rational endeavor. Alchemists regarded lead and copper as seeds not yet fully ripened and sought in their laboratories to accelerate the process of maturation. It seemed no stranger than nature transforming brown acorns into oaks with glorious green canopies. The alchemists were searching for an elixir—the Philosopher's Stone, they called it— that could transmute people as well as metals into a higher existence: lead into gold, people into more nearly perfect beings.

Miners sifted for gold near the heads of streams or searched for telltale threads of white in surface rocks. A streak of rusty brown— iron oxide—was another hint of gold's presence. Miners would break up the surface rocks by building fires there before beginning the drudgery of using picks and shovels. Yet now Michael Lok talked of a land where ore had literally been picked up from the ground.

The rumors infected the court like a fever. Philip Sidney, the queen's favorite courtier-poet, wrote to a friend on the Continent telling of "a certain Frobisher," who had stopped at an island where a sailor picked up a glittering rock that proved to be pure gold—no impurities whatsoever. Another story making the rounds held that the discovery had been made by the wife of one of Frobisher's friends, who threw a fragment of the famous stone into a fire and saw it turn a golden color. Lok's fellow investors felt richer and blessed in every way. Hitherto known only for piracy, Frobisher was welcomed everywhere. Questioned by Elizabeth's counselors, he said his next expedition could find enough ore to fill all the kingdom's ships.

Everyone's confidence was writ large in Lok's account book. Here was an opportunity endorsed even by miserly Elizabeth, through her loan of a ship. Lord Burghley, the Lord Treasurer, doubled his investment to £100. The Earl of Warwick matched him, and the Countess of Warwick invested £50. Philip Sidney doubled his stake, and William Winter invested for the first time. Having seen the black stone himself, the master of intelligence Francis Walsingham ventured £200. Michael Lok pledged £900, and smaller amounts were invested in the name of some of his children. He also advanced £25 on behalf of the polymath of wisdom John Dee. Frobisher contributed £100, and no one knew better than he about the plenitude of ore. Like Lok, he was now akin to an employee of the Privy Council.

Taking orders pleased Frobisher not at all. The commissioners informed him that he would be sharing authority with another officer, Edward Fenton. If they had known Frobisher better, they might have avoided lighting the fuse and suffering the explosion. He responded with "no small raging and outrageous speaking," as Lok remembered the session. Frobisher swore by "God's wounds"— a terrible oath—that he wouldn't sail unless he had sole command.

Edward Fenton, the new man, took him aside and calmed him.

In their formal instructions, the commissioners surrendered by giving Martin Frobisher full authority, along with an impressive title, "captain general." In the orders, the *Gabriel,* the *Michael,* and the *Ayde* were designated as the ships of his fleet, and the combined crew was limited to 120 sailors. The commissioners wanted to control their labor costs, which signaled something new about the work of Elizabethan explorers: "exploration" was to be a quotidian profession, like farming. The investors wanted Frobisher to concern himself with salaries, bills past due, shipping lists, expense accounts—the drab obligations of a clerk. The *Gabriel,* his favorite ship, required new masts; he wanted at least seventy-five sheaves of arrows and thirty-eight dozen bowstrings, the better to fend off the natives. He needed mattocks and shovels for the miners, plus baskets for carrying the ore. One of William Winter's men pressed thirteen miners into service, but six were found unfit and released.

Cheap labor stayed on the commissioners' minds. The formal

instructions ordered Frobisher to take eleven convicts with him and leave them on Frisland with whatever weapons and food he could spare. The convicts—most of them highway robbers—were supposed to befriend the presumed natives of Frisland, the venture's mistaken identity for southern Greenland. Frobisher understood better than the commissioners that the idea amounted to a death sentence. In the end, ten of the convicts bribed Frobisher to let them escape before the expedition began; the eleventh man chose to remain in prison rather than sail with the fleet.

In the instructions, mining took precedence over the search for Cathay. "At your arrival at Hall's Island," the commissioners wrote, "you shall seek a good harbor for the ships as near the same island as may be . . . and from thence you shall repair with vessels and furniture as is apt to the place where the mineral ore was had which you brought hither the last year, and there to place the miners and other men to work and gather the ores."

Finding the five sailors who went missing during the previous voyage was the second priority, but Frobisher was told to maintain a lookout for gold while conducting the search. The orders read, "You shall repair towards the place where your men and boat was taken from you, and in the way going you shall make search both for good harbors, and also for other mines." The commissioners instructed him to be sure the miners were "well settled" before he searched for the sailors.

Reaching Cathay came third, after finding gold and the vanished sailors. Once the first two activities were under way, he could sail up to a hundred leagues west, "so you may be certain you are entered into the South Sea"—the Pacific Ocean. The commissioners no longer doubted that the northwest passage as described by Frobisher was "a truth," but the gold interested them more.

In his contacts with the natives, the commissioners wrote, he should "win both friendship and liking." Yet they also instructed him to bring additional Inuit to England. The company gave him guidelines for choosing desirable candidates. "We do not think it good you should bring hither above the number of iii or iiii or eight or ten at the most of the people of that country: where of some to be old and the other young whom we mind shall not return again thither." He should assume they would remain in England the rest of their lives; the commissioners wanted healthy specimens. It's a mystery how, in their own minds, the commissioners reconciled their warnings about avoiding any offense with the command that Frobisher take natives captive.

If he judged it feasible, Frobisher should leave some of the sailors in Frobisher Strait for the winter, "giving them instructions how they may observe the nature of the air and the state of the country, and what time of the year the Strait is most free from ice." He should assign a carpenter to stay with them and should leave sufficient food, as well as a pinnace. The commissioners, sitting in London, had of course never seen Baffin Island; Frobisher can be excused for not yet having imagined a Baffin winter.

The commissioners were sending Jonas Shutz as one of two assayers to test the ore during the mining. If the ore met the assayers' expectations, the commissioners wanted Frobisher to bring back as much as his ships could carry, "although you do leave out other superfluous things." In other words, the men should strip the ships of all possible gear to make room for the maximum amount of ore.

There was a backup plan in case the mining proved disappointing. No one expected it to happen, but in those circumstances Frobisher should send the *Ayde* back to England, protecting Queen Elizabeth's investment, "and therewithall you shall proceed towards the discovering of Cathay with the barks." Not much attention was given as to how he could obtain enough food for the sailors aboard the *Gabriel* and the *Michael* if they headed farther west, but those were the orders.

The voyage seemed a wager worth taking. Frobisher had found the new waterway with Christopher Hall and the little *Gabriel,* and had survived every storm. He had all that knowledge and Christopher Hall to accompany him again as chief pilot. They could enlist many more sailors, plus the queen's bankroll. They had discovered Frobisher Strait in the northwest by sailing due west along a measured 60 degrees north latitude; weather allowing, they would repeat the strategy. Failure didn't seem a possibility. There was also the gold. They judged the odds far better than just a roll of the dice. Frobisher could find his way back to that cool, auriferous territory inhabited by a people who paddled boats made from animal skins and ate raw flesh. He could be England's Midas and its heroic knight conquering new lands.

CHAPTER THREE

A Cold Addiction

Charles Francis Hall was a man of many enthusiasms. The Arctic was the latest.

During the 1850s he and his wife, Mary, resided in the heart of Cincinnati's commercial district, at 14 West Fourth Street, a half mile from the Ohio River, in a building that also housed the business known as Hall's Engraving Rooms. He specialized in seal engraving—the engraving of metal dies that embossed banknotes and court documents. His firm also manufactured the desktop presses that performed the actual embossing. Hall's advertisements described what the user should do after inserting a document beneath the working face of the press: "STRIKE the apex of the Press a QUICK and QUITE SEVERE blow with the hand—a Seal is thus instantly made."

His interests extended far beyond the engraving business. He was fascinated by plans for laying the transatlantic telegraph cable. Then came an ardor for hot-air ballooning. Cincinnatians read about each of his enthusiasms in his newspaper, the *Cincinnati Occasional,* another of his avocations. The first issue, published

August 5, 1858, contained two short dispatches signed by Cyrus
W. Field announcing the successful laying of the Atlantic cable.

True to the paper's name, Hall published the paper only when
he believed the occasion merited it. He displayed unpredictable
bursts of energy as editor. A week might pass between issues or he
might publish two wholly different editions in a single day. In
October 1858 the paper announced its first (and only) Balloon
Edition, as a balloonist floating above the city distributed a thousand copies to the wind. Most issues of the paper included a one-
sentence stock market report from New York, the local train
schedule, and crime shorts. He liked the blaring of capital letters.
The paper printed thumbnail-size ads from Mrs. W. L. Hudson,
milliner; Beggs & Smith Jewelers; J. Tod, oyster agent; and other
businesses from the Fourth Street neighborhood. Readers also
received the publisher's dollops of philosophy. "Our sentiment has
been, now is, and we hope ever will be—'DO GOOD,'" Hall editorialized. "We trust the *Occasional*'s record proves this."

"There is no time so proper for replying to a letter, as immediately upon receipt."

"SCIENCE may be *truthful*—IT *may err*—God—*never!*"

"Parents should engrave this line in their memories—If young
people are not properly instructed (by control of the passions) before
the age of fifteen, little can be done afterwards to any purpose."

In December 1858 he announced plans for a new, more ambitious newspaper: the *Daily Press* would replace the *Occasional*,
appear six days a week, and instead of being distributed free would
cost a penny a copy. It would also require much more of his time,
especially after he dismissed the experienced editor he had hired
and took the position himself. Hall seemed to need a newspaper
wholly his own for tracking his cornucopia of interests. The *Daily
Press* editorialized in favor of the introduction of horse-drawn
trolleys, discussed at great length Napoleon III's war against
Austria for the liberation of Italy, and seamlessly worked mentions
of Livy and Tacitus into the news columns. On the issue of slavery
in the United States, in 1859, Hall mysteriously stayed silent. The

slave state of Kentucky lay within sight of Fourth Street, on the opposite bank of the Ohio River, but the topic failed to interest him. Compared with Italy it wasn't exotic, and unlike trolley service it seemed wholly beyond his influence. The newspaper reflected *his* world, as if he were transcribing conversations at his dinner table—his curiosity, his mild jokes, and his moralizing.

"In the Chicago Post office there are now ninety-two employees with forty-six mail trains arriving and depositing daily."

"Vanity, like laudanum and other poisonous medicines, should be indulged in very small quantities."

"The population of St. Louis is 190,000, as by a census just completed. This is a gain of 50,000 in two years."

"A gentleman having a horse that ran away and broke his wife's neck, was told by a neighbor that he wished to purchase it for his wife to ride upon. 'No,' said the wretch, 'I intend to marry again myself.'"

Publishing, though, did not offer much adventure, and by the time the *Daily Press* was six months old Hall felt terribly restless. He was thirty-seven and had lived in Cincinnati ten years, but he sensed that true excitement lay somewhere beyond Ohio. His attention began to wander. A brief article in the old *Occasional* gave the first hint of his newest interest. The story in question was printed in small type on the last page of the *Occasional*'s last issue. In it, Hall urged every schoolchild in Cincinnati to visit a traveling panorama commemorating the Arctic exploits of the late, heroic Elisha Kent Kane, M.D.

Everyone knew of Dr. Kane. No other American, it seemed, had crammed so many adventures into a life lasting a mere thirty-seven years. He had served as a navy surgeon in China during the 1840s; sketched the interior of a volcano in the Philippines by having himself lowered by rope into the smoking crater; braved great dangers as a diplomatic courier in Mexico; and in general established himself as traveler extraordinaire. In the 1850s he had become the first American explorer of the Arctic, emerging as a celebrity after writing two stylish accounts of his adventures in the north. He had helped feed the American public's new appetite for all things Arctic, a fascination that could be traced back to the mystery surrounding the fate of a British expedition led by Sir John Franklin.

And the person who "made" John Franklin and "made" the Arctic a topic of popular interest was Sir John Barrow.

John Barrow had the power to make a British naval officer's career. Rather severe in appearance, never known for humor, he served as second secretary to the Admiralty for nearly forty years, beginning in 1804. The second secretary, in theory, served the first secretary and the seven lords of the Admiralty Board but, in practice, knew far more than they did about the workings of the Royal Navy.

As a young man, Barrow had sailed to Greenland aboard a whaling ship and brought home a whale's jawbone as a souvenir; the great arc of bone was used as a gatepost at his parents' cottage. He traveled in China as an interpreter for the British ambassador, worked as a colonial official in South Africa, and married. But the Arctic became his passion. Appointed second secretary, he dedicated himself to finding tasks that would glorify the world's most powerful navy. India, he could see, was going to be an army affair. So was Africa. But in the Arctic, and in the sketchy maps of its guessed-at waters, he saw a suitably large playing field for his officers.

In 1818 Barrow wrote *A Chronological History of Voyages into the Arctic Regions*. He pressed the book into service like a weapon, in a cleverly fought campaign to persuade the Admiralty and the public to think as he did about the Arctic's innate *Britishness*. It was based on connections he traced 240-odd years back, to Martin Frobisher.

Frobisher had wanted to find a northwest passage. Now John Barrow did too. The search itself, the second secretary said in his book, was "peculiarly British," as glorious an inheritance as Shakespeare's plays, belonging by right to the kingdom as much as did the Thames or the Tower of London. One could hear an echo from the sixteenth century on almost every page of the book. George Best, Martin Frobisher's supporter, had described the search as "the only thing of the world that was yet left undone." Two hundred and forty years later, John Barrow proclaimed it "almost the only interesting discovery that remains to be made." Later, the same would be said of reaching the North Pole and the South Pole (Ernest Shackleton called Antarctic travel "the last great journey left to man"). The public became fascinated with each great "undone" as explorers turned to it. From the reign of Elizabeth I, when Frobisher reached Baffin Island, well into the reign of Queen Victoria, the search for a northwest passage satisfied the strong craving for something left to be done.

Barrow relaunched the quest in 1818 by sending two ships north along the coast of Greenland. He anticipated that they would cross an ice-free Polar Sea to the North Pole. The mission failed. A second pair of ships, meanwhile, sailed across the Davis Strait from Greenland to Baffin Island, exploring northern waters for a passage leading farther west. The strategy repeated Martin Frobisher's plan at a higher latitude.

No one doubted the bravery of John Ross, the commander of the expedition sent across the Davis Strait. A veteran of the Napoleonic Wars, he had been wounded in battle thirteen times. But travel in the north seemed an endless war fought against ice and dense fog, the enemy never stopping its harrying. On Greenland's northwest coast, in 1818, his party encountered some Inuit, who regarded the ships as large animals. They believed that a ticking watch was another living creature. Numbering about two hundred, the Inuit there had assumed they were the only humans in the world. Through an interpreter Ross brought from southern Greenland, they asked whether their visitors had come from the sun. This encounter helped cement the officers' opinion that Inuit were simpleminded primitives who were best ignored. Ross sailed west and indeed found a passage—Lancaster Sound, north of Baffin Island. Then he mystified the junior officers by declaring that mountains he alone reported seeing in the fog blocked the way farther west. His ships returned to England.

In 1819 William Edward Parry wintered in the Arctic after finding Lancaster Sound to be a strait. He tried a different route on a second voyage, and was lucky to survive a third after one of his ships was wrecked. John Ross returned to the region in 1829 in a paddle-wheel steamer that became trapped in the ice. His party survived four Arctic winters, thanks to help from Inuit hunters. But this experience failed to change the Admiralty's opinion of the Inuit. Their talents and assistance made less of an impression than the hardships borne by the British crew: surviving four years in the north was seen as proof of British mettle.

The Royal Navy's search for a northwest passage became something of a national sport, as gentlemanly as cricket, and then turned into a morality play. Reading the understated chronicles written by each commander upon his return, the public adored the romance of the search. A hostess couldn't hope for a more interesting guest in her drawing room than someone whose vessel had been trapped by ice for an entire winter. This select group of officers, in company with members of Parliament and writers of a certain sort, became *society*. Parliament promised a £20,000 reward to whoever first reached the Pacific through a northwest passage.

The last of the three expeditions led by John Franklin was a class apart. His was the drama that captured the largest audience. Franklin permanently linked Arctic exploration in the public's imagination with heroism—as long as you credited heroic suffering. He suffered for his reputation during his own lifetime and then, with his 128 officers and men, endured more hardship than any person should have to bear.

In the first Arctic expedition under his command, in 1819–22, Franklin mapped part of Canada's northern coast. His party of Indian guides and French-Canadian voyageurs was plagued by terrible planning and bad luck. In charting five hundred miles of Arctic coast, half the party died of starvation or exposure. By the end of the second winter, the survivors were subsisting on shoe leather and lichens. One member of the party murdered another, and the murderer was executed; some of Franklin's men suspected others of cannibalism. If not for a rescue party, Franklin himself would have died. He summed up the experience as "long, fatiguing, and disastrous."

His second Arctic command enjoyed better fortunes and, from

1825 to 1827, mapped more of the Canadian north. By the time he returned home only a small portion of the northwest passage remained unseen, but even the lowliest clerk in the Admiralty already knew the route would be frozen over for most of every year. Everyone reading the London newspapers knew it too. Commercially, the northwest passage would be worthless. It had the value of trinkets, like the cowbells Martin Frobisher had carried in the *Gabriel*. But the Admiralty wanted it for Britain.

After being turned down by his first choices, John Barrow appointed Franklin in 1845 to serve as commander of a third expedition. Voices at the Admiralty whispered that Franklin, at age sixty, was too old. He informed his critics that he was, in fact, fifty-nine. Other doubts concerned his dated naval experience. He had most recently served for eight cheerless years as governor of Van Diemen's Land (the future Tasmania)—a vast penal colony off the Australian coast. But for lack of any other acceptable candidates, the Admiralty gave him the responsibility for completing the northwest passage.

When tugs pulled his two ships into the Thames, on May 19, 1845, Franklin waved a handkerchief toward the receding dock. The *Erebus* and the *Terror* carried 129 officers and men and three years' worth of supplies: canned meats and vegetables, nearly seventy tons of flour, twenty tons of biscuits, five tons of chocolate, and about four tons of lemon juice to combat scurvy. Officers brought aboard silverware engraved with initials or crests. The Admiralty provided mahogany writing desks.

A whaling ship made the last known sighting of Franklin's ships, in July 1845, moored to an iceberg while waiting for a break in the pack ice blocking the entrance to Lancaster Sound. Later that summer they steamed west through the sound to Devon and Beechey islands. During the expedition's first winter, three of the men died. In the second summer the ships reached the northern shore of King William Island. The winter trapped them there, and the ice refused to release them. Franklin could not have known that a vessel caught there could remain frozen in place through any number of summers, in ice cemented by extreme cold. As suggested by ice cores, the mid-1840s were exceptionally cold or had unusually heavy snows. He had arrived at the worst place at the worst time, and could not escape.

In Britain people knew only that the expedition had vanished.

No other drama of the time captured a more rapt audience or stayed on stage longer. Where were John Franklin and his men? And what could be done for them? Gentlemen sat in the paneled libraries of their clubs and imagined the ice pack—its loud grinding, its groans of motion—pressing against the flanks of the *Erebus* and the *Terror*. Everyone caught the fever of ice.

Five rescue expeditions sailed to the Arctic in 1848; a year later three more sailed. Another ten went in search of the Franklin expedition in 1850. Lady Jane Franklin, the missing admiral's wife, outfitted some of the vessels at her own expense. Search parties sounded gongs in hope that Franklin's men would respond, released carrier pigeons carrying messages announcing that relief had arrived, and added new territory to the maps. Each new expedition coined new heroes in their own narrow escapes. But still no trace of John Franklin.

The ships engaged in the search carried muscular names. HMS *Rescue*, the *Resolute*, the *Advance*, the *Diligence*. The *Assistance*, the *Enterprise*, the *Investigator*. Just pronouncing them gave the public a little Arctic frisson. In the course of the otherwise fruitless search, Robert McClure, of the *Investigator*, found the last links in the northwest passage. McClure and his men were frozen in for three winters until, miraculously, another of the Franklin search parties rescued them, only for the ice to trap them all for another year.

Credit for finding the first clues about Franklin's fate belonged to John Rae of the Hudson's Bay Company. Employed by the company as a surgeon, Rae had already mapped more than a thousand miles of Arctic coast, and had made a point of learning from Inuit. Leading compact expeditions, he traveled as Inuit did, with dogs and lightweight sledges. Searching for Franklin, he thought to ask Inuit if they had seen other white men.

In 1854 several Inuit told him that they had heard stories about a large number of whites dying in some distant place. Other informants told Rae that some families had encountered about forty whites dragging a boat over the sea ice. Gaunt and weak, the whites had traded some of their possessions for seal meat. Sometime later, Inuit had found the corpses of thirty or so of the whites near a ship's boat. In his report to the Admiralty, Rae relayed what the Inuit had told him about the finds:

> Some of the bodies had been buried (probably those of the first victims of famine); some were in a tent or tents; others were under the boat, which had been turned over to form a shelter; and several lay scattered about in different directions. Of those found on the island, one was supposed to have been an officer, as he had a telescope strapped over his shoulders and his double-barreled gun lay underneath him. From the mutilated state of many of the bodies and the contents of the kettles, it is evident that our wretched countrymen had been driven to the last resource—cannibalism—as a means of prolonging existence.

Long after the event, knife marks from the butchering remained visible on the bare bones; Franklin's men had cooked some of their fellow sailors. In addition to hearing the gruesome story, Rae obtained from the Inuit some of the officers' silverware, a gold band from an officer's cap, a medal that had belonged to Franklin himself, and enough other artifacts to convince him that the Inuit had indeed encountered some of Franklin's men.

What offended the English public most was that John Rae chose to believe the Inuit. He had accepted their word that Franklin's men, rather than the Inuit themselves, were the cannibals. The writer Charles Dickens was sufficiently enraged to declare in print what seemed obvious to him—that Inuit were the horrid eaters of raw flesh that Martin Frobisher had described in the 1570s, untrustworthy and uncivilized. "We believe every savage to be in his heart covetous, treacherous, and cruel," Dickens said. So they were capable of having murdered weakened members of the Franklin expedition and concocting a grossly offensive tale about members of the Royal Navy resorting to cannibalism. As for his countrymen, "it is in the highest degree improbable that such men would, or could, in any extremity of hunger, alleviate the pains of starvation by this horrible means." Rae, he insisted, had wrongly accepted the word of a "gross handful of uncivilized people."

After appeals from Lady Franklin, the United States Navy joined the search. The New York shipping magnate Henry Grinnell financed the outfitting of two ships, and the navy loaned the expedition a captain. This first Arctic search party from the United States included Elisha Kent Kane, who came aboard as a volunteer surgeon. In his chronicle of the sixteen-month trip, Kane rendered his experiences as a boy's extended winter lark. In 1850 the United States Grinnell Expedition, as it was called, found the site of Franklin's first winter camp, on an icy island littered with empty food cans, but no further clue as to Franklin's fate.

Kane himself commanded the Second Grinnell Expedition, which embarked in 1853. He sailed north along the west coast of Greenland in hope of discovering an open Polar Sea but encountered mostly ice. His ship was frozen in for a winter, a summer, then a second winter and a second summer. All those months, the workday always began at 6:00 A.M., though the necessary tasks filled only a few hours.

> The decks are cleaned, the ice-hole opened [for drawing fresh water]. . . . At half-past seven, all hands rise, wash on deck, open the doors for ventilation, and come below for breakfast. . . . Our breakfast, for all fare alike, is hard tack, pork, stewed apples frozen like molasses-candy, tea and coffee, with a delicate portion of raw potato.

Lunch would be more potatoes. Dinner was the same as lunch except the portions were smaller. Repairing sails and skinning birds sometimes took up a few more hours of the winter darkness.

We have cards sometimes, and chess sometimes. . . . Our fuel is limited to three bucketfuls of coal a day, and our mean temperature outside is 40 degrees below zero. . . . Our lamps can not be persuaded to burn salt lard; our oil is exhausted; and we work by muddy tapers of cork and cotton floated in saucers. We have not a pound of fresh meat.

Whenever some of the Greenland Inuit befriended the party, everyone feasted on caribou and seals. One Inuit hunter caught enough game on his own to feed all the Americans. Kane interpreted every act of kindness as evidence that members of the Franklin party could still be alive. Thanks to the natives, the land could seem rich in game. Kane could still believe that a "lost" expedition could easily survive. Isolated for two years, he knew nothing of the grisly stories that other Inuit had told John Rae.

After a third frozen-in spring, Kane's ideas about the Arctic darkened. He ordered everyone to prepare to abandon the ship, which was still trapped by ice. By then he had faced two mutinies and the death of two of his men, and during the last winter the ship's bulkheads and rigging had been burned to keep the crew warm. The sailors made boots from sealskins and walrus skins, as the Inuit had taught, and loaded their remaining supplies into the ships' boats. Then the Americans dragged the boats across three hundred miles of ice to open water. After eighty-four days in the boats, sailing more than a thousand miles, exposed to the elements all that time, Kane and his men reached the safety of a Greenland settlement in August 1855.

Kane's *Arctic Explorations: The Second Grinnell Expedition,* published in two volumes, was favorably compared to *Robinson Crusoe;* Washington Irving praised it as "one of the most extraordinary instances of the triumphs of mental energy and enthusiasm." Kane described the hardships with a minimum of bombast, though engravings showed his ship trapped at a twenty-degree tilt in broken plates of ice, and polar bears playing with barrels as if they were toy tops. With sixty-five thousand copies printed in 1856, it was the best-selling book in the country.

Exhausted by his travels, Kane died that same year in Havana. When the steamboat carrying his casket reached New Orleans, crowds lined the banks of the Mississippi River. The funeral cortege went upriver and then by rail to Philadelphia, and people mobbed the tracks at every stop for the chance to glimpse the body of a hero.

In Cincinnati, Charles Francis Hall watched steamships chug their predictable course on the Ohio River. In 1859 his neighbors included the dentist Dr. Wardle, a shirtmaker, and a purveyor of upholstery. The *Daily Press* failed to satisfy Hall: as a publisher, he could speculate about the world, but he believed that only explorers fully experienced it. How many times did he visit the panorama illustrating the exploits of Elisha Kent Kane that he had recommended to every schoolchild?

He immersed himself in books about the Arctic. He read the chronicles by Kane and John Rae, coming to know the missing John Franklin and his crew as if they were neighbors in distress. He procured a copy of John Barrow's *A Chronological History of Voyages into the Arctic Region.* He diligently clipped newspaper articles about the north, pasting them into a book of navigational tables. He found a copy of the Franklin family crest, and that too was pasted into the scrapbook.

Hall became addicted to the Franklin story, and the *Daily Press* began to emphasize Arctic news. "Does Sir John Franklin Still Live?" the newspaper asked in an editorial. The writer sounded nearly overcome by emotion from the loss of Franklin and his men even as he held out hope that they remained alive. Hall was in despair for the Englishmen's suffering, yet invigorated by his own strong feelings for them. In June 1859 an editorial praised Lady Jane Franklin for sponsoring new search expeditions. ("All men must feel a lively interest in the fate of those bold men, and be most desirous to contribute toward their restoration to their country and homes.") In its weather reports, the paper confidently blamed the Arctic ice pack for a local cold spell.

Smitten by this new passion, he wanted a new role for himself. He hungered for an important task. Since no one else had learned the full truth about the Franklin expedition, Hall volunteered to try. The chronicles of the Arctic and the pictures seen by his mind's eye moved him more than did anything on West Fourth Street. Here was a chance for him to bring relief to men in terrible distress in the far north. On July 15, 1859, he announced, "The *Daily Press* is about to pass into other hands. . . . I retire to private life, with cheer around me, having now accomplished the noble undertaking of establishing a successful DAILY PENNY PAPER in Cincinnati."

"In one word, then," he said years later with undiminished fervor, "it seemed to me as if I had been *called,* if I may so speak, to try and do the work."

Hall had never traveled on an oceangoing ship or ventured north of New England. None of that troubled him. He reasoned that anyone competent enough to have learned a succession of trades could teach himself Arctic exploration.

He began by trying to raise money from Cincinnati businessmen to outfit a ship. The petition he authored proposed a two- or three-year expedition with a well-trained crew dedicated to finding Franklin survivors, an effort he grandly named the New Franklin Research Expedition. Now that he had assigned himself a cause, he was wholly single-minded: if contributions fell pitifully short of paying for a full-fledged expedition, as they did, he was willing to search the Arctic by himself. Since no ship was offered, he would settle for traveling the first leg north aboard a whaler. If necessary, as it proved to be, he would come aboard as just one more item of freight. He revised his strategy without compromising his goals. So the New Franklin Research Expedition consisted solely of himself.

Then word came that the Franklin mystery had been solved.

The hero was Captain Francis Leopold McClintock. Lady Franklin herself had chosen him as commander of the steam yacht *Fox*. She had paid for the outfitting because the Royal Navy—having spent twice as much money searching for her husband as on the search for a northwest passage—now preferred to forget the Franklin expedition. In September 1859, McClintock returned to Britain with the story of the terrible last days of John Franklin's men.

Inuit had again provided the most important clue. They told McClintock about having seen two large ships off the northern coast of King William Island. Whites had abandoned the vessels, the Inuit said. Searching there, McClintock's second in command found a written message the Franklin party had deposited in a cairn. One of Franklin's lieutenants had neatly inked the vessels' latitude and longitude on a standard Admiralty form, plus the date, "28 May 1847." He had added two words: "All well." In April 1848 another of Franklin's men had retrieved and amended the paper. In about 150 words crowded in the margins, he reported that the party had three days earlier abandoned the *Erebus* and the *Terror*. The ships had been trapped in ice for a year and a half without any prospect of freeing themselves. John Franklin, the note continued, had died on June 11, 1847. In still smaller script the officer who had inherited command countersigned the message, adding that the men would travel south on foot to try to save themselves. Their destination was a Hudson's Bay Company post 1,200 miles from the cairn. Eleven years later, McClintock read the message.

The Franklin expedition had used men rather than dogs for hauling sledges. That was the Royal Navy way. As the Admiralty saw it, men automatically followed orders, while dogs would have to be trained like new recruits; officers thought it better that sailors exhaust themselves hauling the sledges loaded with supplies than depend on animals. Even when it was unnecessary, hard labor seemed a badge of honor. Standard practice called for eleven men to pull a sledge loaded with food and fuel weighing, in all, about a ton—roughly two hundred pounds a man. A prayer for sledging parties began, "O Lord of life and death. . . . Have mercy upon those that are appointed to die." So British sailors in the Arctic (and later the Antarctic) obediently harnessed themselves to sledges, and the custom helped doom Franklin's men after they abandoned the frozen-in ships. McClintock himself did things the same hard way.

On King William Island, McClintock discovered a boat from one of Franklin's ships. Franklin's men had mounted it on an oak sledge and dragged it across the ice before abandoning the effort. Two skeletons were inside the boat, along with an assortment of shoes, several copies of the Bible, silverware, forty pounds of chocolate, saws, and oars; McClintock found a third corpse closer to the island's northern shore. He picked through a pile of clothing four feet high left near the boat and found a scattering of shovels and rope—the leftovers of the expedition's land base. The weakened men had lightened their load before they headed south. They had apparently starved one by one along the route.

The headlines declared the Franklin saga over. "There will be no more Arctic expeditions to discover the fate of Sir John Franklin," said the *New York Sun* in a long report reprinted in Cincinnati by the new proprietors of the *Daily Press*.

> All hope that any of Franklin's party survive is at an end. It is over eleven years since they abandoned their ships, and they doubtless all perished within a short time after the abandonment in the vain attempt to escape from the perils which surrounded them. Their noble commander did not live to see them reduced to the last terrible extremity.

Almost everyone accepted that Francis McClintock had solved the mystery.

Charles Francis Hall thought differently. Thanks to McClintock, he now knew where his own field investigations should begin.

McClintock had discovered the right locale—King William Island. Someone who had studied every detail of the Franklin story, Hall believed, should now travel there, befriend the Inuit, and determine what they knew.

All those months of reading Arctic books convinced him that Inuit knew more about Franklin's men than any expedition had learned so far. Inuit had directed search parties to a small number of bodies, but where were the rest? Hall considered it supposition but not fact to say that everyone in the Franklin party was dead. He was obsessed with the missing sailors. He persuaded himself that some of them could be living with Inuit, awaiting a savior. A self-made man could envision himself in just such a role. "Why should not attempts be made, again and again," he wrote in explaining his new mission, "until the whole facts were properly known?"

Given a chance to explain himself, Hall displayed remarkable powers of persuasion. Rutherford B. Hayes—recently elected city solicitor in Cincinnati, and future president of the United States—signed Hall's petition for the New Franklin Research Expedition. So did Cincinnati mayor R. M. Bishop, and the governor of Ohio, and Senator Salmon P. Chase.

Merchants either donated what he sought or sold him the items at cost: rifles, pistols, a keg of powder, thermometers, pocketknives, tobacco, compasses, a copy of *Principles of Zoology.* Wytte & Co. in Cincinnati supplied beef at a favorable price for the making of pemmican, the staple food for every Arctic explorer. Geo. H. Hill & Co. provided beef suet for it. A Mr. Robinson provided the kiln where the mixture was cooked and dried before canning. H. W. Stevenson supplied the tin cans. The merchants either believed in his grand project or were exhausted by his pleadings.

The most important endorsement came from Henry Grinnell in New York. In the business world, his word was the gold standard. He was the scion of a New England family which had learned at an early date that it could make more money selling whale products obtained by others than by going whaling itself. Whale oil lubricated industrial machinery, provided light, and was an ingredient in soaps and paint. Baleen—the long, flexible strips of bone from the whale's mouth—was rendered into carriage springs, chair bottoms, and hoops for women's skirts. At first the Grinnell family specialized in the oil. By the time Henry joined the family firm, Grinnell, Mintum & Company was the agent for packet ships relaying freight between New York and Liverpool. Then the Grinnells built ships of their own. Grinnell, Mintum & Company became known as a rich, conservative house that was as moral as unregulated business allowed, and Henry Grinnell as its successful director. He had bankrolled the expeditions of Elisha Kent Kane, which in Hall's eyes made him all the greater.

Hall traveled with his petition from Cincinnati to New York. He had the gumption to seek an audience, and he interested Henry Grinnell as a worthy charity. To Hall's great pleasure, Grinnell shared the belief so dear to him that members of the Franklin expedition could indeed still be alive.

From New York, Hall went by train to New London, Connecticut, to talk with whaling captains. The ticket agent of the Norwich and Worcester Railroad gave him free passage after Hall described the nobility of his mission. In the journal he began to keep, the next weeks are portrayed as a fierce battle against a hundred treacheries. Captains promised help only to desert him; humiliations assaulted him. It is the first time we catch a glimpse of his suspiciousness, a dark conviction that betrayal lurks everywhere. He moodily lurched between unbounded excitement about his plans and extreme anger at delays.

Captain Sidney O. Budington rescued Hall from disappointment: Budington offered him passage aboard the *George Henry*. It was about to sail to the whaling grounds of Baffin Island, from where Hall might be able to make arrangements with Inuit to travel farther west. As Hall envisioned it, the Inuit would teach him their language as they made their way to King William Island, where Franklin's men had begun their trek south. In his imaginings this was an economical, simple plan: travel with a half dozen natives and rely on their skills and on Providence. His limited means now seemed a virtue, freeing him to travel light. Budington also volunteered the services of Kudlago, a Baffin native the captain had brought to New London. So Hall now had a guide.

The business cards Hall squirreled away record his rounds in New York: F. L. Kneeland, No. 159 Front Street, purveyor of DuPont's Gun Powder. Giuseppe Tagliabue, Barometer and Thermometer Maker. Thinking ahead to his dealings with Inuit, he visited an importer of beads, M. P. Brown on Pearl Street. Penciled on the back of a card from Baker & Co., importers of toilet articles from Paris and London, is a reminder in his hand: "Rifle—(see about Bayonets)."

His alliance of supporters in Cincinnati cooked and canned the pemmican. Another consortium built him a sledge, to a design based on one used by his hero Elisha Kent Kane. Captain Budington generously supervised construction of a twenty-eight-foot boat for Hall's hoped for explorations at King William Island. The American Express Company paid the cost of sending the sledge, a half ton of pemmican, and a case of books by train to New York; Adams and Co. Express waived all charges for transporting the cargo from there to New London. Henry Grinnell made the largest cash contribution: $343, roughly a third of Hall's total budget. About to disappear as an important figure in her husband's life, Mary Hall donated $27. Her husband placed Grinnell first in the printed list of supporters, and her last. The New Franklin Research Expedition filled him with importance; what people thought of him did not seem to matter, for he was wholly self-absorbed.

On May 5, 1860, the *George Henry,* Captain Sidney O. Budington in command, sailed from New London, Connecticut. The owners, the whaling firm Williams & Haven, waived all charges for Hall and his personal cargo, including his new skiff and enough stores to last at least a year. He also brought his library of books about the north, including *A Chronological History of Voyages into the Arctic Region,* by John Barrow.

It was a dreadful time for whalers. Whaling ships had first reached the northern part of Baffin Island in the 1820s. After depleting those waters, the whalers extended the hunt south down the Baffin coast. Then some vessels began to spend the winter there—the wooden ships willingly frozen into position. They would arrive in midsummer and hunt until the freeze-up in October, then endure ice and darkness for six months in order to resume work at the first sign of breakup, and stay through most of the second summer. The whalers hailed from a large catchment basin of New England towns—Dartmouth, Falmouth, Mystic, Nantucket, New Bedford, New London, Provincetown; and from Scottish ports—Aberdeen, Dundee, Hull.

A glut of whalers had driven down the price of oil. Then a terrible dearth succeeded the glut. It helped convince New Englanders to steer their money into less volatile investments, such as textile mills. No one had yet given much thought to the oil well that E. L. Drake had just drilled in Pennsylvania—the importance of petroleum still seemed small. But whalers said that a man would be better off "painted black and sold to a southern planter" than as a member of a whaling crew.

By the 1850s captains were hiring Inuit for the six-man whaleboats. In some waters, in the mid–nineteenth century, sailors could encounter Inuit as isolated from the ways of whites as the Powhatans had been at the beginning of the seventeenth century, when they watched whites building a settlement the intruders called Jamestown. The Inuit would touch the sailors' faces to see if the white would come off. Inuit were offered what looked to be a dried meat, which the sailors called tobacco. Swallowing a brown leaf, the Inuit found it disgusting. The two cultures needed time to appreciate each other. Young men who relied on hunting for every meal quickly proved more expert whalers than young men from played-out New England farms, so more Inuit were hired for the boats. The Inuit were lookouts, harpooners, and boatheaders, steering the thirty-foot boats in pursuit of *Balaena mysticetus*.

A mature bowhead whale weighed forty tons or more. Wounded by a harpoon attached to nine hundred feet of rope, a whale could tow a one-ton boat with six men aboard for half a day, if the rope didn't break. Or if the boat wasn't swamped by a rogue wave, or wasn't dragged onto rocks. The whalers would let the rope play out as the whale dived, draw it back when the animal resurfaced, increasing the drag until the whale exhausted itself. A quick movement of its flukes—twenty feet across—could capsize the boat. Rope speeding through the chocks would sometimes smoke and set a boat on fire; a kink could let the whale draw the rope taut and take control. Someone stood with a hatchet aimed at the rope as the whale's forward motion uncoiled it, just in case. The danger peaked when the men rowed close enough to use the lances. Whoever handled them needed enough strength to stab through the blubber to the heart.

Everyone was a slave to the whale once the harpooners towed the carcass to the mother ship. The senior men would take charge of the flensing, the peeling off of great strips of blubber with a long-handled spade, as if plowing rich soil for a garden. The strips of blubber, called "blanket pieces," weighed as much as a ton. Everyone worked in shifts at the "making-off," chopping the blanket pieces into morsels small enough to fit into the kettles. During the "trying-out," the blubber was boiled off, leaving the oil to be drained into casks. The personnel included krengers (who did the initial trimming), clashers (who carried the blubber to the next station), skinners, and choppers. A fifty-foot whale could yield twenty tons of oil. The men stank from oil and struggled to keep their footing on the greasy deck. They prayed they wouldn't be crushed if a blanket piece slipped from its chain.

Whaling remained a dangerous profession even in the absence of whales. Of the eight whaling ships that had left New London the previous year, one had disappeared off Baffin Island. Another had been wrecked near Mozambique, and a third vessel had been lost in the Pacific. No word had come from a fourth, presumed to be in the Indian Ocean.

For the first twelve days aboard the *George Henry,* Charles Francis Hall was horribly seasick. ("A miserable time I have had of it—ill nearly since we left; and now, as I write, my head is like a mountain of solid rock.") He was also depressed by the sudden lack of activity. After the exciting months of preparations, he was merely a passenger among the whalers. "I have felt myself swung, tumbled, jammed, knocked, struck, rocked, turned, skewed, slewed, warped, pitched forward and backward, tossed up and down, down and up, this way and that way, round and round, crossways and kit-a-cornered, in every possible manner." It was an apt description of both his seasickness and his moodiness.

Once the seasickness ended, euphoria overtook him. Seeing his first whale exhilarated him. So did the gale the ship passed through. He believed that the hand of a benevolent deity guided every wave. When a member of the crew began calling him Captain Hall, his spirits improved even more. Two weeks at sea qualified him, in his thinking, to offer advice about sea conditions to the indulgent Captain Budington. Hall considered himself to be undertaking an especially noble mission, and he would attempt to part the waters himself if that might help save John Franklin's men. "I felt myself to be in the performance of a duty I owe mankind—myself—God! Thus feeling, I am strong at heart, full of faith, ready to do or die in the cause I have espoused." That was how far he had traveled from his life in Cincinnati. He was ready to die for this.

Sidney Budington tolerated his passenger's quirks. As captain, he worried mainly about finding whales; profit and loss were more important than Hall's reveries. Unlike some captains, he usually kept his temper in check and controlled his taste for alcohol, and he was experienced in the north. Nine years before, in 1851, he had voluntarily spent a winter in Cumberland Sound, the richest whaling grounds at Baffin Island. His experience there had helped demonstrate that whaling crews could survive a winter and then have a head start on the next year's hunt.

The *George Henry* was accompanied by a schooner, the *Amaret*. Hall revered the *Amaret* because it had also accompanied Elisha Kent Kane on his first trip north, under the name *Rescue*. In Hall's emotional state that name seemed a talisman, so in his journal he called the schooner the *Rescue*. The *George Henry* and the *Rescue* carried a total of twenty-nine officers and sailors, plus Hall, his new skiff, and Kudlago, the Inuk from Baffin Island who had agreed to be Hall's guide.

In a sense, Kudlago was a descendant of Martin Frobisher's Inuit "stranger" of 1576, whom Frobisher had forcibly taken to England as a token of the new territory. In the nineteenth century, the number of Inuit who willingly went south would barely fill a whaleboat. Kudlago was one of the few who entrusted themselves to whaling captains and ventured in that direction, to see the white man's world. Now he was on his way home and in Hall's company.

Unlike Frobisher, the whalers recognized the Inuit's skills. In 1839 the Scottish whaler William Penny had met a young Baffin Island man who talked about a bay teeming with whales, and drew a map showing those waters. The young man's name seemed strange to southerners: Eenoolooapik (in modern spelling, Inulluapik). Captain Penny took young Eenoolooapik to Scotland, in hope of organizing another trip to explore those unseen whaling grounds. The visitor from Baffin Island found Scotland's trees and lighthouses especially interesting. The Scots were struck by his treating everyone the same, as if a class system were not essential for navigating life. Until his hosts insisted, he resisted wearing caribou skins and putting himself on display. An illness of some kind confined him to bed for several months, during which time he objected to being bled as strongly as he had objected to wearing the caribou skins. But his hosts again prevailed. In 1840, Penny returned to Baffin Island with Eenoolooapik as his pilot and "discovered" Cumberland Sound. The new waters assured the whaling industry of a decade of relative prosperity.

In 1847, hunting whales in Cumberland Sound, Captain John Parker had encountered Inuit who were starving to death. Either the ice had formed late the previous autumn, making it impossible for Inuit to begin the seal hunt, or disease had killed their dogs, which would have had the same disastrous effect on hunting and would also have prevented families from moving to other hunting grounds. Or perhaps the caribou had failed to arrive. Parker brought an Inuit couple to England to help raise money for relief.

Seventeen-year-old Memiadluk, dressed in furs, would sit in a kayak on stage in company with his wife, fifteen-year-old Uckaluk. Parker would meanwhile address the audiences about the Inuit's desperate living conditions.

The young couple was regarded as charming domestic pets—"gentle, docile, grateful, and evidently much attached to Captain Parker," the *Times* said, in a description suitable for a basset hound. "One of those outlying varieties of the human family," reported the *Guardian*, which claimed to see hints of Africa and the South Seas in the Inuit. They were as marvelously strange as the man brought back by Frobisher, but more pliable. Uckaluk was taught how to wash laundry and clean dishes—skills thought suitable for a good-natured savage.

Aboard the *George Henry,* Kudlago was now heading home to Baffin Island, after exploration of New York and New England. He remained a cipher. "He never expressed surprise at any thing," Charles Francis Hall said of him. They were an ill-matched pair. Hall rarely disguised his strong feelings, while Kudlago was watchful and controlled. A drawing of him from his days in the United States shows a strikingly handsome man, perhaps in his forties, with a chiseled face as hard as a statue's. His dark hair is neatly parted on the right, and he wears a bow tie and topcoat suitable for Henry Grinnell's parlor in New York. He gazes straight ahead. Hall said that Kudlago uttered not a word at seeing a locomotive for the first time. "He looked upon the works of civilization with interest, but never with wonder."

Kudlago seemed to have a cold, which worsened during the voyage. His decline was obvious to everyone aboard. He preferred staying in a tent on deck rather than in his bunk, and repeatedly asked in Inuktitut if anyone had sighted ice. It would mean the ship was nearing Baffin Island. Before dying, he asked many times, "Do you see ice? Do you see ice?"

Hall sounded more upset by the need to find a new guide than by the death itself. He offered a few remarks at the shipboard funeral, but always portrayed himself as the center of attention. "I must say that never did I participate more devoutly in what I consider the most solemn scene of my life," he wrote. It was a bright Sunday morning, and the blue-white glaciers of Greenland were visible in the distance. At Captain Budington's signal, the sailors let Kudlago's body slide into the water.

The *George Henry* anchored at Holsteinborg, on Greenland's west coast. For the next three weeks, Hall toured every building in the settlement, learned from the Danish governor the population figures for the region, recorded the results of the previous year's hunt (number of caribou killed, pounds of seal blubber secured), made a census of the inhabitants by profession, studied the wage scale, inventoried the contents of the general store and the community's warehouse, which was stocked with two years' worth of staples in case the annual supply ship failed to arrive from Denmark—that is, he gathered *facts,* because he wished to know everything about the Arctic. Writing them down made him feel that the north was more nearly a part of him.

He could never resist moralizing. Climbing a mountain with a sailor from the *George Henry,* he battled mosquitoes on the way to the summit, where he and the sailor found a crystal-clear lake. They used their hands to catch three small trout, which they cooked using moss as fuel for the fire. There he was, atop a mountain in Greenland, with a carpet of heather as the table for a meal he had secured himself. It became the occasion for another of his sermons: "There is philosophy in every thing, especially in eating. The world eats too much. Learn to live—to live as we ought. A little food well eaten is better for any one than much badly eaten."

Every experience seemed to him useful in some way. He talked with the Inuit and unsuccessfully tried to recruit a new guide. Invited aboard the *George Henry,* the governor examined Hall's library of expedition reports and flattered him by asking questions. Queried about the United States, Hall reverted to one of his earlier pet causes by extolling the marvels of trolleys. The governor was entranced. When Hall decided to buy a dog team, the governor himself helped select the animals: Kingok, Flora, Ei, Melaktor, and Hall's two favorites, Barbekark and Merok. The dogs cost five dollars a half dozen; two bushels of dried fish to feed them added twenty-five cents.

The three weeks in Holsteinborg convinced Hall that Inuit were "glorious good fellows." He extrapolated his findings in that well-ordered town to include all of the Arctic. Honest, good-natured, hospitable—Inuit seemed to him to be cheerful creatures devoid of vice. "This is just their nature," wrote Hall. Some months later, during his travails on Baffin Island, they would be rendered as "untamed children," a "treacherous people." He had assumed they would always carry out his orders. He admired them for their independence and later would despise them for it.

After another bout of seasickness, Hall made himself almost drunk with sensation. He ran out of words for naming the colors in an evening sky that never turned dark—how to describe fifty purples? One morning, as the *George Henry* headed west, a line of icebergs very distinctly hung upside down in the sky. Dead ahead was an inverted mountain range too, somehow suspended from the clouds. The mountains dipped when the ship rolled, just like real mountains, and grew larger as the ship traveled in their direction, just as they should. He knew it was a mirage, a trick of air bending light, but struggled to believe it. He judged it an excellent display of God's creativity.

The *George Henry* stood off the Baffin coast for a week because of fog. Boats from the *Rescue* and another whaler towed it the last few miles into a bay. Hall was brimming over with emotion.

> I look over the bow of the George Henry every now & then, & what a pretty sight! Every now & then, I cast my eye westward, & *glorious* is the scene!! I turn toward the star-board side, & *grandeur* stands before me!!!

He promptly named the anchorage Cornelius Grinnell Bay, for the son of his patron Henry Grinnell.

Inuit began coming aboard even before the ship dropped anchor. A man named Ugarng arrived first, as befit his status as the best hunter in the area. His thirteen wives, including three at present, further confirmed his standing. A gifted hunter needed a large household to sew the sealskins obtained during spring into tents, to butcher the caribou hunted in autumn, and to tailor the fur into clothing. On an earlier voyage, Captain Budington had been sufficiently impressed to offer Ugarng passage to the United States. Ugarng remembered New York as a place of too many houses and too many horses but was greatly impressed by the women. "He had several excellent traits of character," Hall wrote, "besides some not at all commendable."

On that first day, Ugarng took Hall ashore to an Inuit camp. The American peered into the sealskin tents and exchanged a few words of greetings. He was dismayed to see the corpse of a woman no one had taken the trouble to bury, lying on the ground as if her body were just another boulder. ("This inattention to the *sick & dead* is a blot upon the otherwise noble people," he wrote.) Yet he approvingly noted that the Inuit had left untouched a mountain of supplies left by whalers the previous years.

He thus began a new career as an ethnographer, closely observing and recording the habits of this band of Inuit. In the months to come, he wrote down the stories the Inuit told, compiled a small glossary of Inuktitut, and traveled with them. "His" Inuit were the Nugumiut, who in summer lived in sealskin tents along Baffin Island's southeastern coast and fished for char. They hunted caribou in autumn, and during winter and spring lived in igloo villages, from which they ventured out to hunt seal, walrus, and polar bear. The Nugumiut moved according to the season and the hunt but usually camped in the same places every year. Hall had planned a different kind of exploration, but his powers of improvisation were truly remarkable. If he was a sometimes bumbling amateur in these investigations, there were as yet no professionals. In his notebooks he mapped a culture along with a geography that no white person—no southerner—had explored since the days of Martin Frobisher.

A week after reaching Cornelius Grinnell Bay, the *George Henry* and the *Rescue* sailed south. Most of the Inuit, including their extended families, stayed aboard as the newly hired whaling crew. In exchange for their skills they received three meals a day in the ship's main cabin, as well as guns, ammunition, and tobacco. Two intertwined societies made themselves at home aboard ship. Some of the women skinned a large brood of ducks with their teeth and gave the carcasses to the ship's cook for the whites. The Inuit meanwhile feasted on the layer of fat attached to the skins; whole families, satiated with duck fat, slept on the deck. After a few hours' travel, the *George Henry* anchored in the waters Captain Budington intended to make his headquarters for whaling. Hall called the second anchorage Cyrus Field Bay, in honor of another of his heroes.

He never tired of naming things. The Inuktitut place-names described the topography or animal life and guided the hunter. Pangnirtung was "Where the Caribou Bulls Are" and for that reason, among others, is now a town. Learning the place-names, a boy could remember the terrain and understand where to expect seals. A location was marked by a name because ice or winds there were treacherous in some way, or because of a dependable abundance of animals. Names served as both map and survival guide.

Hall bestowed on the geography the names of benefactors and people he admired. James Lupton of Cincinnati, who had contributed thirty dollars, a pocketknife, and books, was the namesake of Lupton Channel, at the southern end of Cyrus Field Bay. East of Lupton Channel lay Sylvia Grinnell Island, named for Henry Grinnell's daughter. From there Hall saw a high tower of rock, which became Jones' Tower, in honor of George T. Jones.

History is greatly indebted to Jones, superintendent of the Cincinnati office of the American Bank Note Company. He and a Thomas Newell gave Hall two of the notebooks that became the diaries of his adventures. The paper is made of the linen ordinarily used for banknotes. Hall sketched islands in the notebooks, recorded his interviews with Inuit, and listed compass readings. His handwriting changed, depending on his level of excitement.

Some entries were written as he traveled in a whaleboat, the words rising and falling like the water, because he couldn't wait to record a new experience. Some of the other notebooks fit a shirt pocket with room to spare; as the months passed, he was famished for paper. He used school tablets, cannibalized navigation tables and ledgers, and only later turned to the handsome notebooks presented by Jones and Newell.

He did not forget to honor Thomas Newell: Newell Sound lies east of Eggleston Bay (in appreciation for thirty dollars from Benjamin Eggleston) and south-southeast of Fletcher Island (in recognition of Lowell Fletcher of Cincinnati, provider of ten gallons of alcohol).

He practiced for traveling to King William Island by making increasingly ambitious excursions from the *George Henry*. Using his new skiff for the first time, he outpaced the *George Henry*'s whaleboats—"Truly glad was I to find my boat so good"—and visited other whaling ships to gather more intelligence about the north. On one of his ventures ashore, he hiked to the top of a ridge and stared at the waterway whalers knew as Frobisher Strait. The waterway was littered with remnants of icebergs, like bobbing white steeples. No one from the south knew the strait's length or had sailed all the way through it. Hall looked through a telescope at the waterway's southern shore. He knew the land's name, Meta Incognita, from his books about the north. In late summer the land is a rampart of steel-gray mountains crowned by a glacier beneath a wide-painted stripe of blue. Still gazing through the telescope, he faced south, then slowly scanned west to follow Meta Incognita's coast. In the distance the land seemed to curve north; the image wobbled in the darkness of the lens. The scene entranced him— "beautiful and exciting in the extreme."

A day later he met Koojesse, a hunter who stood second in status only to Ugarng. Together Koojesse and Ugarng offered Hall a geography lesson after examining one of his maps. On the map, Frobisher Strait trended northwest until it reached space left blank. Cartographers in the United States and Great Britain were unsure whether the empty space was land or a frozen sea.

Koojesse and Ugarng guided Hall's hand over the map's outline of the waterway. They traveled, so to speak, west along the southern shore and then turned north. The land curved there, they said. The route of their hands showed that Frobisher Strait was closed on one end. It was not a strait but a bay. This was something only Inuit knew. Their knowledge of geography was "truly wonderful," said Hall; their intelligence was "of a surprisingly high order" when it came to describing topography. One of Ugarng's wives, supporting everything the men said, described how she had traveled on both shores all the way to the land at the western end of the waterway. Koojesse himself drew a map showing dozens of islands scattered in the bay, and inlets and sounds unknown to the whalers. "In what they related to me about Frobisher Strait," Hall wrote, "there could be no doubt."

He filled the weeks making social calls among the Inuit. A gray-haired woman named Petato came aboard the *George Henry,* talked of her twenty-five children, and impressed him with her memory. The women spending their days aboard ship busied themselves chewing sealskins to soften them for sewing into boots, or sewed caribou skins with sinew. The men, when it suited them, worked in the whaleboats, and some of the children attended classes organized by Hall. He also tried to persuade Koojesse to lead him to King William Island in the new skiff, to obtain word of John Franklin's men. When Koojesse and Captain Budington insisted it was too late in the year for such a trip, Hall resigned himself to waiting until spring.

Depending on his mood, he found the Inuit either endearing or dreadfully unruly. They infuriated him when they failed to take schedules and plans as seriously as he did. They lacked restraint, he concluded; they were debased due to the bad influence of whalers, men who drank and cursed. He wanted them bound by his own sense of time, and his anger exploded whenever they forced him to change plans. All his good feelings about Ugarng evaporated into a rage when Ugarng left without him on a hunting trip. Hall interpreted every difficulty as an attempt to thwart the New Franklin Research Expedition.

On September 26, his plans were changed again. Snow began falling at noon, and by early evening the seas rose in a strong gale. It soon felt like a hurricane. The winds tore Hall's skiff from its moorings and slammed it onto rocks, and the storm pounded it for another day until nothing was left except the sternpost. The *Rescue* turned broadside into the waves, lost her masts, and suffered the same fate on the rocks. Lacking a boat, Hall would not be able to travel to King William Island. Yet he considered these events only a setback, rather than the end of his mission. He quickly consoled himself with the prospect of learning more about the Inuit. If one plan failed, he would make another. His self-centeredness nurtured his resilience: he had decided nothing could stop him.

He could count on having a whole winter and spring for his explorations among the Inuit. By mid-October, ice had already closed the Davis Strait. It was too late for Captain Budington to sail home. The *George Henry* would winter in Cyrus Field Bay.

On a November day, while writing in his cabin, Hall was startled to hear the voice of a woman. Her soft, sweet "Good morning, sir" might as well have been a sudden kiss, so great was his pleasure at hearing her speak. He thus met Hannah. She was wearing a bonnet and a ruffled dress, over caribou skins. Her politely extending an ungloved hand made her all the more endearing—"a *lady* Esquimaux!" Her real name was Tookoolito, as Hall chose to spell it. Later that day he met her husband, Ebierbing, whom the whalers called Joe. Hall had found the guides who would become his companions for much of the rest of his life: Hannah and Joe.

Hannah was about twenty-two, and Joe twenty-four. They were the most worldly of all the Baffin Island Inuit. In 1851, they had met Captain Budington in Cumberland Sound; a year later, a Scottish shipowner had taken them to Britain in company with an Inuit boy, where they stayed for three years. Hannah and Joe wed in the shipowner's house and went on display in exhibition halls, in company with stuffed seals and a kayak, as a sort of *tableau vivant* of Baffin Island.

Dressed in their furs, Hannah and Joe had been presented to Queen Victoria and Prince Albert at Windsor Castle. "Had seen before luncheon 3 Esquimaux, a married couple, & a little boy," Victoria wrote in her journal. "They are my subjects, very curious, & quite different to any of the southern or African tribes, having very flat round faces, with a Mongolian shape of eyes, a fair skin, & jet black hair. They are entirely clothed in skins." On her part, Hannah found the queen "very kind, very much lady."

Hannah returned to Baffin Island with a liking for bonnets and silk dresses. Other women imitated the new fashions by sewing caribou skins into dresses, and Hannah taught them how to knit. In a photograph taken some years after she began aiding Charles Francis Hall, she wears an unflattering plaid dress with a small ruffle across her bosom. Her face is square and somewhat mannish. She stands very straight with her shoulders back, perhaps at the instruction of the photographer. The look is that of someone who will do anything that is asked, and then will inquire if, sir, she can do something more.

Joe, in a different photograph, is incongruously posed in full winter gear in front of a painted backdrop of leafy trees. Baffin Island has no trees. He looks slightly built even though he wears a caribou parka with the hood up, caribou trousers, and fur boots. His long face is without much expression.

Hall's relationship with Joe seemed relatively straightforward at first, as that of employer and employee. Before guiding the American, Joe had expertly piloted whaling ships along the Baffin coast. His skills as a hunter were such that, more than once, he had kept entire communities alive in desperate situations. In the months to come, he would push himself literally to exhaustion for Hannah and Hall, out of love for her and a powerful mix of loyalty toward the American and self-abnegation. Joe was not especially fluent in English, and one senses Hannah hovering nearby whenever Hall records a conversation with him.

In the one image that shows the three of them together—an engraving rather than a photograph—they all wear caribou skins. Hall stands between Hannah and Joe, with his hands paternally reaching behind them. Their postures reflect the relationship that Hall told himself was true: here was Father Hall with his arms embracing his dependent children of the north. He towers over them, and even his caribou skins seem finer. A handsome shock of hair and a thick long beard highlight his very large face. He stands with feet wide apart—powerful, steady.

Hannah bewitched him. Being in the presence of an intelligent Inuit woman who spoke English gave him almost more pleasure than he could bear. A day after the shock of her sweet "Good morning," Hall visited Hannah and Joe in their caribou-skin tent. She was knitting socks when he entered the tent, and she offered Hall tea, for which she had developed a taste during her stay in Great Britain. Every friendly gesture was magnified by his having spent the last six months mostly in the company of whalers. As it happened, she fully shared his dislike of swearing and gently complained about the language of the whalers. "Her words, her looks," Hall wrote in his notebook, "her voice, her tears, are in my very soul still."

When winter set in, the Inuit began drifting away from the *George Henry*. The hunters and their families left when the sea ice became thick enough to support travel by dog team to the sealing grounds. Eager for adventure, Hall joined Hannah and Joe when they headed north in the company of a hunter named Koodloo and ten dogs. To live on the frozen bays, in his view, would be excellent preparation for the travels he wished to make later.

On this first sledge trip, Hall acted the professor and judged Joe "a capital dog-driver." They traveled over the sea ice toward Ugarng's winter camp. At the end of the first day Joe and Koodloo needed just an hour to build an igloo.

Igloo building—like making tools from stone, like shaping a pot from clay—is learned rather than intuited. For a long chapter of human history, it was as important as knowing how to use a flint to spark a fire, and in the Arctic that chapter is not over. Igloos belong to the same broad category of unheralded, significant objects as bows shaped with stone tools and (in the south) bark canteens. Those anonymous inventions helped keep people alive.

A person building an igloo needs a long-bladed knife, compacted snow, and a felt sense of geometry. Ideally, the first blocks cut in the snow are large enough to make the builder stagger when he lifts them, and the entrance is best sited at right angles to the prevailing winds to prevent it from being buried by drifts. A traveler could create a safe haven at every stopping place if, in addition to food and fuel for a fire, he had a snow knife. Hall thus passed his first night in an igloo, dining by the light of a seal-blubber lamp. The flame melted ice for drinking water and dried everyone's clothes.

After two more days and nights—much of that time spent pinned down by a violent gale—the party reached Ugarng's camp. Ugarng and one of his wives welcomed everyone with a meal of fresh seal. Then a blizzard confined everyone to the igloos. The storm lasted until the only remaining food was some uncooked whale skin intended for the starving dogs. Almost all the seal blubber—the fuel necessary for light—was gone. Hall had read about hunger in other explorers' chronicles, but the sensation was much worse than what he had expected. His thermometer registered twenty-five degrees below zero Fahrenheit.

He sometimes slept between Hannah and one of Ugarng's wives for warmth. Hannah had suggested it when his feet became especially cold. With such intimate treatment, his foot ailment disappeared. It was a small, pleasureful clash between conventional American behavior and the practicality of the Inuit, and he began to favor the practical. Men and women needed each other not for sex but, literally, for warmth.

When the weather finally broke, Hall asked Koodloo to travel back to the *George Henry* for supplies. Hall, the least experienced person at the camp, portrayed himself in his notebooks as being in command. Koodloo was better qualified to appreciate conditions and refused to make the trip alone. Hall volunteered to travel with him.

Even in the privacy of the notebooks he refused to admit to making mistakes. Every problem was attributed to other people's giving up, their simplemindedness, their lack of energy. As time passed, there were also treacheries that only he could detect. For months his only serious conversations had been with himself. A person feeling so alone can become infected with righteousness, can accumulate a list of secret grievances and see betrayals everywhere. Hall had the company of the Inuit, of course, but he was never truly one of them and did not want to be. He was an American; they were—he believed—talented primitives. Inuit subsisted, Americans accomplished. So to take command seemed the natural order of things, and to admit weakness would be to lose sense of who he was. In his version of events, not even the dogs worked as hard as he did.

But the first miles with Koodloo must have badly frightened Hall, given his own account. With great difficulty he and Koodloo helped the dogs wrestle the sledge through ice as rough as boulder fields, only to reach treacherously deep snow.

Koodloo was the first to express second thoughts, in Hall's telling. "Koodloo seemed to think of giving it up," he wrote later, "and I was so weak as to be hardly capable of dragging myself along." He preferred to attribute any thought of turning back to Koodloo, not himself; after Koodloo, he blamed the dogs. For the dogs to haul the sledge in such deep snow "would be impossible."

Joe had been watching them from a distance and snowshoed to the sledge. Understanding the problem, he volunteered to take Hall's place alongside Koodloo. Perhaps Koodloo had considered turning back because he saw the American's fatigue and knew that a long sledge trip could be fatal for both of them. Hall accepted Joe's offer and retraced his way to the igloos. And in the conditions that he had found impossible, Joe and Koodloo coaxed the dogs forward in the direction of the *George Henry*.

Hall waited for their return with Hannah, Ugarng, and a hunter nicknamed Jack. Still lacking seal blubber, the camp was without heat or light. Ugarng stood over a seal's breathing hole in the ice for a full day, a night, then a second day. On that second day, as if part of a test of faith, a seal rose beneath the breathing hole but disappeared after taking a single quick breath and without giving Ugarng a chance to throw his harpoon. Ugarng shrugged it off as normal winter luck and, with Jack, resumed hunting.

One tatter of whale skin remained in Hall's igloo: it was one and a quarter inches wide, two inches long and three-quarters of an inch thick. It refused to grow larger no matter how long he stared at it. His thermometer showed zero degrees Fahrenheit in his igloo; it recorded minus fifty-two outside in the wind. For extra warmth, he invited the dog named Merok into the igloo.

Then Jack returned to camp with a seal. As was the custom, he divided the catch into portions for every household, and he walked to Hall's igloo with a thick blubbery meal on his harpoon. Shaking himself awake, Hall sensed that Jack was outside the entry tunnel with superlatively rich, warm, odorous blubber. Merok sensed it too. As soon as Hall pushed away the snow block to unseal the tunnel, Merok leaped.

Hall tried to force open Merok's jaws, even jammed his hands into the dog's mouth in his attempt to wrestle back the blubber, but other dogs arrived howling and jumping, refusing to be beaten back. They devoured every morsel.

The heroes during that difficult time were Joe and Koodloo— especially Joe. On the long trek to the *George Henry,* one of his dogs sniffed out a seal hole; Joe marked the place in a landscape of endless white by erecting a small pillar of snow and capping it with a squirt of tobacco juice. Everyone aboard the *George Henry,* including Captain Budington, was surprised by their reaching the ship. The sailors had long ago assumed that all the members of Hall's party had died in one of the storms. Koodloo's wife had believed she was already a widow. After a short rest, Joe traveled back toward camp on his own with the dogs pulling the sledge piled high with supplies. He found the seal hole marked by his pillar of tobacco-stained snow. After standing there an entire night, he speared a seal, then resumed traveling without having slept.

His navigation through a landscape that wind and snow changed every day was a special skill of the Inuit, and remains so. You cannot depend on the stars, for example, to set a course at night, because they can be hidden by clouds. In any case, a star high in the sky would force you to look up, not at the ice, while guiding

the sledge—an invitation to disaster. A blizzard might hide everything beyond the reach of your arm. The Inuit relied on snow-
drifts shaped by the prevailing winds, drifts carved into subtle
pointers as reliable as a compass needle in announcing direction.
Usually, the drifts are bulkier on the windward end and taper away
from it. So they literally point: if the prevailing winds are west-
southwest, the drifts (usually) taper east-northeast. If they were
buried in fresh snow, then the hunter stopped and used his snow
knife to find the form underneath. A hunter who knew the direction of the prevailing winds could set his course by those drifts; in
bad weather, they were his only guide.

With a two-hundred-pound seal on his sledge, and utterly
exhausted, Joe came within sight of the igloos before he collapsed
in the snow. Hall and others helped him cover the last distance. Joe
was the bringer of food, heat, and light.

Traveling by snowmobile, Meeka Mike guided us to camp shortly
before midnight. Navigating in a nearly all-white landscape,
whether aboard a snowmobile or a dog-pulled sledge, is not significantly easier now than in the era of Hannah and Joe. Meeka
could accurately read the ice that covered Frobisher Bay, find
detours around the largest fissures, and, despite the apparent same-
ness of the ice, recognize the entrance to one of the bay's frozen
inlets, which led to a particular snow-covered hill. Every feature
looked the same smooth white in the moonlight. We walked
rather than rode up the slope because of the fissures there. A half
dozen dogs, leaping over the fissures, raced down to greet us.
There, on a natural shelf at the midpoint of the hill, stood the
house of Goola and his wife, Paniloo.

They were the potentates of the hill. Goola was neither tall nor
bulky but was very strong. The skin at his cheekbones was burned
nearly black by the sun's reflection from the ice. As the hunter, he
commanded deference. Mealtime was when Goola was hungry;
the menu was whatever Goola carried home from the hunt. He

trained the dogs, hunted, and took care of the butchering. Paniloo, a less intimidating presence, kept house, sometimes accompanied Goola on the hunt, could tailor the skins into clothes, and, if need be, could perform the shooting and butchering herself.

Their house was a low rectangle of weathered plywood. A small door opened into an anteroom containing the carcass of a caribou, the room functioning as a freezer and airlock. A rack of antlers was half-buried in the snow outside.

The hut for visitors was a few steps away. It had an igloo's converging walls and flat-topped dome, built in straight lines rather than curves. Goola and Paniloo had draped the wood frame with layers of canvas, plastic sheeting, and carpet remnants. The interior walls were cardboard. For ingenuity in the use of low-cost materials, you could hardly improve upon it. You crouched to enter a short tunnel used for food storage, went through a low doorway into a small space for boots and parkas, crouched again to enter the living area. At the rear was the platform for sleeping—one step up, into warmer air. There were two skylights, fashioned from heavy plastic, and the walls and ceiling were papered with pages torn from magazines and government reports. Every night you could go to sleep by reading another paragraph. The dogs woke us in the mornings by climbing onto the roof to paw at the skylights. The hut could accommodate twelve people, very intimately.

Goola wanted to go seal hunting in the morning, so seal hunting it would be. His preferred companion was Boy, who was chief dog. Boy had spent several hours lounging lengthwise on the seat of Goola's snowmobile, brown tail at the handlebars and black muzzle parked atop the backrest. He was blessed with a sensitive nose. Under way, he trotted ahead of the snowmobile until he smelled a seal's breathing hole in the ice. He changed course to sniff it more closely without making a sound.

The instant Boy stopped, Goola leaped off the snowmobile and ran to a small dome of crusty ice, kicking hard at the dome with his heel. He broke through into the den. It was the season for pups. You hoped to burst into a den where a pup was too young to swim away, or to surprise both the pup and its mother. Every winter, as Frobisher Bay began to freeze, the seals broke through the ice with their heads to create networks of breathing holes. The seals are ringed seals, *Phoca hispida,* the adults five feet long. As the ice thickened during the winter, they scratched and gnawed the breathing hole from below to keep it large enough for a nose. A little water sloshed out whenever a seal rose into that small dome to breath, and the dome became a mille-feuille made of ice. Given enough patience you could hear the scratching underneath the ice, or a deep wet breath. The mother would nurse her pup underneath in the den; the den led to a form-fitting tunnel, which was the animal's escape route into deeper waters beneath the ice.

The first den was empty except for slushy water. We all took a turn wriggling headfirst far enough into the den to sniff at the tunnel.

Boy led Goola to a dozen breathing holes. No one spoke. For a very long time seals played as large a role in Inuit life as buffalo had played in the lives of Plains Indians in the south. Seals provided food; their blubber was fuel for cooking and for light; their skins were made into clothes and into summer tents. Ten sealskins were enough to make a kayak. The Inuit rarely suffered from scurvy, despite the lack of fruit and vegetables in their diet, because seal meat was exceptionally rich in vitamin C. Charles Francis Hall, unlike the finicky whalers, adopted the Inuit practice of eating seal meat—cooked and uncooked—and derived all the benefits.

In the era of Joe and Ugarng, long before the snowmobile, a hunter would catch seals by standing on a scrap of fur placed on the ice, upwind from the animal's breathing hole. Or he stationed himself on a seat made from a block of ice with the scrap of fur on top. The fur prevented the cold from drilling into his feet or his bottom. Then he remained as nearly motionless as possible with a rifle or a harpoon until he heard a seal scratch at the underside of the hole or heard the puff of its breath. Polar bears played the same waiting game. The wait could last fifteen minutes or overnight, as Joe experienced during his trip back from the *George Henry.* A seal under the ice could hear a hunter shift his weight from foot to foot; it could see the movement of a shadow, and would swim away.

There is a sizable literature about traditional seal-hunting methods, including a remarkable step-by-step analysis by the anthropologist Richard K. Nelson. In the 1960s Nelson subjected the hunt to something akin to a time-and-motion study. He concluded that the only way for a novice to catch a seal by traditional hunting methods was to work with a hunter who was already proficient. It simply couldn't be mastered except with help from an experienced hand. An instruction manual would not work for sealing, any more than one could learn how to drive a car by reading an anthropological account of Detroit.

When a seal arrived at the breathing hole, the hunter remained silent on the ice. He would wait through the seal's first short breath, while the animal tested the air for danger, and then through the pause. Then through a second deep breath. There was time for just one attempt: one shot or one strong thrust of the harpoon, which had to strike the animal's head or neck. A cough, a shift in the wind so that the hunter's scent wafted across the hole—the seal would be gone.

The meat was like sweet stringy lamb, the blubber as rich as warm cream. Everything from the hunt was put to use. A seal's intestines—cleaned, inflated, and each end tied in a knot—served as a Slinky-like toy. Goola wore sealskin boots. His mittens were made of polar bear fur lined with Arctic hare, faced with caribou skin, and trimmed with a big ruff of dog fur. In his house, the broom was made from the feathered wings of a ptarmigan, spread wide as if ready to fly.

He spent the afternoon talking with other hunters via a battery-powered radio. They traded information about the winds and the look of the sky, assembling a personal daily weather report. Depending on the wind, the floe edge would move, the ice would fracture or become more stable. By altering the ice, wind moved the animal life.

Goola's possessions did not extend far beyond necessities. A hunter-gatherer could load onto a dog-pulled sledge everything needed for obtaining food, making clothes, and building his family a new shelter. The snowmobile and the radio could be left behind. Inuit adhering to a traditional way of life concentrated their energies on securing food for their family's next meals and accumulating a small cache. At night, the men shared their catch. They told what they had observed of the animals and the ice, a pooling of intelligence that made the topography safer for everyone. Inuktitut was especially rich in phrases for ice conditions, the habits of wildlife, changes in weather—all the environmental factors influencing the hunt. Without that full sharing, families couldn't survive. Sometime later during the night, the adults traded old stories about the doings of white people, the *qallunaat*. Thanks to their guns and a wealth of food, the first *qallunaat* had seemed all-powerful though not very skilled. In the many retellings, the stories attached encounters with *qallunaat* to one or another place, and they too became part of the geography. Then it was time to sleep. Then it was morning and time to hunt. The more possessions a person had, the harder it was to follow the migration of the animals. The Inuit called this life "living on the land," and Goola and Paniloo were among the small number of them who retained the skills for it.

"You have too many conveniences in the south," Meeka Mike said one night when dinner was under way. "In the south, people don't help people as much." She had used the radio to invite all the other hunters in this part of the bay to share the meal, and four were on their way. Outside, the moonlight combed and groomed the ice. Cold air seeped into the hut, a vaporous white ghost snaking along the floor. When the hunters arrived, they pulled off their boots and browsed the magazine pages pasted on the walls.

After a discussion of the day's hunt, everyone offered family news. There was talk of parents, many stepparents, and many children. One of the hunters asked whether I too was related to some-one he knew. I looked familiar, he said, as Meeka translated the Inuktitut. It is worth knowing that I have an unruly fringe of brown hair but am mostly bald. I lost track of what was being said, but Meeka burst out laughing. The hunter had realized who I must be—recognized my family from having watched television in a settlement, he said. From TV, he knew the *qallunaat* named Larry, Moe, and Curly.

Did I know Curly? Was I related to Curly?

Frobisher Bay and the hills were draped in the moonlight's white silk. The landscape was frozen into white curves and sensual whorls. The bay, in the moonlight in spring, was a plausible setting for a perpetual afterlife—cool and spare, economically lit, every-thing so finely tuned that you heard, or thought you heard, the flapping of a bird's wings as it flew by, and heard the bird's breath.

In February 1861, Charles Francis Hall returned to the *George Henry* after having spent forty-three days in igloos with Hannah and Joe. His cabin felt almost too comfortable now, too warm, the bedding too soft.

Captains wintering at Baffin Island always prepared for the worst from the crew. They gave pep talks about the need to keep a cheerful countenance in the darkness and the importance of stay-ing active. They lectured about the dangers of alcohol. Do not mope, they advised. Do not leave the ship to venture onto the ice except in the company of your shipmates, and only after inform-ing an officer. Beware the terrible consequences of frostbite.

For months the only dependable activities would be sleep, gam-bling, and worry. Worry that the groaning plates of ice would crush the hull; that a gale would snap the masts, which were frozen into icicles; that other members of the crew were pilfering the best food. Captains organized shipboard dances, to which the Inuit were invited. There were calisthenics and dramatic readings. Sailors played endless games of dominoes. On the unrulier vessels, the crew celebrated holidays by consuming stupefying amounts of alcohol. "We had twelve bottles of brandy mixed up for toddy, four plum puddings, half of a pig and brandy sauce and many other things," the boatsteerer aboard the Scottish whaler *Emma* recorded for December 26, 1859. "Four P.M. dancing and singing in the 'tween decks, some drunk &c. Kept it up till midnight, both masters among the crew." But on every ship, the men suffered from cramped quarters, the lack of any real comfort, and the darkness and cold. Moodiness overcame almost everyone. So the winter lengthened aboard the *George Henry*.

Some of the sailors were suffering horribly from scurvy. The disease accounted for their gums' painful swelling, their teeth falling out, and the dark blotches covering their legs—their limbs "as black as coal tar," Hall said. Wintering in Canada in the 1530s, the explorer Jacques Cartier had seen his sailors' legs swell and turn black; their breath "became stinking." The disease induced a terrible lethargy, which was far worse than the cold. Its victims talked of a deep-seated soreness, as if some force had beaten every bone, before the disease killed them. In 1576, Martin Frobisher had returned home without any explicit complaints about scurvy. His experience seemed to support the theory that the disease was caused by prolonged exposure to sea air, for he had been at sea a mere four months. Physicians cited idleness as another possible cause, as well as melancholy, excesses of black bile, and splenetic blockages. As early as Frobisher's day, a few captains recognized the curative effects of lemon juice, oranges, fresh vegetables, and fresh meat. No one would hypothesize until 1912 that an entire category of hitherto unknown nutrients tentatively named vitamins might exist. In 1932, researchers identified the antiscorbutic common to citrus fruits and fresh food; they named it ascorbic acid—vitamin C.

Having lost thirteen men to scurvy on an earlier voyage, Sidney Budington agreed with Hall that the best available remedy was fresh meat. Two of the ailing whalers went onto the ice to live with the Inuit for a diet of seal and walrus. Unfortunately, eighteen-year-old John Brown, feeling strengthened, shook off his guides when heading back to the *George Henry*. His tracks in the snow showed the search party every place he had fallen as he wandered, lost, in a large circle. The search party found the body before animals had the chance to nibble it. Budington and Hall covered him with snow, leaving the corpse to sink into the water come summer. "But oh, what a finding!" said Hall, who took the death very hard. "Spare me from the like again!"

Well into spring, the whalers and Inuit passed the time telling stories. The hunter Koojesse had months before drawn a map of Frobisher Bay for Hall. Now he told an odd tale of some *qallunaat* who a long, long time ago had left behind wood as well as "small red pieces" on an island not far from the *George Henry*. He talked of their having built a ship there.

The Inuit were playing dominoes in the main cabin as Hall chewed over Koojesse's story. Half the jottings he made that night described a gale blowing outside, the game of dominoes, and the fact that the pregnant wife of one of the Inuit hunters had fallen down the forecastle steps. Then he wrote a few lines that linked Koojesse's story to Martin Frobisher.

"In a few days I hope to be exploring Frobisher Bay," he wrote. "I may thereafter have something to add to the matter above referred to."

First he made a sledge trip with Koojesse, during which he devoted much of his energy simply to introducing himself to other Inuit. "My sleep last night was a sound one tho I was tightly squeezed—the sleepers being numerous & all in the same bed!" he wrote on April 23. "There were nine of us beside *the infant at the breast* . . . !" In any case, his limited knowledge of the language turned everything into a garble. A few weeks later, Hannah came to his rescue as a translator, but Hall preferred to believe that his own understanding of Inuktitut had suddenly improved.

Joe was one of the people he interviewed. Joe remembered, as a child, playing on an island with the "small red pieces" and with lumps of coal; he had arranged the red objects in rows, built towers with them, and been fascinated with the red marks they made on rocks. During his sojourn in England he had learned they were bricks.

His grandmother knew the stories of the region much better. Indeed, the Inuit said she was the oldest person alive on Frobisher Bay. Her name, as rendered by Hall, was Ookijoxy Ninoo, and Hall guessed her to be at least a hundred. Her sons included Ugarng, the virtuoso among hunters; Joe was the son of one of her daughters. In the mid–twentieth century, Inuit considered one of Ookijoxy Ninoo's great-great-grandsons to be the best hunter of their own time; that man's son was later judged the best hunter of *his* time.

Ookijoxy Ninoo invited Hall to crowd into her caribou-skin tent. It accommodated a goodly supply of walrus skin and blubber and one small lamp. She lay on her stomach, elbows propped up, her chin cradled in her hands. A grandchild cried outside in the bitter cold of May, occasionally interrupting Hall's questions. He began by showing Ookijoxy Ninoo the map of Frobisher Bay drawn months before by Koojesse.

Yes, she knew the inlets and islands there. She remembered seeing bricks and the like on one of the islands. Here, on the map. She had heard from the elders about white men coming to the island by ship many years ago. They had killed several Inuit and taken away several others, she remembered hearing. Hannah translated the old woman's responses and made sense of them, interpreting the memories, as when Ookijoxy Ninoo recalled seeing stones different from all the rest. They had been heavy and black—pieces of iron, Hannah said.

Some of the Inuit had been injured, and so had some of the whites, the old woman continued. Five whites had stayed with the Inuit for several seasons. Later, the five *qallunaat* built a large boat, in which they placed a mast with sails, but they tried to sail away too early in the year, and some of the men suffered frostbitten hands. Finally, their boat reached open water, which was the last seen of them.

Lacking a written language, the Inuit transmitted their history through the stories told by elders. To be useful, the stories had to convey accurate information about their important points, such as where to find wood and how such a memorable quantity of it came to be at a particular place. Through the stories, the Inuit preserved a memory of the arrival of outsiders along with a catalog of the dangers they brought. A precise chronology was less important than information that helped you make sense of the world, explained an oddity of the landscape, or helped you navigate the present. The stories could vary from telling to telling. Ookijoxy Ninoo answered some of the same questions differently the next time Hall talked with her, and other Inuit directed Hall to a different island from the one she first named. But textbooks change as well, are revised when the information they contain no longer seems important. As the repository of knowledge, the elders received as much respect as the best hunters. Thanks to the stories, a young person could know something about the material wealth of *qallunaat* before encountering them. The critical knowledge of the Inuit was right there, in the kernel of the stories.

Hall asked Ookijoxy Ninoo how many ships had arrived. Hannah translated only the first part of the old woman's answer. "They came every year." After some reflection, she offered the rest: "First two, then two or three, then many—very many vessels." So the ships had arrived three times in different numbers: first two ships, the second time two or three ships, the third time a much larger number of ships.

Hall recognized the outline of the story. He returned to the *George Henry,* and the sky remained bright enough at midnight for him to reread John Barrow's *A Chronological History of Voyages into the Arctic Regions.* He found the section telling the story of Martin Frobisher. Barrow told of Frobisher's three voyages to Baffin Island, and Ookijoxy Ninoo had told the story of three visits a long, long, long time ago by whites. Barrow told of the five sailors Frobisher lost during the voyage in 1576, and the old woman had described the fate of five lost whites. It was as if Hall had found the five missing men himself.

He admitted in his journal to having had some skepticism about the link with Frobisher but added, *"No longer have I doubts!"*

His excitement about Frobisher quickly extended to John Franklin's men. If the Inuit had preserved an account of Frobisher for nearly three centuries, Hall judged that they would surely know after a mere sixteen years every detail about the Franklin party.

"I was now convinced, more than I ever had been, that the whole mystery of their fate could have been, and may yet be easily determined with even the smallest well-directed aid," he wrote some years later. "At all events, I felt that, while life and health should be spared me, I would devote myself to this undertaking."

But first he wanted to visit the island said to be littered with wood and brick.

CHAPTER FOUR

Treasure Island

Martin Frobisher's second northwest voyage enjoyed a more auspicious start than the first. He was now a respectable earl rather than just another pirate, and his three ships left port in May 1577 without colliding. Queen Elizabeth had loaned him the two-hundred-ton *Ayde* as his flagship, and he again had the little *Gabriel* and the *Michael*. The sailors were expecting to harvest gold.

Michael Lok, the treasurer and chief promoter, had supplied them with mining equipment: pickaxes, mattocks, crowbars, shovels, and baskets for carrying the ore after it was worked from the ground. In consideration of the previous skirmishes with the natives, he approved the purchase of additional guns and arrows. The new expedition also gave him an opportunity to improve the previous voyage's dismal balance sheet, by selling some of the supplies left from the first voyage to the new one—the navigation instruments, for example, for forty pounds. That is, he fiddled the accounts. New investors became responsible for the old expenses. The knives and cowbells intended for trade in Cathay were handled that way, shifted from one page to another in Lok's ledger. A change in cost centers, in modern parlance.

The investors worried about the expenses, especially wages. Frobisher had crammed the three ships with assayers, miners, and soldiers, as well as the sailors, and at least a dozen "gentlemen" expecting a splendid adventure. Perhaps he thought that the larger the number of men, the more gold—and glory—he could bring home. When the ships stopped at Harwich to load provisions, a letter arrived from Queen Elizabeth's Privy Council reminding him that he had agreed to employ a maximum of 120 men. He discharged a few at Harwich and continued onward with 140-odd. He was always headstrong, and gold would excuse anything.

Christopher Hall, aboard the *Ayde,* was again his pilot. Hall's log from this trip has disappeared, but in the chronicles written by others he seems the same calm, reflective person. George Best— eventually the author of a pamphlet flattering to Frobisher—was aboard the *Ayde* as both "gentleman" and Frobisher's lieutenant. Enthusiastic and awestruck, he never faults Frobisher, who has the title of captain general. Edward Fenton, considered and rejected as co-commander of the expedition, was captain of the *Gabriel;* Gilbert York captained the *Michael.*

When the ships reached the Orkneys, in early June, the sailors made an especially boisterous landing. Some of the islanders mistook the sailors for an invasion force and fled. George Best went from cottage to cottage reassuring people that the visitors intended to buy their food, not steal it. The Orcadians, valuing leather more than English money, took old shoes in payment.

For the next month the ships traveled without sight of land. George Best marveled at how the northern sky provided enough light for him to read late into the night. He noted too the "many monstrous fish." A fishing line lowered without any bait brought back a halibut that fed everyone aboard the *Ayde.* The north seemed wonderfully rich.

On July 4, Frobisher sighted the southern coast of Greenland, "Frisland" to him. On the 16th, he became convinced they were nearing Frobisher Strait. On the morning of the 17th, he saw land from the maintop. By noon he could make out Hall's Island, where, a year before, Christopher Hall had landed with the sailor who had picked up the famous black stone. Best meanwhile stared at the "huge quantity of great ice," so much ice "that we thought these places might only deserve the name of *Mare Glaciale.*"

Frobisher was all business now. He set an altogether different tone on this voyage, exactly as the investors overseen by the Privy Council wanted, by concentrating from the start on searching for gold, at the expense of searching for a passage to Cathay. A day after sighting Hall's Island, he rowed a pinnace there with assayers in hope of finding black ore, while a second party explored land elsewhere. Hall's Island is a scant square mile of territory, just a little bean of rock. Frobisher examined the whole of it without finding any black rocks, not even "so big as a walnut."

This was worse than scurvy. Given the expectations in London, it was almost worse than dying. Fortunately, the second party found promising outcrops on other islands. George Best interpreted the mixed results as a sign of God's special blessings on England. It was an Englishman who a year ago had found the only black ore on Hall's Island—surely a miracle, Best reasoned—and now Englishmen had found black ore on other islands. A second miracle.

Frobisher, the next day, took about forty gentlemen and soldiers ashore by pinnace. On a modern map, this new landfall is Christopher Hall Island. The land where the ore was first found is, in nomenclature, reduced to Little Hall's Island. On Hall's Island, the Englishmen hiked to a summit that Frobisher named Mount Warwick, for the Earl of Warwick, his first patron on the Privy Council. After piling stones into a high column, and after a trumpeter sounded a few notes, everyone knelt and prayed.

It was an oddly subdued ceremony, this first ritual gathering of Englishmen in North America. Frobisher and his men came ashore without a grand show of flags and assumed they were without an audience. If Frobisher proclaimed Queen Elizabeth ruler of the new territory, or left a flag on Mount Warwick, no one recorded the event.

In 1492 Columbus had flown a royal banner as he stepped ashore in the New World. The Spanish, beginning on the beach that Columbus called San Salvador, always put on a brash show to make their authority unmistakable. They tried to make the foreign seem familiar by simply declaring their own rules as law. At each first encounter with a new people, conquistadores would read aloud a document in Spanish, telling natives who knew nothing of the language that Spain now possessed complete authority over them. They were warned that disobedience was punishable by death, for which the Spanish absolved themselves in advance. What mattered to the Spanish were the legalisms, and every step was planned. There was always a notary among the officers, and the ceremony concluded when he stepped forward and affirmed that the audience was thus properly informed of its obligations.

It's hard to know what the audience made of the Spaniards' show, other than bewilderment. For societies that knew of such things, it could seem some sort of theater or a religious event, the notary perhaps a holy man.

Modest ceremony done, Martin Frobisher marched his men down Mount Warwick, toward the pinnaces.

These sixteenth-century Englishmen were very terse. George Best's first impression was that the territory contained nothing worth discovering other than black ore. What he reported seeing was water, rugged mountains, and ice.

They are the phyla of the north. In summer, depending on the evening light, the ice floes glow pink. They float on a sapphire sea. The land is hardened gray steel. The palette is narrow: gray or gray-brown with patches of purest white. It looks unfinished because of the dearth of vegetation, as if some furnishings were still to come. The landscape is largely unexamined and unwalked-upon except, occasionally, by caribou. The unnamed lakes number in the hundreds at least, formed when the ground caved in after a melting of the ground ice. In geology, it is called thermokarst topography. In describing the scenery, Dionites Settle, a soldier aboard the *Ayde,* was more forthcoming than George Best. Settle would write a pamphlet rendering the 1577 voyage as a stirring adventure worthy of the greatest knights. (His account opened with verse equating Martin Frobisher and his travels with mythical Jason of the Argonauts and the search for the Golden Fleece.) The landscape, though, left him unmoved. He saw only bareness except for patches of dense low plants that reminded him of moss. He noted the bleakness from the lack of trees. The word *tundra* had not yet entered the language, so he lacked a name for the scene. "To be brief," Settle reported, "there is nothing fit or profitable for the use of man, which that country with root yields or brings forth."

On their way back to the pinnaces, the Englishmen saw several Inuit atop Mount Warwick. The Inuit waved a pennant and mooed like bulls, or so it sounded to the Englishmen. Martin Frobisher mooed in return. The Inuit laughed and danced when the trumpeter played his horn. Frobisher and Christopher Hall stepped away from the other Englishmen—just the two of them. They raised two fingers as an invitation for the Inuit to send two men of their own.

The Inuit understood the gesture. They understood too that the meeting was a gamble, and tried to minimize the dangers. They behaved, in fact, as if they were practiced at encounters with potentially hostile bands from distant places. In sign language the Inuit told the Englishmen to place on the ground whatever they wished to trade, then to step back. Two Inuit came forward, picked up the trifles, and left things of their own for the Englishmen. Everything having gone well, the two Inuit approached Martin Frobisher and Christopher Hall.

A more trusting commander would have tried to nurture good relations.

In 1584, seven years after this second voyage by Frobisher, Arthur Barlowe was in command of an English bark coasting North Carolina on a reconnaissance mission for Walter Raleigh when he saw Roanoke Indians for the first time, in a canoe. Barlowe rowed with two other men to a point of land where one of the Indians had stepped ashore. The Indian waited for them without any show of fear. He willingly went with Barlowe to the

Englishmen's ship, sampled the food and wine, and accepted a shirt and hat as gifts before being ferried back to land. He retrieved his canoe and began to fish, filling it to the gunwales within thirty minutes. He divided the catch—half for the whites, half for himself. A day later, another of the local dignitaries presented himself with an entourage of forty or so men and exchanged deerskins for kettles and pans. From then on the Indians supplied the Englishmen with deer, rabbits, fish, nuts, cucumbers, and maize— every necessary supply—every day. Along with the trade goods, trust was the common currency. "We were entertained with all love, and kindness, and with as much bounty, after their manner, as they could possibly devise," Barlowe said. "We found the people most gentle, loving, and faithful, void of all guile, and treason, and such as lived after the manner of the golden age."

Martin Frobisher, on the other hand, assumed the worst of every stranger. As the two Inuit men approached, he already had a plan for kidnapping one of them, and gambled that he could make peace with the other by offering him more trinkets. This is an example of an explorer's belief that the native people will value their liberty as little as he does. One of the Inuit cut off the tail of his parka and offered it to Frobisher, a generous gift if you realized the tail was part of the necessary protection against the cold.

Then Frobisher gave the signal to Christopher Hall.

The Inuit kept fighting even when the Englishmen seemed to have hold of them. Everyone else stood too far away to do anything but watch the struggle, and the Inuit broke free. They picked up their bows and arrows and chased the two unarmed Englishmen toward the pinnaces. There would have been a few quick shouts and the sound of feet scuffling over rocks. An arrow hit Frobisher in the buttocks. More arrows flew by, and arrows were aimed at the boats.

Frobisher ran as fast as he could but feared that an Inuit army would emerge from behind the rocks. The Englishmen at the shore fired a gun as they watched everything go wrong. Nicholas Conger, a muscular soldier from Cornwall, gave chase when the

Inuit retreated at the sound of the shot. He wrestled one of the Inuit to the ground in such a way—demonstrated "such a Cornish trick"—that the captured man's sides ached for the next month. The other native had escaped, and Frobisher was wounded in a particularly humiliating spot. But he had the captive he desired.

A gale pinned down the Englishmen for the rest of the day, giving Frobisher time to consider his situation. He thought himself in enemy territory and knew his ships were waiting out the gale amid ice floes every bit as dangerous as uncharted shoals. The land around him offered nothing but rock and gold, both inedible. He believed that his men were surrounded by people who would rather eat them than give them food.

"And thus keeping very good watch," George Best reported, "they lay there all night upon hard cliffs of snow and ice, both wet, cold and comfortless."

On July 22 the *Ayde,* the *Gabriel,* and the *Michael* sailed west into Frobisher Bay. The sailors named their first anchorage Jackman Sound, after the master's mate Charles Jackman, the first to see it. The assayers went ashore and reported finding silver on one island. They examined four kinds of rock that appeared to have promising quantities of gold, and then explored another island where the sands and cliffs literally glittered. "But upon trial made, it proved no better than lead," George Best said, "and verified the proverb. All is not gold that shineth."

They saw too a dead narwhal with a long spiraled tusk.

Two seagulls a long, long time ago had seen a girl with her hair in lovely long braids, went one of the stories Inuit told around fires of seal oil. Seizing the girl's braids in their beaks, the gulls carried her into the air. Her braids twisted themselves into a tight spiral as the birds flew. When the girl screamed, the gulls let go. Her braids stayed entwined in that spiral as she fell into the water—the girl turned into the first narwhal and her twisted braids into the animal's spiraled tusk. A narwhal tusk, seen close up, could be mistaken for something precision-manufactured rather than grown.

The tusk is a tooth exclusive to the males and grows, complete with nerves and blood vessels, up to eight feet long, its spiral always right to left. Males are thought to advertise themselves with that tooth and brag about the length.

The Englishmen identified the creature as a sea unicorn. Its ivory tusk was added to the cargo.

On July 26, the *Gabriel* and the *Michael* sailed toward the northern shore of Frobisher Bay while the *Ayde* stayed near the southern shore, in Jackman Sound. Despite having been in those waters for more than a week, Frobisher had yet to find a significant quantity of ore. His temper grew short. When Christopher Hall addressed him without first removing his cap, Frobisher cursed Hall, threatened to hang him, and moved to strike him. Edward Fenton intervened just in time. As captain general, Frobisher had nearly the authority of a king but seemed blind to anyone's efforts except his own.

On the 29th, the *Gabriel* and the *Michael* entered a sound protected from drifting ice by a chain of small islands, as if by a fence. At one of the islands, the assayers went ashore by clambering up a cliff. They examined outcrops of black rock, George Best reported, "which in the washing held gold plainly to be seen." The island was sheltered from the force of the tides and offered views of the mainland, to the north, and the main waterway, to the south. Frobisher concluded that he could find no better headquarters than this ore-rich island, and ordered the tents to be unloaded from the ships.

Countess of Warwick Island, he called it, in Countess of Warwick Sound.

He set an example by starting to work the ground himself with a pickaxe. From that moment on, the miners bent over the veins of black rock. They were visible on the surface and went deep. The Englishmen were mining permafrost that had an overburden of rock. They believed they were shoveling wealth, which they carried away by the basketload. A layer of frost coated the shovels and softened the baskets each morning. The miners could see their breath the whole summer long on the island. It seemed only right, though, that a man had to work hard, as if this were God's compromise—the wealth of black ore in exchange for difficult labor.

London seemed as foreign as a palm forest, the meddling investors less of a presence than the gulls and seals.

From a mile away, Countess of Warwick Island was just a small swelling, browned and hardened, rising abruptly twenty feet above the water. At high tide it was somewhat less than eighteen acres. It had a dusting of grainy protosoil but was mostly rock blooming pink and green with lichens, a pointillist abstraction.

It is a poor camping place, since the island lacks water except for a trickle of melting ice at the shore. There is little protection from the wind. A freshly picked-over skeleton of a seal is evidence that polar bears have come ashore. There is caribou scat, and ducks protecting their glowing yellow eggs.

Frobisher's first mine on the island is a deep gash in the cliff of the northern shore. The trench looks to be a large sculpture from the studio of an artist who works in unpolished forms. Everything was *hewn,* a few inches of rock at a time. The miners had relied chiefly on brute strength. They loosened the surface as best they could with the pickaxes, opening the ground wider with a crow-bar and placing an iron wedge into the gap. They then applied the mattock or a twenty-pound sledgehammer to the wedge. An alternative was to hammer the chisel end of the mattock deeper, force iron plates into the openings, and hammer wedges between the plates until the rock shattered. In the mining profession, it would be known as plug and feather. Two blacksmiths resharpened the tools as they wore. New ones were forged from five hundred pounds of iron and steel the ships had brought from England. The picks left distinct scars on the trench walls, like the beginnings of petroglyphs. The miners whittled the eastern wall into a sharp blade, like the spiny back of a stegosaurus. They kept whittling until the cut was sixty feet long, fifteen wide, twenty-four deep, large enough to serve as a dock or a ramp for loading ore.

Looking across to the mainland, the sailors saw what seemed to be the remnants of an Inuit camp. The dwellings were foundations dug into the ground, over which the Inuit could erect tents. The earthen rooms, as round as great stone ovens, were connected like rabbit warrens. Each dwelling included a platform for sleeping, made of flat stones carpeted with moss. The entrances faced south, and there were trenches that served as gutters to carry away snowmelt from the hills. George Best, examining the interiors, proceeded to write the first English account of a native settlement in the New World. His horror of dirt meant that he was struck most by the uncleanness and the scattering of bones. "They defile these dens most filthily with their beastly feeding," said Best. He theorized that the natives stayed at a given camp until the squalor compelled them to go elsewhere.

Frobisher's captive tried to explain his culture through sign language. His name, as understood by the Englishmen, was Kalicho. When they found a tomb containing the bones of a dead man, their first question was whether Inuit had eaten the corpse. No, the bones had been picked clean by animals, Kalicho explained. What interested the visitors most was the fate of the five sailors who had been left behind a year ago. Frobisher's men would have struggled to make their questions clear; neither side could be sure if it was understood by the other. But on this the Englishmen must have pressed Kalicho for an answer. He counted one-two-three-four-five on his fingers and pointed to a pinnace. That seemed to be the answer: he was aware of the five sailors who had disappeared in a pinnace. The Englishmen pantomimed their being eaten. No, Kalicho said, that was not what had happened to the sailors. But he lacked the signs for describing their fate.

Frobisher's cargo included some of the portraits Cornelis Ketel had painted in England after the voyage. Kalicho was shown a canvas depicting the native Frobisher had kidnapped and taken to England. In the intimacy of Inuit society, the man was surely known to Kalicho. He looked at the painting in silence. All he knew was that the person whose image he saw had been taken captive—much like himself—and had not returned. Frobisher's captive had died in England. But he seemed altogether present to Kalicho, albeit in a strangely flattened form. That, at least, is George Best's description of the encounter. Kalicho talked to the portrait, became agitated, and asked it questions. He touched the surface until he established that the figure was not alive. Then he uttered a terrible cry.

With the mining now under way, the *Michael* sailed back to Jackman Sound to find the *Ayde* and lead it to Countess of Warwick Island. Gilbert York, the *Michael*'s captain, at first anchored some distance from Jackman Sound because of the lack of wind. From that anchorage, York saw Inuit tents. He went ashore, picked through the camp, and found a canvas doublet and various unmatched shoes. They belonged to the five missing sailors, York was sure. In hopes they were alive, he left a note saying help had arrived, and pen and ink and paper for them to write a reply.

York reached the *Ayde* the next morning with a plan of attack already formulated. Forty sailors from the *Michael* and the *Ayde* rowed pinnaces later that day toward the Inuit camp until the order was given for them to stop. Charles Jackman led some of the men ashore for an overland approach. His party marched over the hills while the pinnaces resumed their course.

The Inuit panicked on seeing the strangers. Running to their kayaks, the Inuit left behind some of the paddles. So for once the English boats could outrace them, and they blocked the Inuit's escape. The Inuit were forced back onto their spit of land and used their bows and arrows against the sailors' crossbows and firearms. The Inuit picked up the arrows shot by the whites and fired them back. They pulled arrows from their flesh and fired those too. One sailor was hit in the belly, and arrows struck at least a half dozen natives. Some of the wounded Inuit, preferring drowning to capture, jumped from a cliff into the water.

The sailors named the battleground Bloody Point. "We would have both saved them, and also have sought remedy to cure their wounds received at our hands," wrote Dionites Settle, horrified by the sacrifice. "But they, altogether void of humanity, and ignorant what mercy means, in extremities look for no other than death." Their ferocity, for Settle, seemed proof of their barbarism.

A painting of the battle, made after the expedition returned to England, depicts the sailors surrounded by enemies. The sailors are firing harquebuses from a wide-hipped skiff, aiming them at Inuit wielding bows and barbed arrows atop a cliff. A native paddles a kayak in the foreground, and a flotilla of supporting kayaks floats in the distance. The water is a maze of ice floes. Still more Inuit stand on land in sight of a cluster of skin tents; the background is an endless landscape of bare hills. That sense of being surrounded by a cunning enemy is perhaps what frightened the Englishmen most.

When the fighting stopped, the Englishmen captured a woman. But they thought her so ugly and old that they feared she was a witch, and so let her go. They found a second woman hiding behind rocks with an infant boy who was wounded in an arm. She preferred to lick the wound rather than use the ointments offered by the sailors.

Now Martin Frobisher had three captives: the woman, her infant, and Kalicho.

How Kalicho would behave with her became a matter of titillating interest. When he first met with her as a fellow captive, some of the Englishmen positioned themselves to spy on the expected intimacies. The sailors knew her as Arnaq—"Woman"—and the baby as Nutaraq—"Child." During that first encounter Kalicho and Arnaq silently looked at each other until Arnaq turned away and began to sing. At a second closely watched meeting, Kalicho spoke at great heated length, the watching sailors of course understanding nothing. Over the next weeks she tended to the cabin they shared, butchered dogs for food, and prepared the meals as a woman would ordinarily do for a hunter. But Kalicho and Arnaq, to the great disappointment of the sailors, remained unfailingly modest in each other's presence, even in dressing and undressing.

After some time for reflection, Dionites Settle decided they were more likely cannibals than not. He based his conclusion in part on the Englishman's apparent terror of raw meat. He assumed as a matter of course that anyone who ate uncooked fish and freely drank blood, as the Inuit did, would also eat people. No less offensive to him was the natives' appetite for meat regardless of its

Battle in 1577 between English sailors and the Inuit at Bloody Point, along the southern shore of Frobisher Bay. (Copyright © The British Museum)

odor—"a loathsome spectacle." Yet he admired them for making use of every part of the animals they hunted, their weapons (including arrowheads made of sharpened bone, and bowstrings made of sinew), and their striking watercraft. The kayaks were admirably fast; their umiaks—made the same way, by stretching sealskins over a frame of driftwood or whalebone—could transport a dozen people with their household goods, like a wherry on the Thames. Their sails were made from animals' intestines "very fine and thin, which they sew together."

Settle could not make much sense of their housing. He saw the sealskin tents and the foundations for the skin-and-stone structures used in autumn. Considering the summer temperatures, he reasoned that winter would be very cold and the tents inadequate. "I cannot suppose their abode or habitation to be here, for that neither their houses or apparel are of no such force to withstand the extremity of cold that the country seemed to be infected with." He had never seen an igloo.

In skin color, the natives reminded him of "a sun burnt country man"—the laborers back home who worked outdoors. He remarked that Inuit wore their hair very long; some of the women had tattoos of blue dots on their faces and wrists. The Inuit conception of the world interested him too but, given the language problems, remained another mystery. "What knowledge they have of God, or what idol they adore, we have no perfect intelligence."

In the beginning, two men were born fully grown from a mound of earth. One of them was changed into a woman, and their children populated every coast and island: thus was the world peopled. In that long ago time, a girl trying to escape her incestuous brother flew into the sky and became the sun; trying to follow her, her brother became the moon. Those were the stories that Inuit told their children.

In the south, most peoples abandoned hunting and gathering in favor of more settled life. They built settlements and developed pottery. They recorded their histories by incising mud-brick tablets, or carving stones, or painting scenes of this world and the afterlife in burial chambers. But people in the north lived differently.

In the Arctic, until the early twentieth century, hunting and gathering was the only workable strategy. The earliest ancestors of the Inuit migrated from Siberia or Alaska about four thousand years ago, hunting musk oxen. The Independence people, as they are known, somehow did more than just survive in conditions that, for every form of life, favored the pared down and the modest. They moved east a vast distance through the High Arctic while living in skin tents. When the Independence people turned south they hunted caribou, whose skins the women sewed into clothing with thread made from tendons.

Then the climate turned cooler. Climate is the great engine for change: as the sea ice grows or shrinks, it redistributes animal life—and the hunters who depend on it. They acquired new skills, or they moved, or they starved. A new people, the Dorset culture, arrived from the Bering Sea area by about 500 B.C. with a new tool—snow knives. The newcomers' expertise was hunting from the floe edge. Catching seal and walrus, they farmed the sea ice. They also dug foundations into the ground to build winter shelters made of sod and stone. Each dwelling was large enough to accommodate several families—architecture testifying that the Dorset were a people able to gather enough food to stay put for a whole season. Staying longer in one place, they were able to allocate time otherwise used for the logistics of moving to the making of things, whether better housing or small sculptures that hint at a spiritual life.

The Dorset thrived on the continent's cold edges for fifteen hundred years.

When cold conditions again gave way to warm, in about A.D. 1000, the Thule people appeared in the northwest. The newcomers brought dogs and the technology for hunting whales. They introduced kayaks and umiaks, ideal for the whale hunt now that the warmer temperatures had reduced the sea ice. With dogs and kayaks, they could expand the hunt over a larger territory in every season. With a larger catch, they could support larger communities, and their settlements grew to house perhaps as many as fifty people. By about 1100 the Thule reached Greenland, then went as far south as Labrador.

Their relations with the Dorset people remain something of mystery. There may be a Pompeii somewhere in the Arctic that, in its mix of artifacts, will explain what happened between the Dorset and the Thule, but it has yet to be found. In some places the two peoples coexisted for at least a century. They may have intermarried or clashed violently, probably both. What is certain is the Dorset culture disappeared.

The Thule were the immediate ancestors of the Inuit observed by Martin Frobisher. In the sixteenth century, their most important resources were the snow and cold, and their own attentiveness. Their survival depended on their scholarship of the natural world. When a hunter captured a seal, Inuit tradition held that the seal had chosen to give his life to the hunter, for every resource was shared. The Inuit occupied a small tight niche. They had stone vessels but, lacking clay and fuel for a kiln, they never developed pottery. Since they had no written alphabet, their history consisted of the stories told around soapstone lamps burning blubber.

Frobisher Bay supported the animal life that supported the Inuit. In even the coldest winters, a polynya—an area of open water—could be found near Countess of Warwick Sound. It reliably attracted the entire Arctic food chain. Seals basked right there on the ice edge, and polar bears came to feed on the seals. Once the bears were satiated, foxes arrived to nibble on the carcasses. A polynya served as a breathing hole for whales, as well as a walrus resting place. When the climate turned cooler in the 1500s, the polynya is believed to have survived, which is why the Inuit built the camp that George Best saw in 1577 on the mainland.

In 1990 Inookie Adamie, an Inuit hunter then in his mid-sixties, led archaeologists from the Smithsonian Institution in Washington, D.C., to the site.

Inookie is the son of Adamie, who was the son of Nowdlak, who was the son of Soudloo. Soudloo was a son (or perhaps grandson) of one of the most important informants of Charles Francis Hall's, the elderly woman named Ookijoxy Ninoo. Growing up, she had heard the stories about whites who arrived three times in an ever-greater number of ships. Five whites had stayed behind, the storytellers said. As a young man, Inookie had heard the same stories. His elders also talked of an island where white men had a long, long time ago dug a trench.

"The southwest wind is pretty strong, and the pack ice goes pretty fast, and one of the ships got damaged and they built a trench on the island," Inookie Adamie said. "That's what I started history with."

He is small and taut, the cords of his neck like cables. In his younger years he was the person who organized the hunt, knew every family's history by heart, and could explain the significance of every place-name. He now spends each winter with some of his children and grandchildren in a one-story cottage in Iqaluit. In summer, the extended family lives on the land along Frobisher Bay. When I visited him in the cottage in Iqaluit in the company of one of his daughters, his hair had turned gray, and he was losing his hearing.

"The first thing was rabbits and ptarmigans," said Inookie, recalling how he learned to hunt. "Then I shot my first caribou, and after caribou I followed my father and caught my first seal." He was the second of nine children and the oldest boy. Most of the stories the elders told had been about the animals and harpoons. "We hardly had any guns," he said.

The family traded their sealskins for supplies at the Hudson's Bay Company store at Cormack Bay, named for John Cormack, the store manager. Bill Mackenzie was the assistant manager in the 1960s, by which time the store had been moved closer to Iqaluit, and he remembered Inookie's father and uncles. The Hudson's Bay Company had loyal customers because it held a near monopoly on the fur trade. No other firm would dependably extend credit for fur or blubber. Dry goods were on the right, groceries on the left, and Mackenzie had two checkout counters. "The sons, including Inookie, were always very, very good hunters," said Mackenzie, a bear-sized figure with a Santa Claus beard. "That's what gave them their stature."

Inookie Adamie refrained from bragging. Questions about polar bears were shrugged off as if the species were beyond his expertise. After all, he said, he had not killed very many. "Probably not over a hundred." During the conversation he excused himself to bring in a set of maps from another room, the better to show the hunting grounds. His fingers traced the way to the peninsula where he was born. His household moved to town in 1964 because his children needed schooling. In the mid-1970s they moved back onto the land. He was, as a descendant of Ookijoxy Ninoo, a descendant of the Inuit who saw Martin Frobisher. Listening to him, one could almost glimpse the sails of the *Ayde* in the distance.

The Smithsonian team excavated the Inuit camp over a period of two summers. The archaeologists' hard labor testified to the difficulties in tracing the lives of Inuit from the 1500s. Kamaiyuk, as Inuit called the camp, consisted of sod-and-stone foundations in which the archaeologists found Elizabethan coal and flint, materials Inuit had scavenged from Martin Frobisher's camps. Deeper down the excavators found evidence that Dorset and Thule peoples had been in residence earlier. Anne Henshaw and several colleagues recovered from Kamaiyuk and two other sites more than twenty thousand bones, the leftovers of long-ago meals. About half the identifiable bones at Kamaiyuk were from seals. The next largest category was dog, followed by caribou.

Henshaw, then a graduate student in anthropology at Harvard, traced the social arrangements of Kamaiyuk's past residents through the bones. Bones were sorted by genus, species, and skeletal part. Cataloging them by anatomy was how she determined that the Inuit had hauled back whole seal carcasses from the hunt to Kamaiyuk so the meat could be shared, rather than butchering the animals where they were killed and starting to eat them there. Almost every part of the skeleton, not just the tastiest parts, was accounted for in roughly the right proportions in the mix of bones. The sharing cemented ties between the households and averaged out the risk of starvation for all.

Henshaw intended to take this one step further by, in effect, reassembling individual carcasses from the puzzle of twenty thousand parts. Putting part of a skeleton back together—assuming you had recorded precisely where each bone had been found—could show how the meat had been parceled out. You would learn the "trajectory of cuts," the details of how food was shared—whether, that is, the best parts all went into one dwelling. One had to make allowances for the several centuries of people who had camped at the same place and sifted the debris. In any case, the attempt to reassemble the bones from Kamaiyuk had limited success: two anklebones were identified as being from the same seal, and the researchers matched the halves of a single pelvis.

The focus, however, could be narrowed to teeth. During a caribou's life, the animal's teeth gain layers of cementum each year, and the layers alternate between the translucent and the opaque. With great effort, a person could count the layers, like tree rings, to estimate the animal's age. In the case of ringed seals the researcher could read teeth for both age and the season in which the animal died: opaque dentin was deposited between July and March, and translucent layers were deposited between the end of March and the end of June. (The alternation may be related to diet or to hormonal changes during the season of molting.) Know the season of the kill, and you would know the season people lived at the camp. Learn the age of the animals that were killed, and you could deduce the preferences of the hunter or the nature of the herd. The research required more than just a casual look. The teeth were pulled from the jawbones found during the excavations, cleaned with ultrasound, cut lengthwise by a high-speed saw, polished by a grinding wheel, and thinned to a depth of about a hundred microns before going under a microscope.

An anthropologist could then know that a hunter from Kamaiyuk had captured ringed seal No. 160-59 in summer or early autumn, year unknown, when it was seven years old. You learned more about the seal, however, than about the hunter.

The Inuit were always few in number and widely dispersed: Frobisher Bay could support a maximum of about two hundred people living as hunter-gatherers. The population probably remained about the same size from Martin Frobisher's arrival in the 1570s to Charles Francis Hall's in the 1860s. In that period London grew from 100,000 to 2.8 million. Famine, extremes of cold, or a sudden dearth of dogs helped limit the numbers in the north. Then explorers and whalers brought influenza, measles, and tuberculosis.

The Nugumiut, the Inuit of Frobisher Bay, numbered about 80 in 1883-84. An Anglican missionary who went tent to tent in 1913-14 counted 86. In 1941 the Canadian government counted 183. The land could support no more.

George Best was at first horrified by the Inuit, especially by their eating habits. Later, the Inuit impressed him as a nimble, clever people with a great talent for fighting. They had experience with bartering, since they had acquired metal for their harpoons ("their darts"), and the women wore copper ornaments, as ladies-in-waiting at Greenwich Palace adorned themselves with pearls. Yet he always described the natives as merely a species of exotica, like a narwhal tusk. The presence of the three captives—Kalicho, Arnaq, and Nutaraq—did not change his opinion. He regarded them as individuals only to the extent that a busy gentleman would make distinctions among a litter of puppies—charming little beasts, but not important in their own right. That the kidnappings had given the Inuit sound reasons to fear whites did not much interest the Englishmen. In any case, puppies couldn't be trained unless they had fear.

In his chronicle Best complimented the natives for their knack with sign language, and for their imitating Englishmen. "They will teach us the names of each thing in their language, which we desire to learn, and are apt to learn anything of us," he noted approvingly. Christopher Hall had made a list of Inuktitut words during the first voyage, and it's easy to imagine the sailors and captives pointing to one another's clothing or their bodies, as each person listened intently to the odd sounds uttered by the other. "They delight in music above measure," continued Best, "and will keep the time and stroke to any tune which you shall sing, both with their voice, head, hands and feet, and will sing the same tune aptly after you." Paddling kayaks, the Inuit synchronized the strokes with the sailors' oars in the pinnaces, "and seem to take great delight therein." He believed that they used witchcraft, as when they tied a string to a stick and chanted certain words, then lifted a boulder as if it were weightless. "And they made us by signs to understand, lying groveling with their faces upon the ground, and making a noise downward, that they worship the Devil under them."

In that setting, the Englishmen were the true primitives. They misunderstood an environment that, due to the cold, would become more threatening the longer they stayed. The Englishmen were helpless but for their guns. The Inuit, dressed in caribou fur and sealskin, possessed the more appropriate technology, and had by far the better skills. A person dressed in Yorkshire woolens could not stay alive through a winter with just a gun. Anyone squeamish about eating uncooked meat or ignorant of igloos would meet the same fate as poor Hugh Willoughby, frozen to death on his ice-bound ship north of Russia. During the summer, George Best was complaining about the "intolerable cold air" even as he expressed optimism that vessels sailing farther west in Frobisher Strait—toward Cathay—would encounter warmer weather. The whites did not yet truly know where they were.

As Martin Frobisher's lieutenant, Best oversaw the fortification of Countess of Warwick Island after the clash at Bloody Point. This was in early August 1577. With the mining still under way, he established a lookout post called Best's Bulwark on a cliff jutting into the sound. Even before the soldiers finished building it, they saw Inuit men on the mainland, shouting and waving a flag of some kind.

From that moment on Frobisher took charge, as befit a commander in dangerous territory. He wanted to find the five missing sailors, and the Inuit wanted to rescue Kalicho, Arnaq, and her infant. On Frobisher's orders, Arnaq walked to the highest point of Countess of Warwick Island so the Inuit on the mainland could see she was alive. Then Frobisher rowed a skiff to the mainland with Kalicho.

At first Kalicho cried so hard he couldn't speak with his countrymen. He finally talked while handing over the trinkets he had received from the Englishmen. For once, the Englishmen recognized the natives' humanity and saw their sadness. "They are very kind one to the other," George Best wrote, "and greatly sorrowful for the loss of their friends." In sign language, Frobisher promised to free his three captives and be generous in his gift-giving in exchange for the return of the five sailors. Frobisher, that always impatient man, energetically performed as a mime, held up five fingers, pointed to himself—acted out the idea of "exchange."

Kalicho talked with his countrymen for a long time before responding. They drew lines on the ground; Frobisher's men understood this to mean that at least some of the five sailors were alive. Frobisher was encouraged too when the natives acted out the motions of writing a letter. The Inuit lacked writing in their own culture, having no alphabet and nothing to write on except fresh snow. They were either imitating what they had seen sailors do or asking for a letter.

Kalicho, captured in 1577 after being wrestled to the ground. (Copyright © The British Museum)

Kalicho. Frobisher's sailors decided the Inuit were more likely cannibals than not. (Copyright © The British Museum)

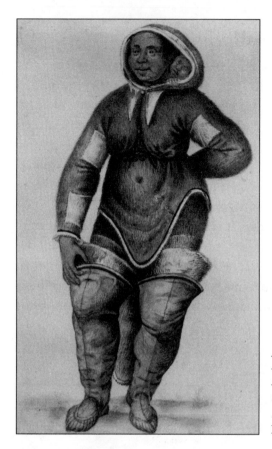

Arnaq ("Woman") and her son Nutaraq ("Child"), captured after the battle at Bloody Point. (Copyright © British Museum)

A second meeting took place the next day. The Inuit made the same motions of writing, and Frobisher had a hastily written letter ready. With great economy it told the missing sailors everything they would have wanted to hear. Here, in his few lines, was information useful for negotiating one's freedom, and here also was a bracing promise of revenge:

> In the name of God, in whom we all believe, who I trust hath preserved your bodies and souls amongst these infidels, I commend me unto you. I will be glad to seek by all means you can devise, for your deliverance, either with force or with any commodities within my ships, which I will not spare for your sakes, or anything else I can do for you. I have aboard, of theirs, a man, a woman, and a child, which I am contented to deliver for you, but the man I carried away from hence the last year

is dead in England. Moreover, you may declare unto them, that if they deliver you not, I will not leave a man alive in their country. And thus, if one of you can come to speak with me, they shall have either the Man, Woman, or Child in pawn for you. And thus unto God, whom I trust you do serve, in haste I leave you, and to him we will daily pray for you. This Tuesday morning the seventh of August. Anno. 1577.

Yours to the uttermost of my power

MARTIN FROBISHER

I have sent you by these bearers, pen, ink, and paper, to write back unto me again, if personally you cannot come to certify me of your state.

Everything was handed over as the Inuit wanted. A sailor placed the papers and ink and pen on the ground and stepped back, letting the Inuit then walk forward. In leaving, they held up three fingers and pointed to the sun, as if to set a time for the next meeting: three fingers, three days.

For the Inuit, the meetings served as a way of bargaining for time, an opportunity to collect intelligence for planning a rescue. Their pantomime about the five missing whites was just that—a well-acted play to hold the sailors' attention. On the third day, all the Inuit stayed out of sight and no conference occurred. The five missing sailors, a year after they rowed away from Frobisher's *Gabriel,* were never produced. Probably they were long dead. The urgent appeals for a letter were, it seems, a sham by a community determined to free the man, woman, and child held by the Englishmen without putting more lives at risk.

The Inuit twice tried to tempt Frobisher close enough to be kidnapped. On August 11, three natives called out from the mainland. He headed there by skiff and had a man leave a telescope as a gift. When lookouts spied many more natives hiding behind rocks, Frobisher rowed away without learning any more about the missing sailors. A few days later the Inuit tried a second time by waving a pennant made of animal guts. Three Inuit stood there in full view, but others did a poor job of concealing themselves. Each side greeted the other in sign language. Offered a gift of raw meat by the Inuit, sailors snagged it with a boat hook without coming closer. One of the Inuit tendered himself as another gift by hobbling a few ostentatiously lame steps, until he was hoisted onto the shoulders of another man, who deposited the fellow at the water's edge. He remained right there, like another cut of meat ready for the taking, if the whites would row closer.

At Frobisher's order a soldier fired a musket at the man. He forgot the limp as he ran away.

As the man retreated, other Inuit rushed from hiding places with bows and arrows and slings. The natives had decided that rescuing the captives was worth desperate measures, and they showed no fear of the Englishmen's guns. But the Inuit's arrows fell well short of the boats; Frobisher and his men safely rowed away.

Both sides were disappointed. Frobisher had just a hint that the five missing sailors might be alive. The Inuit knew that Kalicho, Arnaq, and Nutaraq couldn't be rescued.

The mining on Countess of Warwick Island exhausted the men. Some were lamed or had ruptured themselves, their clothes now reduced to the style worn by London paupers. Carrying the heavy loads of rock had seemed endless work. With twenty days' labor they had mined 160 tons of ore. On August 21, the men loaded the last of it onto the ships. The water was beginning to ice over at night.

They held a leave-taking ceremony on the 22nd, a Thursday. Miners and sailors lit a bonfire atop the highest point of the island, marched everywhere as if a war had just been won, fired a volley of shots—a loud, rowdy time. On Friday, the wind died before the vessels could clear Countess of Warwick Sound. They made much better progress on Saturday, beginning at about three o'clock in the morning. By nine o'clock that night, the winds sent them past the mouth of Frobisher Bay.

So strong were the winds, the *Michael* lost sight of the *Ayde* and the *Gabriel* and was forced to set its own course. Snow six inches deep covered the hatches of the *Ayde*. The seas were rough enough that William Smith, master of the *Gabriel,* suffered through a nightmare in which he saw himself falling overboard, being grabbed by the boatswain, but drowning when the boatswain lost his hold on him—a terrible dream that disturbed him so much that he described it to Captain Edward Fenton. That was August 29. On August 30 William Smith, master, was washed overboard along with the boatswain, who grabbed hold of a rope with one hand and held Smith with the other as long as he could manage. William Smith drowned.

The *Michael* lost its mainmast. The rudder of the *Ayde,* George Best reported, was "torn in twain, and almost ready to fall away," requiring a half dozen men lowered by ropes to lash planks to the underwater stump of it, the men reemerging from the water "more than half dead." To escape the storms Christopher Hall steered the *Ayde* south for several days, then resumed his course east. The little *Gabriel* had the hardest time, since without William Smith, the ship lacked a pilot.

By good fortune, the *Gabriel* encountered a ship from Bristol when approaching the English coast. The escort safely led the *Gabriel* to that port, some days after the arrival of the *Michael* and the *Ayde*.

Queen Elizabeth smiled upon Martin Frobisher after hearing his report. She accepted the narwhal tusk as a gift, and the tusk—six feet long—went into the Royal Wardrobe for use as one of her phallic jokes.

Michael Lok, the keeper of the account books, failed to see the humor. Indeed, he regarded the captain's generosity as a nasty business. Frobisher had presented the tusk in his own name, reaping the queen's favor just for himself rather than in the name of the Cathay Company, the pool of investors Lok had been cajoling and pampering now for two years. He calculated that the ivory tusk,

given away without a word to him, was worth a rather rich
£1,000. Queen Elizabeth's good wishes, shining now on
Frobisher, had even higher value. A fawning retinue attached itself
to the captain, who had the pleasure of hearing compliments
everywhere he went. Lok was thus finding more and more reason
to dislike him.

The queen bestowed a name on the new territory: Meta
Incognita. It was fittingly open-ended, as if she sensed Frobisher's
uncertainties about the geography. Her Latin sounded better than
would the English. Meta Incognita was "Unknown Shore," or
"Unknown Limit." How far the new territory extended was left
unsaid, other than that it went beyond a starting point called
"Unknown." Frobisher had given her the first opportunity for an
English monarch to name a landscape, to stake an English claim to
something wholly new, since John Cabot's travels in the long-ago
reign of Henry VII, Elizabeth's grandfather. Now she had done it.
At about this time John Dee, one of her pet intellectuals, sketched
Meta Incognita onto a large map of the Western Hemisphere.

The map is gray with age, as if from the soot of the candles at
John Dee's writing desk. The parchment resists being unfurled.
Either Dee or a draftsman supervised by him used a fine-point
quill to outline Europe and the bulge of Africa. North America
was placed at the map's center. He took up a less fine quill to add
hypothesized mountains and rivers to the North American interior, and sketched the grid of latitude and longitude. Greenland
("Groenland") is a long narrow finger south of an Arctic continent. Imaginary Frisland is rendered in great conjectured detail.
Near it are the imaginary lands Duilo, Florini, and Neome. North
America has an east-west mountain range at roughly the latitude of
St. Louis; cartographers abhorred empty space and invented features to fill it.

Dee used the map to advertise his conviction that the English
monarchy needed an empire. It was, at the time, a novel idea.
British Empire was a newly coined phrase, and Dee was one of the
first writers to use it. After researching the matter in his library at

Mortlake, he wove together evidence that supported, or could be twisted to support, an English claim to the North Atlantic, to the waters and lands above Russia, to most of North America, and to Iceland, Greenland, and lands presumed to reach to the North Pole. His inventiveness is breathtaking. He first made his case in four volumes written at great speed, beginning at about the time he was tutoring Martin Frobisher and Christopher Hall in mathematics and navigation. Frobisher's adventures seemed to give Dee the confidence to seek a larger audience. About half of this work is lost—Dee decided against publishing the second of the four volumes, and burned the text of volume three for reasons he kept to himself. The surviving parts, though, included a well-argued proposal for building a navy to create an empire.

His *General and Rare Memorials Pertayning to the Perfect Arte of Navigation,* the first volume, spelled out how many vessels of what tonnages a proper navy should have. Dee lobbied for sailors to be "liberally waged"; money should also be set aside to support sailors' widows, he advised. He proposed the hiring of senior pilots equipped with the best available instruments. He went so far as to outline a taxation system to pay for this and described how the tax rates should differ for foreigners and servants. And he wanted part of the navy's annual budget devoted to voyages of discovery. This was less about military strategy than economics. It was "most certain," Dee wrote, the expeditions would find "great riches of lead, tin, copper, silver, gold and divers kinds of other very commodious and profitable mineral materials." Martin Frobisher's exploits were proof of it.

A woodcut used on the book's title page made Dee's arguments allegorically. Originally sketched by Dee himself, the image shows Queen Elizabeth enthroned on the sterncastle of a ship. A shining disk bearing God's name beams in the sky behind her—she is at the helm of the monarchy and enjoying God's favor. A figure labeled "Lady Occasion" stands to one side on a mountain, with a crown extended toward the queen, and a fleet of ships waits in the west.

John Dee was urging Elizabeth to look west for building an

empire. He intended the message specifically for her and a handful of her advisers, depicted facing the queen on that ship. The woodcut, of course, was meant to flatter her.

He also flattered himself. The book, in one of its detours from the subject of empire, informed its readers that no other English intellectual had accomplished so much in so little time as the author. This was his opportunity, he believed, to relive every grievance and to correct the record. That, apparently, is why he reviewed at great length the accusations of conjuring that had followed him since his student days in Cambridge.

His hunger for recognition helped fuel his sense of having been wronged. Dee suffered seeing men of far less learning receive greater favors from the queen, for money was as much a worry for him as was his reputation. Judged by his patchy diary for 1577, the worries were never ending.

> 18 June. Borrowed £40 of John Hilton of Fulham. . . .
> 19 June . . . Borrowed £20 of Bartylmew Newsam. . . .
> 20 June. Borrow £27 upon the chain of gold. . . . 18
> Nov. Borrowed of Mr. Edward Hinde of Mortlake £30.

Yet his many admirers included Elizabeth.

"22 Nov. I rid to Windsor, to Q. Majesty," he recorded. During his audience, he informed Elizabeth that his research showed her to be the rightful owner of Greenland. He further declared, unfortunately for his later reputation, that his investigations found her to possess title to Frisland.

Some years passed before he presented her with his large parchment map. On the back of it, he summarized the evidence for England's claims to various seas and territories. He conjured ownership by transmuting legends into historical facts. Greenland, in his judgment, was properly English territory because King Arthur had conquered it in about the year 530; such was his interpretation of the tales of Arthur. They were further interpreted to suggest that Arthur's conquest had extended to all the waters between Greenland and Russia. So "it is probable" Frisland too was rightfully England's.

He said England could claim North America, thanks to the purported exploits of Prince Madoc of Wales. Madoc was said to have sailed west with Welsh colonists in the 1100s. Dee chose to believe the general outline of the story and concluded that Madoc had successfully colonized North America. This story enjoyed a remarkably long life: in 1805 Meriwether Lewis, hearing the rough-sounding language of the Salish Indians of western Montana, wondered in his diary if he had found the descendants of Prince Madoc's colonists.

Dee's belief in an ancient British empire helped make empire building seem a rational project. His point was that England had a great destiny. He argued that it could best be achieved through overseas exploration followed by the building of colonies, which he justified by invoking that glorious, mystical, imperial past.

Elizabeth was never much impressed by the argument. She was always reluctant to invest money in overseas adventures. The learned Dr. Dee, one imagines, handled himself well during his audience as he described her ownership of territories that she knew only as interesting shapes on a map. She may have listened intently until he reached the matter of cost. A grand design interested her only if it were inexpensive. Her frugality—her conservatism in all things—helped define the age. Her ministers were constantly frustrated by her reluctance to *spend* and by her slowness to reach decisions. She did, though, allow her courtiers to spend themselves into ruin. They entertained far beyond their means or lost fortunes gambling or risked everything in their own efforts to establish colonies. She granted patents for colonies as long as their purpose was to harry the Spanish or mine gold, a practice that began with Martin Frobisher in Meta Incognita.

A few days after the ships' arrival in Bristol, Kalicho entertained the townspeople by paddling his kayak on the Avon River and spearing a brace of ducks. The mayor and other citizens, being English, were fascinated by the Inuit's diet. Kalicho and Arnaq preferred meat that was either raw or barely cooked, ate enormous portions, as if England were not well populated with ducks, and even ate the innards. No less fascinating was that the man and woman knew nothing of bread. It was thought strange that they preferred to live as Inuit rather than civilized Englishmen. One of the English phrases they learned was "God give you good morrow," though one can't be sure they knew its meaning. "Farewell" was another. It was said that Kalicho, on his first attempt at riding a horse, positioned himself facing the animal's tail. Which, if true, was more entertainment.

In a watercolor painted at about this time, Kalicho is wearing a parka made of sealskin with a hood and a long tail. His sealskin trousers are tucked into sealskin boots. He has a mustache and a small, trim beard and lightly grips a wooden bow with his left hand. The painted detail is such that the seams in his clothing are visible, including patches at the crook of the elbows. In other renderings Kalicho is shown from the back or holds a long paddle in addition to his bow, like a hitherto unknown species being examined from all angles. The watercolorist was, almost certainly, John White, the future governor of Walter Raleigh's colony at Roanoke. During his sojourn in the New World during the 1580s, White sketched Indians, their campsites, and animals and vegetation hitherto unknown to Englishmen. His studies of exotica apparently began with the portraits of Frobisher's captives.

Arnaq, in another of White's drawings, carries her baby on her back, inside her parka, so that his face peers out from the hood, alongside her own. A cord cinched around her middle keeps him from falling off. She poses with one of her arms at her back as if to hold him. Her face is decorated with tattoos of blue dots in the gentle curves the Inuit found beautiful.

The Cathay Company wanted to commemorate Frobisher's exploits with more formal portraits in oils. It again enlisted Cornelis Ketel, the artist who had painted the native captured the year before. Ketel this time was commissioned to paint four canvases—two full-length, plus two smaller ones—of Arnaq with her baby. Michael Lok dispatched two of the paintings by carriage as a present to Queen Elizabeth. He finally had a gift to match the narwhal tusk presented by Frobisher.

Kalicho was the first of the captives to die. He had been short of breath, had begun suffering from deafness, and had complained of terrible head pains. Dr. Edward Dodding examined him during his last hour, but the physician seemed less upset by losing a patient than by the worry that Queen Elizabeth would be disappointed by not having seen the man from Meta Incognita. In his autopsy report, Dodding said he had wanted to bleed Kalicho but was overruled by the patient and, it seems, by Frobisher. Dodding blamed some of the symptoms on the patient's having been too liberally fed, a situation brought about "by the utmost solicitousness on the part of that great man, the Captain." The physician had several times warned that Kalicho was dying, "but nobody would listen."

At autopsy he found two badly broken ribs. Probably the injury dated from when Nicholas Conger had wrestled Kalicho to the ground until his sides ached. One of his lungs was infected, perhaps from the unknit ribs, and the lung had collapsed; it explained Kalicho's breathlessness. His brain showed signs of injury, but sixteenth-century medicine was ill-equipped to describe or diagnose them.

Dodding insisted on showing Arnaq the body. He also forced her, on November 8, to watch the burial at St. Stephen's Church in Bristol. He assumed her own people ate human flesh and wished to prove that her hosts did not.

Arnaq was buried four days later at the same church. If Dodding performed another autopsy and described his findings, his report has not been located. Arnaq's baby boy survived long enough for Michael Lok to hire a nurse to take the infant from Bristol to the Three Swans' Inn in London. One suspects that the Cathay company was rushing to present the baby to Queen Elizabeth. In the end, the cost of lodging was minimal. The child died in eight days. For the nurse and the burial, one pound and small change.

The cargo of black ore quickly generated gossip. A few days after Frobisher reached England, the French ambassador in London wrote King Henri III that a man "named Forbichet" had come home with a great quantity of gold. In a second letter he informed Catherine de' Medici, the king's mother, that the ore came from lands vast enough for France to send its own expeditions. "It will be quite easy," he said.

The newly appointed ambassador from Spain took the gossip seriously. No one proved more resourceful in gathering intelligence. "As the business is managed with great secrecy, and any person connected in it who divulges the details is to be punished with death, I have had much difficulty discovering particulars," Ambassador Bernardino de Mendoza said in his first dispatch on the matter. Some of the intelligence he forwarded to King Philip II proved incorrect. He reported that three natives in the new territory had defeated a group of thirty sailors in battle; three natives captured by Frobisher were said to have died during the voyage to England. But the ambassador's information was sound on some matters. He knew that Frobisher's miners had worked on an island, and he learned its approximate location: about sixty-two degrees north latitude.

Ambassador de Mendoza recruited at least one spy in Frobisher's party. It was a remarkable feat; Spanish diplomats and their servants were closely watched by informants reporting to Francis Walsingham, master of Queen Elizabeth's intelligence network. (But double agents sometimes complicated the spying game. In one of his dispatches to King Philip, de Mendoza lamented the death of an unnamed informant: "I shall never find another so intelligent and faithful as he. He was employed in Walsingham's office.")

De Mendoza managed to obtain samples of the black ore. "I send them herewith," he wrote the king, "as this letter is taken by one of my own servants, and I have ordered him, in case the ship in which he sails is overhauled to throw the letters and samples into the sea, as I have another similar set of specimens here." By the time of his writing, a small number of metallurgists were assaying the ore, but the circle of intimates remained quite small. The security was extraordinary. Queen Elizabeth had ordered that the ore from the *Ayde* and the *Gabriel* be stored in Bristol Castle in a room newly fitted with four locks requiring four different keys. Ore from the *Michael* went into the Tower of London, behind a similar set of new locks. De Mendoza's secret agent had served him well.

He was tentatively identified in the late 1990s. Two researchers—Bernard Allaire and Donald Hogarth—traced information backward from one of the ambassador's coded letters and considered who could have gathered it. They narrowed the likely candidates to only one. Robert Denham was an assayer who had sailed with Frobisher aboard the *Ayde* and fit every requirement. He was at the right place, always at the right time, to acquire the information the envoy then passed to Spain. Since the ambassador remained in the dark about some aspects of the voyage, Denham may have been a double agent. Or de Mendoza may have employed more than one informant. The ambassador wrote of plans to obtain a map from the man who was preparing one for Frobisher—a man surely no other than Denham.

Whatever his sources, Ambassador de Mendoza remained keenly interested in Frobisher's endeavors.

The investors meanwhile congratulated themselves on their wisdom. Philip Sidney, the courtier-poet, wrote a friend on the Continent about the optimism reigning among shareholders of the Cathay Company. Frobisher, he reported, was bragging that Meta Incognita contained more riches than Spain's silver mines in Peru; courtiers were already debating how to protect the venture in Meta Incognita from the Spanish and the French.

Sidney's Continental friend was Hubert Languet, a French-born diplomat. Languet wrote back from Frankfurt. He was fifty-nine, his English friend only twenty-three. In his letter Languet offered his young friend a tale about mariners from ancient Carthage. In those long-ago times, he wrote, storms had sometimes blown sailors from Carthage to distant lands of marvelous beauty. Upon returning home, the sailors would describe the near perfection of these newly found territories, and the sailors would attract large audiences. The Senate of Carthage always responded the same way, he wrote. The Senate always ordered the sailors killed. It thus protected the citizens of Carthage from unsettling dreams of impossibly sweet lands. A thirst for untoward beauty or great wealth, he suggested, always brought disappointment.

The stories about Martin Frobisher's success worried him. "Who would have expected that the extreme north would at last supply us with so great incitement to evil?" Languet wrote. Yet even he couldn't help admiring Frobisher for his perseverance and luck—the captain had "hit the mark." And by investing in the Cathay Company, so had Philip Sidney. And whatever Languet's concern about the corrupting influence of gold, he joined the speculation. The brave captain would after all need to secure a suitable harbor, and Languet debated whether the English should build a fort in Meta Incognita or a whole town.

"If that which you say of your Frobisher is true," said Languet, "he will doubtless eclipse the reputation not only of Magellan but even of Christopher Columbus himself."

CHAPTER FIVE

Colonizing Dreams

The investors gambled everything on the assays. An assay of metal usually involved more than guesswork but was always short on precision. Every metallurgist and alchemist developed a method of his own, with varying degrees of success. For the black ore from Meta Incognita, the assayers hired by the Cathay Company ground a sample of the rocks into powder, weighed it carefully, and placed it with a roughly equal amount of lead in a crucible. They also included one or another secret additive, proprietary ingredients that somehow helped the process. After the powdered ore cooked in a furnace for some days, any gold or silver it contained would be a mass bound with lead at the bottom of the crucible; the slag floated on top. That was the melting process. The next step was the refining. Cooked in another furnace, the lead oxidized and left a bead of silver-gold alloy. The assayer separated the two metals with nitric acid to produce a dot of pure gold.

Jonas Shutz was the chief assayer. He had sailed to Meta Incognita aboard the *Ayde,* helped supervise the mining there, and, in England, designed the brand-new furnaces that stood on the property of William Winter, one of the commissioners appointed by Queen Elizabeth to oversee the doings of the Cathay Company. To keep the furnaces hot during the first assay, two men pedaled foot-bellows for a week. Shutz melted a hundred pounds of the black rock with a hundred pounds of lead and was almost suffocated by the smoke. From this first assay, in November 1577, he calculated that a ton of Martin Frobisher's black ore would yield about £40 of gold. But he assumed that some additional gold was in the unexpectedly large amount of slag.

In any case the new furnaces seemed too small, judged by the results of the assay. Shutz believed that something was wrong with the bellows too, since the large quantity of slag indicated that the fires were not hot enough. In melting the original stone a year before, he had determined that a ton would yield £240 of gold, not £40. The £40 was disappointing but—after deducting the sailors' wages and the other expenses—still enough to make the ore profitable.

A select group of other assayers conducted tests of their own while Shutz tinkered with his furnaces. Frobisher himself had a furnace built at his house in London. In December, Shutz performed a second major assay using another hundred pounds of ore. It too generated a cloud of choking smoke, a surfeit of slag, and an estimate of £40 of gold a ton. William Winter believed that the assayers simply needed more experience working with the ore. "And albeit the ore in report do not appear to be of the value which hath been looked for," he informed a member of the queen's Privy Council, ". . . the commodity is such as may content reasonable minds, for in my own opinion I believe it will fall out better than the workmen hath said it does."

Michael Lok, the treasurer of the Cathay Company, showed great faith. He envisioned the investors' erecting something akin to an industrial park for refining the black ore, a project he called the "great works." On behalf of the company, he proposed building a water mill to drive the bellows and to drive stamps for crushing the 160 tons of rock, and a large bank of furnaces for the melting and refining. An army of assayers using the latest technologies would recover the hoped for mountain of gold.

His great works was a necessity. Without it, the Cathay Company lacked any practical way of refining the gold. Without the gold, Lok was struggling to pay the company's bills, including the wages of sailors waiting to be dismissed from Martin Frobisher's three ships. Every few days he sent another letter to Francis Walsingham describing the importance of the great works. "It grieveth me to see so much time lost before we begin to give order for the making of the furnaces," he wrote at the end of November. Six days later he deflected a query from Walsingham about the quantity of gold in the ore, saying he could not predict how much the great works would produce until the furnaces were operating. Success was always said to be very near. As if in passing, he reported that Jonas Shutz believed that the ore from Frobisher's second voyage differed from the original black stone. The latest ore was "of a strange nature" and more difficult to handle in the furnaces, Lok said, conveying Shutz's concerns—"but he doubteth not in the great work he will learn to know it perfectly."

Martin Frobisher tried to take charge by sponsoring an assayer of his own. Like his patron, Burchard Kranich had outsized pride and exceptional confidence in his own expertise. He informed Frobisher that the truly valuable rock from Meta Incognita was *red,* not black. The red ore, said Kranich, contained four times more gold than the black. He proposed taking Jonas Shutz's place as chief assayer and requested a guaranteed-for-life salary. As any investor could have guessed, he and Shutz despised each other. Kranich claimed Shutz had designed the furnaces all wrong; Shutz complained that Kranich was both ignorant and ill-mannered.

For Lok, those were minor details. He was riding through the countryside inspecting potential sites for the great works. The town of Dartford met the specifications he had in mind.

Dartford thrived thanks to the River Darent and the fact that the town was one day's walk—seventeen miles—east of London along the old Roman road to Canterbury. Pilgrims on their way to Canterbury had needed lodging and food, and tavern owners in Dartford had proved happy to oblige. Farmers in north Kent, attracted by the crowds, made Dartford their market town. In the 1540s King Henry VIII had razed a Dominican monastery on the edge of town to erect a royal manor house behind high stone walls. Lok saw that too.

He and Frobisher and Shutz toured a property a mile upriver from town. A man named William Vaughan was leasing the property from the crown and operated two mills there for corn and wheat. The River Darent's current was strong at that spot. Construction materials could be barged from the Thames into the Darent. Dartford itself had ample housing for workers. Lok described all the advantages in a letter to Francis Walsingham ("We think that place good for the purpose . . .").

In January 1578 the Privy Council approved construction of the great works.

The course of the work was recorded in Lok's account book. He returned to Dartford with Shutz, a mason, and a carpenter and measured the exact dimensions of the property. In compensation for the disruptions, the crown awarded William Vaughan a longer lease on his two mills. Then workmen cut a temporary channel for the Darent so they could dig a proper millrace. The workforce grew from nine men during the first week to twenty during the fourth week. By week eight, it numbered fifty-five; one week later, eighty. The Cathay Company wanted everything done at the greatest possible speed, in order to have the furnaces in operation at the earliest possible date. Workers felled, squared, and transported elm trees needed for the mill house. Gabriell Woodaye earned eight pence for cutting some of the trees; a crew led by one John Stace received ten shillings for loading them onto carts; the farmer Richard Clarke transported six tons of elm boards a distance of three miles, as did one John Winde, profession unknown. A different set of workmen felled oak trees and cut them into boards of varying lengths for carpenters fashioning the waterwheels. Even William Vaughan joined the workforce, by transporting oak pilings destined to become the mill wharf.

The workmen shaped earthen platforms for the two new watermills, and for two structures Michael Lok called workhouses, and for the furnaces, and for another building for storing coal. John Winde earned four shillings a day for transporting earth and chalk with his horses and two carts. Richard Clarke, the farmer, transported 280 loads of clay for the mill foundations. Foundations ready, the Cathay Company took delivery of 22,000 bricks brought inland from the Dartford wharf, as well as bundles of lathing. Thanks to support from the Privy Council, the company could acquire enough material to build the equivalent of a prosperous village in record time. Twenty-five bushels of lime arrived for use in making mortar. Six thousand tiles came from London for the furnaces. In the paylists sawyers gave way to carpenters, who were succeeded by bricklayers, who gave way to tilers, followed at last by plasterers. One of the construction managers approved the purchase of ten tanned hides, which a German-born millwright transformed into ten pairs of twelve-foot-long bellows; for the bellows, £17. Michael Lok paid an additional two shillings for the nozzles, plus a small charge for hog grease, and one shilling for three pounds of glue. A Dartford blacksmith supplied an iron hoop that acted as a camshaft for lifting and lowering the stamps.

Lord Burghley, the queen's Lord Treasurer, followed the course of the work. A sketch drawn for him shows men tending a furnace that has chimneys spouting bright daggers of flame and curls of smoke. In the drawing, the furnace has a bank of bellows worked by an overhead jungle of rods and rollers, connected to a cascade of wooden waterwheels; black ore is piled in front of the furnace. The River Darent would power the wheels that would drive the rods that would pump the bellows that would blast the fire that would melt the ore that would make the investors rich. This was the Cathay Company's promise of high technology.

Burghley wrote some figures about the ore. As Lord Treasurer he was not given to wastefulness; his figures were based on what Michael Lok and Martin Frobisher told him. Lok said that the preliminary assays in London were going well. Whenever a melting proved disappointing, he explained that the bellows were

William Cecil, Lord Burghley, Lord Treasurer of England, ca. 1560–70. (Courtesy of the National Portrait Gallery, London)

positioned too low in the furnace or the assayer's assistants had failed to be diligent during the work. He suggested that every problem would disappear once the meltings were performed in the larger, hotter furnaces under construction at Dartford. Meanwhile,

Frobisher promised that he could bring more ore to England if given enough ships, and that he would make the investors rich beyond their dreams.

Burghley performed his calculations on a sheet of parchment. He assumed a miner could dig a half ton of ore a day and work thirty days a month, but then he changed it to twenty-eight days. On the next line he did the arithmetic for a hundred miners working one month, minus some inefficiencies. The product was 1,200 tons of ore. He made a computation for teams of both two hundred and three hundred miners. Allowances were made for wages and freight costs. That is, he calculated the potential profit from Frobisher's making another voyage to Meta Incognita.

A businessman would want to be sure of a commodity's value before going to the expense of acquiring more of it, and Michael Lok was a rational businessman. He believed in the ore and was confident that every difficulty encountered to date could be corrected. There was otherwise no explanation for the course he followed. As of early 1578, he still lacked the money to pay off the crew. Unable to discharge the sailors, he was bearing the expense of feeding them; they were eating money he didn't have. With their rigging deteriorating in the salt air, the vessels themselves cost the Cathay Company money every additional day they sat idle. Added to that was the cost of the London assays.

His solution was to spend more. Queen Elizabeth turned down his request for a loan, but the Privy Council authorized the Cathay Company to require its investors to pay a surcharge. They could either add 20 percent to their investment or forfeit their stake. If you had invested £50, you now owed the company an additional £10, or you lost your original investment and any claim to the flood of profits expected to come once the great works at Dartford opened.

The 20 percent paid off the sailors and the miners. The company levied a second surcharge—another 20 percent—to pay for the construction of the Dartford mills and furnaces. This work proceeded quickly but cost nearly five times more than expected and consumed all the money from the surcharges. Then there were the projected costs of the new, third expedition: if you truly believed in the ore, then the logical response was to find more of it. That was why Lok favored a third expedition to Meta Incognita, and how he convinced Lord Burghley to support it.

Jonas Shutz began another assay in February 1578. On the third day of the melting, when Shutz was already ill from inhaling smoke, Frobisher came to observe. According to Lok, Frobisher—whose temper was extraordinary—rushed at the assayer with a dagger. Shutz's subsequent cool relations with Frobisher seemed to confirm the tale. Determined to return to Meta Incognita, the explorer had wanted to ensure that Shutz reported favorable results.

Shutz completed the assay with the company's commissioners as an audience. They watched him produce a lump of silver-gold alloy and then separate the gold. But the quantities proved disappointing: he lowered his valuation of the ore from £40 a ton to slightly more than £23. As always, he offered assurances that better, hotter furnaces could wrest some additional gold from the slag.

Frobisher's man, Burchard Kranich, conducted an assay of his own for the commissioners. From the same quantity of ore he produced five times more gold than did Shutz, plus a large amount of silver. His methods, though, were unconventional. He allowed the commissioners to watch only the last stage of the assay, when he worked with a hundred pounds of ore in small pots rather than in a true furnace. His audience wondered too about the material liberally added to the pots—his "additament."

The commissioners sought to learn more from Robert Denham, his assistant. Denham had sailed aboard the *Ayde* and, unknown to the Cathay Company, may have spied for Spain. In the presence of the scholarly John Dee and other men considered expert in precious metals, he assayed a sample of his master's additive and found it rich in silver. Kranich had found a significant amount of silver in the ore, Denham explained, because he had added it to the mixture himself. So his impressive results had been meaningless.

Questioned more closely, Denham confessed that his employer had assayed not the hundred pounds observed by the commissioners but just one pound. Before the public performance, Kranich had melted one pound as a test. Then he had secretly added silver and gold coins to the mix his guests saw, to guarantee that the results would please them. As for the additive, Kranich did not know it contained silver. He remained ignorant even of facts as basic as that it took twenty pennyweights to make an ounce. In years past he had introduced new mining technology to England and earned enough money to spend £700—a very large sum—buying houses and gardens in London. Yet as an assayer, he might as well have mistaken copper for gold. In his assistant's telling, Kranich's work as an assayer was a fraud.

Kranich retained faith in both the ore and himself. Even under the best of circumstances, assayers performed difficult work. They used a changing brew of ingredients, were unable to make precise measurements, and could not count on having an even-burning fire; it was not surprising that they found it difficult to duplicate the results of any given assay. There was also the influence of pride and, in working for the Cathay Company, the powerful sway of investors' expectations. The unseen audience included the queen and the Privy Council. This was an opportunity to secure lifetime employment.

To rescue his reputation, Kranich asked for the chance to perform another assay. He proposed that Denham himself—the cause of all the trouble—conduct the work in the presence of eminent witnesses, including Francis Walsingham. "I am informed that your Honour and the rest be displeased with me as though I had made a false proof," he wrote Walsingham, assuring him that the precious metals in question had come from the ore and not his additive. "And if I do not prove it truly comed out then take my body and goods to your own pleasure."

Queen Elizabeth's advisers let hope outweigh their doubts. Walsingham assured Elizabeth that the black ore contained gold, *enough* gold to make the endeavor profitable. Skeptical about so many other projects, he convinced her that the Cathay Company's endeavor in Meta Incognita remained a worthy one. She was persuaded, as he said in a letter, that "the richness of that earth is like to fall out to a good reckoning." The ore was *likely* to prove valuable. Like other investors, he chose to believe the favorable assays rather than the ones that proved disappointing. Without being absolutely certain of the consequences for himself, an adviser would be reluctant to inform the queen she had made a bad investment. Like Michael Lok, the members of the Privy Council were in too deep to oppose organizing a new voyage. If they stopped the enterprise now, they would have only debts. Apparently no one was willing to express doubts. Elizabeth, said Walsingham, "is well pleased that a third voyage be taken in hand."

In March 1578 the Privy Council formally endorsed a new expedition to Meta Incognita.

Frobisher retained the title of captain general. In its instructions the Cathay Company asked him to explore Frisland during the first leg of the voyage, unless stopping there would jeopardize reaching Meta Incognita. In that case, he should visit Frisland on his way back to England. One can hear John Dee—having told Elizabeth that she was the rightful ruler of Frisland—suggesting the Frisland visit to the company.

Mining, however, was the company's overriding interest. The commissioners instructed Frobisher to return to Countess of Warwick Island and resume digging there, and to use the island as a base for searching for ore elsewhere.

Keeping good records was made a high priority, in hope of pinpointing the richest veins of ore for future voyages. Members of the expedition were to record the location and value of everything they mined, their notes to be written in duplicate and attached to well-labeled samples of ore; the two copies should be carried in separate ships. Burghley, the Lord Treasurer, added a requirement that captains prepare reports in triplicate.

Sailing from Meta Incognita to Cathay now interested the commissioners much less. They authorized Frobisher to deploy two ships to sail through Frobisher Strait into the Pacific Ocean—but only in the course of searching for additional mines.

The company wanted everything done on a grand scale. Instead of three ships, the commissioners this time planned to send ten. Instead of 160 tons of ore, the company anticipated 800 tons.

Frobisher's boasts about the great deeds he could accomplish colored all the plans. And who wouldn't consider a new expedition as a vote of confidence in the commander? Who entrusted with the task of enriching the queen could resist having a high opinion of himself? Success was what Frobisher had wished for, and how he achieved it mattered less than the pleasure of success itself. Mining gold could provide as much satisfaction as finding a passage to Cathay.

Michael Lok found him insufferable. "And now Captain Frobisher having the thing he so much hunted for grew into such a monstrous mind, that a whole kingdom could not contain it," he said. The captain general regarded himself as a new Columbus for having discovered new territory, and as a new Cortés for having discovered gold. Everyone knew that the Aztecs had mistaken Cortés for a god. As the list of expenses in the account book grew longer, Lok liked his partner less.

If one believed in the ore, then building a colony in Meta Incognita seemed sensible. A colony provided a way to conduct mining year-round—to act on one's faith that this was a rich, rewarding territory. A colony would pay for itself, assuming the assays endorsed by the Privy Council were correct. Englishmen living in a colony would determine which was the best season for navigating the rest of the way to Cathay; they might befriend the natives and enlist them as guides, even civilize them. An English colony—a mining camp, really—would boost profits. It would add to geographical knowledge and protect England's claim to the territory.

Francis Walsingham wrote to some of his fellow Privy Council members—"if it might please your Lordships," the note said—about the colony's budget. One imagines a shuffling of papers, the lordships or their minions adding the figures, briefly considering the price of rice, adding the price of this many tons of beef at that many shillings a barrel. The Privy Council decided on a hundred as the right number of colonists. Frobisher supported the idea. To add a sense of urgency, he claimed to have a spy's letter describing a French plan to seize Meta Incognita, but he stopped short of letting anyone read it.

The first English colony in the New World thus begins as just another business matter. Laying the cornerstone, members of the Privy Council glanced at the numbers during a session at which other matters were surely discussed. Her Majesty's Privy Council was awash in paper; supplicants wanted to be heard; the ministers constantly worried about money. Burghley, the Lord Treasurer, complained of having to write upwards of twenty letters a day, even on Sundays. Walsingham was overseeing the commissioners who directed Michael Lok, who with difficulty steered Martin Frobisher—one of a hundred tasks requiring the secretary of state's attention. Privy Council members had from time to time interested themselves in exploration. England had fitfully conducted trade in West Africa, nurtured modestly profitable contact with Russia, and let Frobisher search for a northwest route to Cathay. Now they directed Frobisher to transport a hundred colonists and eighteen months of supplies for them. Like all those other ventures, building a colony was a search for revenue.

Edward Fenton was appointed Frobisher's second in command and governor of the colony. George Best was named one of Fenton's aides. Those who volunteered as colonists included forty sailors, thirty miners, soldiers, shipwrights, a carpenter, a baker, a shoemaker, and a tailor. The Cathay Company allotted them three ships for exploration and for sailing home, in case a fleet failed to return to the colony the following summer. Allowances were made for other disasters. In case of Fenton's death, the colonists would find a list of four successors locked away in a box requiring multiple keys.

A carpenter named Thomas Townson designed a fort for the colony. He hammered together part of the building's wooden frame and built the cranes that the colonists would need for assembling it once the ships unloaded the lumber in Meta Incognita. This fort would serve as a headquarters, a building 132 feet long and 72 feet wide with a wing at each end as a dormitory. "Cunningly designed," said George Best. Thanks to the fort, the colonists would "be defended from the danger of the falling snow and cold air, and also be fortified from the force or offence of those Country people"—the Inuit. The Cathay Company paid Thomas Townson £220 for his work.

For the first time, the commissioners drawing up the orders showed some understanding of the true nature of Frobisher's relationship with the Inuit. In their dealings with the natives, the colonists were instructed simply not to make things worse. Frobisher, in a change of policy, was told to err on the side of caution in his contacts and to take fewer risks. In his meetings with the Inuit he should "rather procure their friendship and good likings towards you by courtesies."

Michael Lok was the readiest source of money, and his fellow commissioners asked him to handle all the contracts with outfitters. "We think it most convenient," the commissioners said. He signed the bills in his own name rather than the company's, a policy he would later regret. Money came from his own pocket as loans to the company for buying supplies. Due to the scale of the expedition, he borrowed money too and lent those additional sums to the company, the interest being another expense recorded in the ledger. He purchased twenty thousand bricks for building the walls of the colonists' fort, barrels of lime and sand for making cement, and elm boards for the roof. To feed the colonists once they were left in Meta Incognita, he bought 141 tons of beer—their largest daily source of vitamins. He bought them beef, pork, dried fish, rice, oatmeal, and peas.

Their supplies also included eight tons of sea biscuits. They greatly differed from the light, flaky creations that are today known as biscuits. Sea biscuits were made from two parts coarsely ground wheat flour with one part water, baked at about three hundred degrees Fahrenheit until bone-dry. The dryness was the only guarantee against mold. Taste mattered less than a long shelf life; sustenance took precedence over alimentary pleasure. Sea biscuits could easily be mistaken for rocks and were able to survive months at sea in a tin–lined chest. You could hammer a nail into the wall with a sea biscuit.

Frobisher again took command of the two–hundred-ton *Ayde*. Due to the size of the venture, the Cathay Company asked him to take charge of paying the *Ayde*'s crew and to oversee the vessel's final outfitting—the buying of capstans, cables, pitch pots, and the like. The company authorized a fleet of ten ships, but Frobisher added another four on his own authority, and Lok added one more. Frobisher billed the expenses associated with the extra ships to the company. His argument was simple: when mining gold in a faraway place, prepare to carry home all you can.

So he commanded a fleet of fifteen ships, rather than ten, carrying about four hundred men, including the hundred colonists.

Edward Fenton captained a vessel called *Judith*. Confidence was one of the prerequisites for command, but shipmates complained of Fenton's high-handedness. The chaplain on another voyage derisively called Fenton "our little king"; Fenton was "a very dissembling hypocrite," "a sly crafty, purposeless but vain and immoderate man." Yet he demonstrated skill as a navigator and leader aboard the *Judith*. Along with the *Gabriel* and the *Michael*, the *Judith* was assigned to stay with the colonists.

George Best took charge of the *Anne Francis*. Christopher Hall went aboard the *Thomas Allen*. Supervising the cargo loading, a purser divided supplies for the colony among several ships. Half of the fort's wood frame went aboard a bark named *Dennis;* half the bricks, along with much of the lime, went into the *Thomas of Ipswich;* at least four vessels took on the barrels of beer. Sailors carried aboard mattocks and shovels for the mining. Enough iron went aboard the ships for building three furnaces for assays. There were stoves made of glazed tiles, seven pairs of bellows, and 120 tons of coal for the fires.

To finance the expedition, the Privy Council authorized a daunting 135 percent surcharge on the investors. Lord Burghley had invested £100 in the second voyage and by that reckoning owed an additional £135. Frobisher owed the same, and Francis Walsingham owed double—£270. Michael Lok had loaned John Dee money to invest and advanced him more for the surcharge, recording the loan in the ledger.

Queen Elizabeth may have participated in the deliberations about the surcharge. But the balance sheet of the Cathay Company did not necessarily interest her, as it neither was a divisive matter nor directly concerned foreign relations. In any case, Elizabeth insisted that her investment in the Cathay Company was just a loan, in the form of her lending the venture the *Ayde*. By her optimistic accounting, her loan totaled £1,000. Because of the latest surcharge, she owed an additional £1,350, but she again protected her interests. She met her obligations by requiring Lok to post a bond that guaranteed her own funds. Her arrangement was every investor's dream: any loss would be borne not by her but by Lok and his other partners.

She was distracted all the while by a toothache. Her physicians wanted to extract the tooth but lacked the courage to tell her. It was evidence of how much her moods frightened her advisers that her toothache too came to the attention of the Privy Council. Great lords fretted over the tooth as if it were their own.

Burghley either declined to talk to her about tooth pulling or failed to persuade her that it was necessary. He asked another of her favorites, Christopher Hatton, to do it. What first attracted the queen to Hatton, it was said, was his dancing, and Hatton epitomized the successful courtier. In return for his devotion, Elizabeth had granted him valuable properties, given him a seat on the Privy Council, and promoted him to positions that would have vastly increased his wealth if he had not spent it so profligately on entertaining her.

Hatton, too, apparently declined to talk to her about dentistry, since the toothache still tormented her.

She granted Frobisher and his captains an audience at Greenwich Palace, during her preparations to leave on a brief "progress," one of her stately processions through the countryside in order to see and be seen by her subjects. She gave Frobisher a chain of gold, and his captains kissed her hand. Her generosity interested Bernardino de Mendoza, the Spanish ambassador, whose spies were still at work. "She expressed herself very warmly as to the great importance of the undertaking for the welfare of her realm," he informed King Philip II. "I am persevering in my attempts to get a chart of the voyage."

Frobisher's flagship, the *Ayde,* ingloriously began the voyage at the end of a towrope. Michael Lok paid about three pounds for the hire of oxen to pull the vessel from its anchorage in Bristol. Christopher Hall then piloted her to the fleet's assembly point on England's east coast, at Harwich. He worked like a traffic police-man, bringing the ships together—the *Gabriel* from London, the *Thomas Allen* also down the Thames. This time the fleet sailed west through the English Channel instead of traveling up the coast from Harwich and making its turn. On June 3 the ships reached Plymouth and, within a day, entered the Atlantic.

In his orders to the captains, Frobisher demanded that every ship stay within a mile of the *Ayde.* It's a mystery why he set a stan-dard impossible to keep, except to demonstrate his authority. All the captains were to confer with him each evening at seven o'clock and in no case later than eight o'clock; if weather interfered, they should receive their instructions from Christopher Hall aboard the *Thomas Allen.* In case of fog they should make "a reasonable noise" with trumpet or drum. Their password at night was "Before the world was God"; the required response, "After God came Christ his son." If land was sighted at night, a captain should display two lights and fire two shots; if by day, he should fire one shot, display the flag, and lower every sail.

They reached southern Greenland, or Frisland, after two weeks. Frobisher named the territory West England. There was a sudden riot of naming because, for the first time, the Englishmen man-aged to go ashore. Christopher Hall sketched part of Greenland's coastline in his logbook, squiggles of mountains in green ink. One of the mountain ranges became Dee's Pinnacles, in honor of Hall's tutor, John Dee. The names endured for just the one day. They are in Hall's logbook, but nowhere else. West from Dee's Pinnacles was Frobisher's Cape, then Hall's Needles ("Hawles needels"), then Master Michael Lok's Foreland.

The ships were enveloped in fog as soon as they left the coast of Greenland. They entered ice fields and the mist followed the ships, like an enemy stalking them. At the end of June, some of the sailors glimpsed Queen Elizabeth's Foreland, marking the entrance to Frobisher Strait. They sighted it again whenever the fog allowed.

The foreland today is Resolution Island, and modern captains remain wary of the waters there. Resolution Island is the home of enormous swells that crowd ships toward the shoals. Steel-hulled freighters spend days working through the summer ice. Frobisher sighted the island through the fog again, knowing his waterway was somewhere ahead, but ice blocked the way forward. At meal-time, silence was probably the main course, every meal a reminder that after a month at sea you could have literally nothing to say to your fellow crew members. The logbook recorded unadorned facts—time, visibility, wind, ice; it did not mention roll, pitch, or the feeling in the captain's stomach. Frobisher lacked weather reports, hydrographic charts, and any navigational aids other than what was visible from the maintop. Christopher Hall went from ship to ship and agreed with the other pilots that there was no safe way through so much ice.

On the afternoon of July 2, against all odds, a pinnace threaded its way through the floes, and the fleet followed. That night, the fog became even thicker. Then a southeast wind put the floes in motion. It blew in more ice from the sea, pushed ice into the bay until it was paved white, trapping the ships like ducks in a pond freezing around them. Four of the ships managed to head back the way they came and forced their way into open water outside Frobisher Straight, but the ice field tightened around the others— "So thick upon us that we cannot sail," said Hall.

Sailors hung bedding over the gunwales as bumpers. They wrapped cables around the sides, lashed planks meant for the colony to the sides, took down the topmasts and used them too as bumpers.

June 1578.

from 8 to mydnight the winde at E N E, a fayre
gale, the ship sayled North west ——————— 6. L.
from mydnight to 4 of clock in the morning, the
winde at N E e by E. a fayre gale the ship sailed N W. 6. L.

The 19. day Thursday, from 4 to 8, the winde at N E.
e by E. a fayre gale, the ship sailed N W. ——— 6. L.
from 8 to 12 at none, the winde at N E e by E a
fayre gale, the ship sayled N. W. ——————— 6. L.
from 12. to 4 of clock, the winde at E N E. a faire
gale, the ship sayled W N W ——————— 6. L.
from 4 to, 8, the winde at E N E a fayre gale,
the ship sayled W. N W. ——————— 6. L.

The 20. friday from 8 to mydnight the winde at E N E
a good gale, the ship sayled W N W. ——— 8. L.
And at that present being 2 of clock in the
morning, I had sight of Friseland being from
me 5 Leages in the front

Mr Dee his Pinacles   N N E in the front   Mount Edgecome
west and by north
in the front.   Jun. 1578.

from Dee's Pinacles, being the south end to Mount
Edgcome, being the North point in sight, the
Land lyeth S. S. W. e N N E. being the S E.
parte of Friseland. And note that from the
south Pinacles westerly; from the said Dee's
pinacles to Frobushers Cape, the land lyeth
S. W. and by W, N E and by E. 5 L. And
from Frobushers Cape, to Bordowe's point, it
W. e by S, E e by N. 5. L. having respect
to Hawles nedels by the way, w'ch be certain
Rocks, they it 16 of the lyeth in sight.
from Mr William Bordowe's point, to M' Michael
Locks foreland, it N. W. e S E, 5 L. so
that the land faleth to turneth Northerly

The 20.

A page from Christopher Hall's log, June 1578, including his sketch of the Greenland coast with "Mr Dee his Pinacles." (British Library, Harleian MS, 167/42 f.187r)

They jumped onto the ice with oars and pikes and tried to push away the floes. They prayed. One of the colonists, the Reverend Robert Woolfall, led the prayers aboard the *Judith* when it was cut off from the rest of the fleet. Closed tight by the wind, the ice pressed hard enough against the ships to squeeze them out of the water, like a pip squeezed between your fingers until it jumps. That terrible night, they heard the hulls groan and the timbers splinter.

Striking an iceberg, the *Dennis* sank off Resolution Island. Everyone aboard was rescued, but part of the wooden frame for the colony's fort went down with the ship.

A shift in the wind saved the rest of the fleet. At about mid-morning on July 3, the wind turned from southeast to southwest and loosened the ice pack; the ships slowly gained maneuvering room in the passages opening among the floes. Some beneficent power parted the ice, like God's parting of the Red Sea for the Israelites. "I dare well avouch," George Best said, "there were never men more dangerously distressed, nor more mercifully by God's Providence delivered."

But the fleet was now split into three parts. One included the four vessels that had managed to reach open waters outside the entrance to Frobisher Strait; they were still unaware that it was a bay. Eight other ships, including the *Ayde,* were sailing toward them. The third part consisted of the *Judith* and the *Michael,* which had stayed well to the west inside the bay but were out of each other's sight and out of the others' as well. For the bulk of the fleet, outside the bay, the only choice was to wait until the winds made the bay safe to reenter by sweeping away more of the ice.

In the blanket of fog, pilots could barely see the water. For the lack of sun, they couldn't use cross-staffs to measure their latitude. They searched for landmarks on the coast, but the ice seemed to have reshaped all the familiar forms. The current felt stronger than Christopher Hall and some of the other experienced hands remembered it being, and it twirled the ships like flotsam caught in a whirlpool. The tides sounded exceptionally loud, as noisy as the waterfall at London Bridge. Every day, the officers debated whether the land they half-glimpsed through the fog was Resolution Island.

Hall said the island lay somewhere north, since the coast looked unfamiliar to him. Frobisher insisted that the island lay south of them. Hall argued that the fleet was well south of Frobisher Strait. His captain general maintained that the ships were about to reenter it, straight ahead.

On July 9 Hall rowed a pinnace from the *Thomas Allen* to confer once again with Frobisher aboard the *Ayde*. Said Hall:

> I told him that it was not the Straits, and told him all the marks of both the lands, that it was not the Straits, and he presently was in a great rage & swore by God's wounds that it was it, or else take his life. So I see him in such a rage, I took my pinnace & came aboard the Thomas Allen again.

Frobisher insisted that this was the waterway they sought.

In a way, the fog was a blessing. Each pilot could do as he believed right aboard his own ship and cite the poor visibility to explain his failure to follow Frobisher. Hall steered the *Thomas Allen* east, away from the unfamiliar coast. Two other ships kept him company. Another vessel, George Best's *Anne Francis*, made a wider turn east and found itself quite alone.

Frobisher led eight other ships west into what he assumed to be Frobisher Strait. It was an example of his hubris and of the limitations of sixteenth-century navigation. He was sailing into the waterway known today as Hudson Strait. His part of the fleet traveled west about two hundred miles, toward Hudson Bay, before he admitted his mistake. Then he ordered the ships to reverse direction. Later, his supporters claimed he had known early on it was the wrong course but had secretly had a higher purpose in mind. Once in Hudson Strait, they said, he had been impressed by the strong current and resumed his search for a northwest passage to Cathay. In their version, he could not resist the pull of his original mission. George Best claimed that if not for Frobisher's sense of responsibility for the mining venture, "he both would and could have gone through to the South Sea, which we call Mare del Sur, and dissolved the long doubt of the passage which we seek to find to the rich country of Cathay."

Or he was simply lost. He named the newfound waterway Mistaken Strait.

Frobisher thereby lost two weeks of the short Arctic summer.

He reached Resolution Island again in late July, joining some of the vessels that had decided against following him. That part of the fleet had stayed near Resolution Island because ice had blocked the route into Frobisher Bay. Another part of the fleet had remained in the bay but had not been seen for weeks. As captain general, Frobisher owed no one an apology for his mistake and surely offered none. His return, however, energized the fleet. On July 28, a Monday, the ice again defeated his attempt to enter the bay. On the 29th, he succeeded by keeping the *Ayde* to the middle of the waterway, though not all the ships followed. On the 30th, he argued about the *Ayde*'s position with a trumpeter serving as lookout. The trumpeter insisted they had passed Jackman Sound, along the southern shore of the waterway. Frobisher vehemently disagreed. The lowly trumpeter proved right, and Frobisher wrong. From the topmast, the trumpeter also pointed out Countess of Warwick Sound. Frobisher left his flagship to go into a pinnace, so he could reach the sound sooner.

By then, he had lost three weeks.

His sailors grumbled about his stubbornness and swore they would prefer to be hanged at home for desertion rather than die in this ice. They argued with officers or ignored orders. Frobisher's contempt for anyone who dared to disagree with him had infected the whole crew: Sailors aboard the *Ayde* loudly told the expedition's notary, Edward Sellman, that he should stay in his cabin rather than criticize them for failing to keep watch for ice. Frobisher's surliness fed their own, said Sellman; "therefore all things have fallen out the worse with us."

Too late, the *Ayde*'s officers heeded Sellman's warning about the ice. Orders were given to raise the anchor and hoist the sails, to

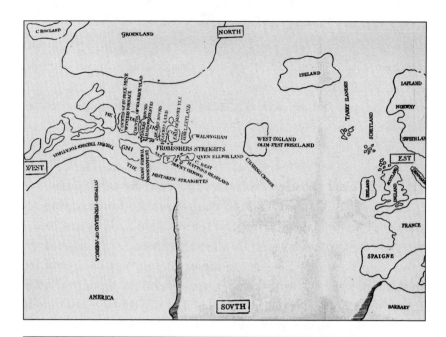

A map from the 1578 expedition showing details of "Frobisshers Streights," including "Countis of Warrick-Ylad." Frisland ("West-Ingland, Friseland") is at the map's center. (Hakluyt Society)

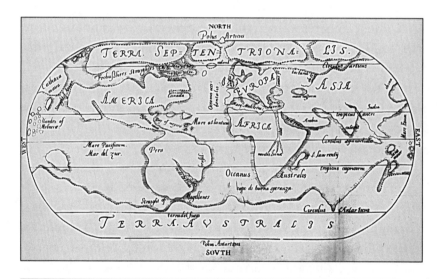

A 1578 map of the world with "Frobusshers Straightes" and "Meta Incognita." George Best used it in his pamphlet. (Hakluyt Society)

avoid drifting floes, but at that moment a floe struck the moving anchor hard enough to ram one of its flukes through the ship's bow, with the same effect as a cannonball. Within an hour, water was four feet deep in the hold; sailors used sides of beef to plug the leak and bailed water for the next nine hours.

Frobisher safely reached Countess of Warwick Sound in the pinnace. He was not the first person there. Edward Fenton—presumed lost along with his ship, the *Judith*—was waiting for him. Fenton had surely assumed the same of Frobisher—that he was long since dead, or already sailing home in defeat. They had last seen each other a month ago, during that terrible night of ice and wind. But here was Fenton in command of Countess of Warwick Sound; and here was Frobisher, bested in his own waterway. They dined together aboard the *Judith,* their pleasure mixed with uneasiness.

Fenton and the *Judith* had first been completely alone, until he had found the *Michael.* While the rest of the fleet had remained outside Frobisher Bay, the *Judith* and the *Michael* had anchored themselves to icebergs, and then sailors had gone into pinnaces and skiffs to try to tow the ships through the ice fields; it had taken nine days to cross just half the width of the bay. The ice and fog had forced the men to devote all their energy to just surviving.

In those conditions, sailing on to Cathay had seemed laughable. Mining gold had been out of the question, since the *Judith* and *Michael* didn't carry any tools. For lack of tools and other supplies, starting construction of the colony had been impossible too. Plus, Fenton now realized, the quantity of ice varied year to year, making a mockery of the investors' assumption that ships could dependably enter the waterway in spring. "And whereas it was supposed we might have got into the straits coming thither in May," Fenton wrote in his journal, "I see it will be much ado to get in there in the beginning of August (as this year we have made dangerful proof thereof), in the end of which month we should return again home." As for performing useful exploration, "it is not likely to be performed where a man shall be both in continual danger of the ice, and also subject to calms and continual fogs." The fog had lifted during only two of the last seventeen days.

Fenton showed great professionalism despite the hardships. After reaching Countess of Warwick Sound, the *Judith* had anchored at Countess of Warwick Island, the expedition's head-quarters from the previous year, "where in our judgement all things remained as we left them." His men had washed their clothes and explored the mainland for black ore. They waited for the rest of the fleet despite the reasonable conclusion that it would never appear. The drizzle sometimes turned to snow; Countess of Warwick Sound froze.

Now, on July 31, Frobisher was on the scene with his pinnace and wanted everything done quickly. On August 1, the *Ayde* and some of the other ships arrived. That evening, some of the miners erected tents on the island.

Frobisher issued a series of orders to maintain close control of the mining. No one was to conduct assays without permission from the captain general or one of his lieutenants. He threatened to fine anyone taking ore for himself; as a quality control, no one was to load ore onto the ships without an officer inspecting it.

Sanitation was another priority. "No person or persons," Frobisher instructed, "shall wash their hands or any other things in the spring upon the Countess Island, where the water is used and preserved for the dressing of their victuals." Since the island lacked a spring, the order apparently referred to the water collected from snowmelt. No one was to defecate ("do his easement") except where the tides could carry away the wastes. Ships would be fined for discharging ballast into the sound.

Swearing was punishable by imprisonment. Anyone drawing a weapon "in quarreling manner" risked being punished with loss of his right hand. He counted on the mixture of threats and hard work to maintain order among the four hundred men, who believed themselves surrounded by gold.

Over the next weeks, Frobisher visited other islands and the mainland by pinnace and approved a dozen new mines. Each one became a small community unto itself, usually with a ship anchored offshore. On Countess of Warwick Island, Frobisher's men built a brick assay shop roofed with tile, as fine an industrial establishment as one would see in London. They also built a smithy and a shelter of some kind. In the fog and drizzle, dozens of men chiseled rock out of a new, deep trench on the island, rock that they carried across the slippery ground to the furnaces, or to the shore for ferrying into the ships. When the fog was thickest, a drummer beat a steady signal on his drum to help the pinnaces and skiffs find their way back to the island. The fog and high seas made commuting to the other mines a terrible trial. One of the captains nearly drowned when sailing a pinnace in search of ore; almost worse, he relived the experience in a dream that night, screaming, "Jesus, have mercy upon me!" and waking Fenton and the other men in the tents. All night, they listened to the wind and rain against the canvas.

George Best endured the most harrowing experience of all. All those weeks, his ship, the *Anne Francis,* remained at the mouth of Frobisher Bay. Two other vessels circled nearby but often disappeared in the fog. Whenever the fog lifted, an unfavorable wind prevented them from sailing west. Whenever the wind shifted, it brought the fog and ice. So the *Anne Francis,* the *Thomas of Ipswich,* and the *Moon* went nowhere.

As senior officer, Best hosted a meeting of the captains and pilots to decide on a course of action. Some officers, led by the pilot of the *Thomas of Ipswich,* favored sailing immediately back to England; others wanted first to look for a safe anchorage, where they could repair the leaks caused by collisions with ice. Best ruled out sailing home as dishonorable but did not insist that they try at once to reach Countess of Warwick Sound. He took care against issuing an order they wouldn't obey. "As true Englishmen and faithful friends," he said, they should first try simply to keep their vessels within one another's sight and search for a safe harbor. If that were accomplished, he proposed, they should then assemble a five-ton pinnace that was lying as a jumble of planks in the hold of the *Anne Francis* and sail it west in hope of finding Frobisher and the rest of the fleet. The officers agreed to his plan. Their agreement lasted until dusk. The pilot aboard the *Thomas of Ipswich*, against the wishes of its captain, persuaded the crew that the wiser course was to sail home rather than remain in a place of ice, fog, and misery. Under the cover of fog, the *Thomas of Ipswich* slipped away.

At daylight, Best coasted along the shore of Resolution Island in search of an anchorage. He spotted a large outcrop of black rock near the island's southeast coast, apparently on another, smaller island. That black rock seemed much like the black ore mined a year ago, but in a quantity so large that he thought "it might reasonably suffice all the gold gluttons in the world." He called it Best's Blessing. The *Anne Francis* struck rocks in approaching it, but the discovery seemed to make up for every hardship. Miners went ashore while Best went farther inland to erect a stone column as a token of possession. The *Anne Francis*'s carpenter meanwhile began trying to assemble the pinnace.

He lacked nails. This problem was solved when a blacksmith used a gun barrel as an anvil and fashioned nails from a fire shovel and a pair of tongs. The carpenter had no such easy solution for the shortage of planks, including the knees to brace the boat's interior. He had little confidence in the finished product. So many planks were missing—some of them broken when used as bumpers against the ice, or by cargo shifting in the hold—that nothing more than the nails themselves were holding the pinnace together. He announced that he wouldn't sail in the pinnace himself even for £500.

"These words," said Best, "somewhat discouraged some of the company."

Best argued in favor of risking a trip in the pinnace to search for Frobisher: find Frobisher and his headquarters; then assayers there could test samples of rock from Best's Blessing. The rock was *like* black ore, but did it actually contain gold? Lacking an assay, they could only guess. When he asked his fellow officers their opinion of the pinnace, they said it just might be seaworthy. Best offered to command it himself, and waited for something more from his officers. He heard the silence. Someone finally spoke—John Gray, master's mate, volunteered to accompany him. In the end, Best had the company of nineteen men.

For three days, this little company rowed west toward Countess of Warwick Sound. Staring at the mainland, Best saw smoke and people waving a flag of some kind but no ships. There were tents, but where was the English fleet? He feared that the small figures in the distance were Inuit—"those bad, cruel, and man-eating people"—or, almost as bad, were a shipwrecked remnant of the expedition and would commandeer the pinnace, dooming all of them. The pinnace sailed closer; Best and a man on shore yelled a greeting—each said, "All is well!" These men were English miners at one of Frobisher's new mines. All the men in the boat and on land tossed their caps into the air.

Frobisher convened a meeting of the officers on Countess of Warwick Island to discuss the expedition's many problems. With the ships having arrived so late, the masons and carpenters had yet to lay the first course of bricks for the colony's fort. No one was even sure what construction materials were on hand, until the captains compared the bills of lading. Part of the fort's wood frame had been lost weeks before with the sinking of the *Dennis*. The *Thomas of Ipswich* had half of the bricks but, still unknown to anyone on the island, had deserted. The *Anne Francis* and the *Moon,* still at the mouth of the bay, carried much of the colonists' beer and other victuals, and many of the timbers on hand were splintered from use as fenders against the ice.

Edward Fenton suggested reducing the number of colonists to sixty, from the original one hundred. He volunteered to stay with them as governor, as originally planned. The carpenters vetoed that proposal by insisting that they would need at least six weeks to build a shelter for sixty colonists, assuming the construction materials were on hand. But the carpenters doubted they had enough bricks and timbers to build housing for even forty.

Frobisher apparently saw the danger in tinkering with plans for the colony. The Privy Council had made a colony one of its goals, yet it couldn't be met since the ships had arrived late and lacked essential cargoes. He was protecting himself by convening the meeting, where the responsibility could be shared. His officers agreed to build a fort or house on the island. But due to the missing supplies and the lateness of the season, they decided against leaving the colonists there. One didn't need a sophisticated understanding of the north to suspect that the colonists might suffer terribly. Frobisher never lacked for bravery and never hesitated to demand that his subordinates take large risks, but even he saw no reason to doom sixty people to starvation. There would be a house, left empty. In any case, he planned on revisiting Meta Incognita in a year, on a fourth expedition. So he could look forward to building a colony in the proper way, next year. Edward Sellman, the notary, kept a record of the deliberations and recorded the fact that all the officers present endorsed Frobisher's decisions.

The Inuit kept their distance. They would sometimes stand in plain sight on the mainland and watch the miners work on Countess of Warwick Island, but they came no closer. Great wooden vessels had come into those waters twice before, and twice the whites had kidnapped Inuit. The Inuit refused to risk further contact; watching sufficed.

The miners gave up on Countess of Warwick Island after a week, the rock being so hard. On August 11 they opened a new mine—Countess of Sussex, they called it—five miles north on the mainland. Over the next two weeks it yielded 455 tons of ore. Edward Sellman recorded the amounts in his role as notary while the chief assayer, Robert Denham, traveled from place to place collecting samples for his meltings. The Englishmen coined twenty-four-karat names for the mines they worked: Denham's Mount, Fenton's Fortune, Winter's Furnace. In the frenzy of work, the orders calling for an officer to inspect the ore were often ignored. Loading the maximum possible tonnage into the ships took precedence over a careful sifting of the rock. "Simple men (I judge) took good and bad together," Edward Sellman noted. "I think much bad ore will be found."

The weather did not improve spirits or help with discipline. On August 19 Fenton recorded, "It was rain with some sleet and snow." He complained to Frobisher about men ignoring officers' orders, but the real problem was Frobisher's failure to back him—that, and Frobisher's stubbornness, and his vanity, and his having wasted three weeks sailing in the wrong waterway. Their argument grew loud enough for others to hear the shouting—"many hot words," Sellman said. Each of those inordinately proud officers suspected the other of scheming to steal full credit for any success.

Frobisher mostly attended to the mining while Fenton oversaw construction of the house. The division of labor helped keep them apart. Barrels of food intended for the colonists were buried on the island, for use by the next expedition and to make room for additional ore aboard the ships. Timbers were buried too. On August 24, the masons and carpenters worked in the rain to begin building what Fenton called his "little watch Tower." The house rose at almost the exact center of the island, and the workmen started by using the local stone. They did the hard, slow work of dressing the stones until the corners were properly straight and tight, built the upper portions of the walls from wood, and topped them with a plank roof. The house was twelve feet wide, fourteen feet long. Roof beams ran the length of the interior, and an oven was in one wall. What Fenton saw was more akin to a stone-and-beam cottage than the great fort that the Cathay Company had envisioned. Here for the first time, though, was something intended to outlast the Englishmen's stay in Meta Incognita. It was the first English house in the hemisphere. More than the mining, the house marked their true claim to the land.

It was "his little beginning," Fenton wrote in his journal. This first house was an experiment to determine "how we should deal in building greater houses." Like Frobisher, he took the prospect of returning to Meta Incognita for granted.

August 28: "Foggy and rain and blew much wind at east-northeast with snow, hail & sleet."

August 29: "Tempestuous with snow & rain."

On the 30th ("very tempestuous weather with great snow and wind") the workmen completed the house. It was furnished, in a fashion, with bells, mirrors, combs, engravings of men and women, and other trinkets that the Englishmen hoped would win the favor of the natives. Baked bread was left in the oven. So little did the Englishmen understand the land that they planted peas and corn. It was a test of "the fruitfulness of the soil," George Best said—as if Countess of Warwick Island possessed soil.

Most of the ships began sailing toward home on August 31. Before reaching the mouth of Frobisher Bay, Frobisher went into a pinnace to oversee the loading of a last few tons of ore. He wanted every vessel filled to capacity. High swells were making travel difficult and should have warned him away, as should have the darkening sky. But he considered the cargo worth every risk.

The gale—the fiercest yet—arrived in full force at about the time he reached shore. Waves nearly swamped pinnaces carrying miners trying to reach the ships, yet in the winds the fleet could not approach land or the boats. One of the *Judith*'s skiffs sank even as sailors tried to haul it aboard. Another of the *Judith*'s boats split in half at the end of its towrope, then disappeared. There was ample time for fright, despite everything happening very fast. Waves swept men overboard, tore away sails, shattered masts. Rotted by the months in the salt air, lines gave way like twine. Sailors on the *Ayde* cut the towline to a skiff. The *Ayde*'s anchor tore lose. Captains sought to save the ships by heading out to sea, rather than closer to land and to the pinnaces.

All this for just a few last tons of ore. Sailors cursed Frobisher in the roaring of the storm—"The General is condemned of all men for bringing the fleet in danger," Sellman said. George Best climbed aboard the *Anne Francis* just as the pinnace that lacked all its bracing sank under his feet. In another pinnace, in that chaos, Frobisher could not find the *Ayde* but reached the *Gabriel,* already over-crowded with men unable to reach other ships. The *Emanuel*—one of the vessels Frobisher had insisted on filling to the gunwales with ore—was trapped among rocks. The *Ayde* kept a fire burning at the end of a pike in the vain hope of guiding some of the missing sailors to safety.

On the evening of September 3, in fog and snow, the *Gabriel* headed east with Frobisher aboard. The *Gabriel* left the *Emanuel* to work its way past the shoals on her own.

. . .

Queen Elizabeth spent the summer traveling in relative comfort on her "progress," the slow procession from one courtier's estate to another. Her toothache still troubled her, though, as did pains in her cheek. When the royal party crossed into Suffolk, the sheriff led a welcoming committee of two hundred gentlemen wearing white velvet, three hundred dressed in black velvet, and fifteen hundred lesser figures on horseback. The visit caused a local shortage of velvet and silk. One of her hosts, William Cordell, showed his devotion by remodeling his manor house into the shape of an *E.*

The queen expected extravagance. The dinner menu for a single sitting could include beef, veal, mutton, fish, and a dozen species of fowl. Her hosts provided everything at their own expense. Over the years, Lord Burghley received her at least a dozen times at his own estate. He was an excellent record keeper. His kitchens served her capon, chicken, goose, pheasant, pigeon, quail, rabbit, beef, lamb, and venison. And bream, carp, eel, lobster, oysters, prawns, pike, salmon, sturgeon, and trout. At that time, Frobisher's sailors were eating sea biscuits.

Her toothache was little better when she returned to Greenwich Palace. Her counselors worried that the pains might be symptoms of some more serious illness. Members of the Privy Council decided to dispatch the most learned man in the kingdom to consult physicians on the Continent about her condition. They sent the scholarly John Dee.

Most of Frobisher's ships had sailed west with just occasional sightings of other ships from the fleet. Aboard the *Ayde,* the crew lost the main yard and fired a shot to get help from the *Thomas Allen.* But the *Thomas Allen* sailed on. Officers had been scattered among different ships during the last chaotic days in the bay, which further tangled the chain of command. Frobisher unwillingly sailed aboard the *Gabriel* rather the *Ayde.* It saved him, though, from seeing storm waves flood his quarters aboard the flagship. "The sea let in at my general's cabin," Christopher Hall wrote in the log "& burst from the cabin floors to the windows all the timber and boards, into him who was [at] the helm—his name is Francis Austen."

The *Emanuel* remained well behind the other vessels. Thomas Wiars, identified in the pay lists as "passenger," wrote of the ship's passing Frisland, the Englishmen's mistaken identity for southern Greenland, and then passing a hitherto unknown second land. He went so far as to describe the coastline of the new territory. By the time the story was told by George Best, the land was said to be "fruitful, full of woods, and a champion country." The *Emanuel* was a buss—a broad, inelegant fishing vessel—and the presumed new land was christened Buss Island in its honor.

Thomas Wiar's report could be explained by his seeing two fog-bound capes of Greenland. Greenland was wrongly placed far to the north on the ship's charts. Seeing land, the sailors could have wrongly believed that it was undiscovered territory, and that Greenland lay elsewhere. Wiars described his find in about two hundred words, enough to make Buss Island seem real. In 1606 an English pilot serving the king of Denmark sighted territory he confidently identified as Buss Island; Captain Thomas Shepherd in 1671 reported exploring the island's coast. A map was duly published showing Buss Island as diamond-shaped, with three harbors and a mountain range. In 1675 the Hudson's Bay Company secured a royal charter granting it ownership of the island, plus a monopoly over its trade, plus rights to precious metals there. It was a champion, illusory land.

Frobisher did not learn the fate of all of his sailors until the last ships reached home. About forty of his four hundred men died during the expedition to Meta Incognita. George Best judged the figure as impressively low, "considering how many ships were in the fleet and how strange fortunes we passed." Some of the deaths occurred during the last, tumultuous gale near the mouth of Frobisher Bay. Some men had drowned and—almost certainly— others had been left behind in the confusion. At least five men were buried on Meta Incognita while the mining was under way. The *Ayde* buried five others at sea during the voyage home; on the subject of casualties the accounts from other ships were mostly silent.

The *Emanuel* lost her masts in a storm and was wrecked on the coast of Ireland. By early October, all the other ships safely reached England. Frobisher brought home 1,136 tons of ore—40 percent more than the commissioners of the Cathay Company expected. It was, strangely, more than the company could afford. The company was unable to pay the vessels' owners the agreed-upon fee of £3 per ton. Nor could it reimburse the outfitters, not even for food that was long since eaten. Michael Lok, the chief financier, had spent all the money—on building the great works at Dartford, on assays of the ore, and on organizing the fifteen-ship fleet. The company had no money. It had ore presumed to contain gold, but the company lacked the money to pay for refining it in the new Dartford furnaces.

Elizabeth rescued the Cathay Company by granting it permission to levy another surcharge. It was the fourth surcharge on the investors in little more than a year. The first had paid the sailors' wages at the end of the previous voyage, and the second had paid for the construction at Dartford; the investors had been assured that the third would be sufficient to finance the latest expedition, bring home a wealth of ore, and refine it. Now that the fleet was home, Elizabeth authorized raising an additional £6,000 to save the enterprise from collapse.

Her commissioners instructed their colleague Michael Lok to obtain written reports about the expedition from Frobisher and his officers. He was also instructed to obtain their maps of Meta Incognita to prevent anyone else from learning the route.

Last, as if he needed to be told, his fellow commissioners asked him to determine, as soon as possible, the value of the ore.

"Her Majesty," they said, "hath very great expectations of the same."

CHAPTER SIX

Kodlunarn

In the summer of 1861, Charles Francis Hall prepared himself for exploring Frobisher Bay. His energy level was high. During the long winter and spring, he had collected stories from the Inuit, reread his shipboard Arctic library, and analyzed his findings in a growing stack of notebooks. Martin Frobisher's expeditions seemed as familiar as the deck of the *George Henry*. For guides, Hall was counting on the hunter Koojesse and five other Inuit men and women, all of them agreeable to showing him the places where they said whites had come a long, long time ago. The boat for his travels—"an old, rotten, leaky, and ice-beaten whale-boat"—was a castoff from the *George Henry,* replacing the brand-new skiff that had been destroyed by a gale. The *George Henry* by then had been in the north a full year. No one aboard knew that Abraham Lincoln had won the presidential election back home the previous November. In April, when the Confederacy fired on Fort Sumter, the ship was still trapped in ice. It was July, about the time of the Confederacy's first victory at Bull Run, when the *George Henry* finally floated free, ready to resume whaling. At about the same time, Hall's party rowed away on its own.

His little company, after three days, reached a large cove that he recognized from his reading as Countess of Warwick Sound. Martin Frobisher had left those waters 283 years ago. The Inuit knew the waters well. But no other whites—no *qallunaat*—had come since Frobisher's time or known where to find the sound dotted with islands. It was considered lost and was absent from maps. The site of Frobisher's would-be colony had been lost, too, from the time his fleet made its disorderly leave-taking.

Unlike any other visitor, Hall arrived obsessed by history. No one had assigned him the task of exploration, nor was anyone truly expecting any results from his travels. His fervor seemed as odd to the whalers as to his Inuit guides. Regardless of the number or identity of his companions, he was always alone in his purpose, but his sense of being apart increased his zeal.

All the clichés he had heard about the independent spirit of the Inuit proved true in the whaleboat. Clichés about Americans' liking for well-ordered plans proved no less true. He valued promptness and a straight-ahead course. His guides went where the animals led them. He wanted efficiency, orderliness, and speed from his companions, whom he expected to perform whatever task he assigned. The Inuit interested themselves mainly in hunting; indeed they considered themselves born to be hunters.

Hall was steering the boat toward one of the islands when Koojesse saw a polar bear. Their chase through the water covered at least two miles. While the men aimed their rifles the women rowed and shouted and screamed—"horrible noises," Hall said— until the animal turned to gaze at the source of the commotion. In that way the bear slowly lost ground as it swam. After the first shots its white fur ran red in the water. The Inuit butchered the eight-hundred-pound carcass on an island they called Oopungnewing, where everyone lunched on the bright-red meat.

That evening, one of the women rowed Hall north to an island the Inuit called Niountelik; some of them said they had seen objects left there by whites. On a modern map Oopungnewing is Willows Island; Niountelik is Newland Island. Wide at each end and narrow in the middle like a well-knotted bow tie, Newland was home only to ducks. In late summer the loudest sound was the trickle of snowmelt from the last outcroppings of ice.

His guide, whom he knew as Suzhi, said she had seen bricks on Newland Island. Every few steps he asked her where the bricks lay. He saw tent rings—circles of stones where hunters had pitched tents anchored by the rocks—and a scattering of animal bones, and he walked past what appeared to be black moss. With Suzhi, he hiked the island's perimeter until they came again to the black moss. Looking closer through a low tangle of vegetation, he saw that the black moss was coal. Never lacking for energy, admirably deductive in his thinking, Hall examined the coal and concluded that the fragments were embedded deeply enough in the ground to prove they had lain on the island for many years. The coal, he concluded, was from Martin Frobisher's camps.

"Great God," he wrote in his notebook, "Thou has rewarded me in my search!" He asked Suzhi how the coal had come to be there. "A great many years ago," she said, "white men with big ship came here."

Charles Francis Hall, from a photograph taken in 1870. "It seemed to me as if I had been called, if I may so speak, to try and do the work."

He danced and laughed and made a somersault atop the coal. At least that was the behavior Suzhi later described to him. In his excitement he entered a sort of reverie and remembered very little except that exhilarating coal. There was Charles Francis Hall, as stern as a New England parson, dancing. "I *felt* like dancing—like turning a dozen of somersaults!"

Hall spent the night and the next day on Willows Island, writing up the finds. Except for Suzhi, his guides went onto the mainland to hunt caribou. He tentatively decided that Newland Island was where Martin Frobisher had built his colony. It would explain the coal, though the stories he heard from the Inuit had led him to expect something more impressive than just a few black lumps in the earth. That was on August 12. On the 13th, his party resumed rowing west in Frobisher Bay with the bladder of the polar bear mounted on a stick as a good-luck charm. Koojesse sketched the northern coastline while Hall took charge of steering, kept a record of distances, and determined latitude and longitude. Every channel and cape was charted by Koojesse. "My assistant draughtsman," said Hall.

At each camping place, Hall asked the Inuit about sightings of coal and bricks. Koojesse's father-in-law, one of his hosts for a night, recalled seeing such objects on Newland Island from the time he was a boy. He also remembered examining pieces of iron; he called them "heavy stones." One was so heavy that hunters had competed to try to lift it. He remembered too hearing stories about whites who had built a ship on another island. Every detail went into Hall's notebooks.

Hall flew an American flag from the whaleboat's bow as his party traveled west. Just the sight of the colors in a new territory gave him a sense of higher purpose. A second boat of Inuit kept his guides company, paddling on what seemed a smooth dark mirror. Meta Incognita, from the water, was a thin hard line of gray-blue hills. If a seal raised its head above water, both boats would give chase; if a school of ducks came into sight, half a day might be lost to the hunt. "They meant not ill," said Hall, "but the Innuits are like eagles—untamable."

On August 22 Koojesse announced that they were one day's travel from the head of the bay. On the 23rd, they reached a river that Hall called Sylvia Grinnell River, in honor of the daughter of his patron Henry Grinnell. The supply of animals there far outstripped everyone's appetite. In a span of three days his guides killed eleven caribou, and the seal population supplied another feast. Dining on caribou steak, Hall decided he preferred caribou fat to butter. The fat also served as salve for painful boils on his shoulder; his beard offered some protection against the mosquitoes. He tasted wild blueberries and blackberries, and noted the abundance of succulent hares.

In all that comfort, his judgment temporarily abandoned him. "I never saw in the States, unless the exception be of the prairies of the West, more luxuriant grasses on uncultivated lands than are here around, under me," he wrote. After a year in the north, including an interminable winter that had erased every color, he saw the wisps of greenery along the riverbanks as a tangled jungle. The land near the river's mouth seemed to him as rich as the best Ohio farmland. Each morning was "splendid," each night "glorious." The animals were "fat as butter." He judged that the riverbanks would be a fine setting for a colony of whites who could plant true civilization among the natives, in place of the whalers' bad influence of alcohol and foul language.

Work never completely stopped. He coaxed one of the women into sketching a map that showed both shores of Frobisher Bay, as well as Hudson Strait. As proved by his comparing her efforts to his own charts, she possessed greater knowledge of the geography than did the British Admiralty or the U.S. Navy. Holding a pencil for the first time in his life, the hunter Tookookaah drew another map for Hall and told him the Inuktitut place-names in exchange for tobacco. After sketching each feature, Tookookaah would jab his patron with the pencil and wait for the name to be recorded.

Hall intended to take a different route back to the *George Henry*. Traveling toward the head of the bay, his guides had rowed along the northern shore. Now, looking ahead, he wanted them to reach the bay's end and then travel along the southern shore, back to the ship.

It seemed a strange idea to his guides. The Inuit knew *qallunaat* were sometimes foolish. This white man could see the head of the bay and the southern shore quite well from where he camped yet insisted on traveling there. Like all *qallunaat,* he knew nothing of the shoals along the southern coast or of the dangerous tides. Plus, the sky hinted that snow was within a few days of overtaking the glorious sunshine. Already, the shallows were freezing at night.

When the whaleboat was under way, Koojesse pointed to an island from where the American would surely be able to see everything he wished. "I answered that this would not do," Hall wrote later. *"I must go where I wanted to."* They rowed to the southern shore just as he demanded, the women as usual then lugging the tents and cooking gear from the boats to the new campsite. He climbed a hill and raised an American flag. But on the morning he intended to explore the head of the bay, Koojesse went caribou hunting without a word to him. Another guide left too. They evaded his orders without explicitly rejecting them or risking a confrontation. Determined to press on, Hall rowed into a river at the western end of the bay, waded through knee-deep mud, and stepped onto land. "A day of trials and discovery," he wrote. "At last I am where I have long desired to be."

He saw for himself that the waterway lacked a western outlet. It proved beyond doubt that the passage Martin Frobisher had explored was a bay, not a strait. "From my own vision, 'Frobisher's Strait' is a myth," he wrote. "It only exists in the minds of the civilized world—not in fact." For Frobisher, the one comfort would have been that white explorers had needed nearly three centuries to prove him wrong.

Hall lost his good spirits back at camp. For three days he barely left his tent because of terrible pain in his shoulders. Doing nothing while a new landscape was waiting outside to be explored only made him feel worse, a misery compounded by a new outbreak of boils. Marooned in the tent, he berated himself as a failure for having nothing more to show for his work than pieces of coal from

Newland Island. His sense of accomplishment evaporated, replaced by self-reproach for not having fulfilled his mission to search for John Franklin's missing men. What were his small pains compared to the sufferings of men lost for thirteen years? Each night was colder, his mood darker. "Another terrible night of struggle with pains," he wrote on September 6. "When shall I be well again?"

His party resumed rowing that same day along the southern shore. To Hall's annoyance, Koojesse rejoined them three days late after a last caribou hunt. But when he rowed Hall to a lookout point, the American forgave him for every misdeed. Hall found the speed of the boat exhilarating, was impressed by Koojesse's skill as a sailor in the roaring tides, and once again felt grateful for the company of the Inuit. At camp, Suzhi served him coffee that tasted better than any drink he remembered from Cincinnati. Hall's moodiness sometimes allowed for such overwhelming happiness, and just then his good feelings extended to everyone. If only he could know whether his companions loved him as he now loved them. His loneliness was nearly unbearable. "Innuits are Innuits, and such they ever will be," he wrote. "They are independent of every other human being, and will never brook control, no matter what engagements they enter into." He considered himself the only civilized person in camp but needed the company of the Inuit. They seemed as untamed as the animals they hunted.

Snowstorms were visible in the distance. Koojesse at first steered the whaleboat along the southern shore. Then a gale confined the party to the tents, and the winds seemed to dissipate every good feeling. There were the long silences of people who have tired of one another's company. Hall saw treacheries in the silences and in every gesture. "I was completely at the mercy of Koojesse and his companions," he complained. "He especially would do just as he pleased; and if I attempted to show opposition or express a determination to do as *I* might wish, ominous looks and sharp words met me."

Under way again, Koojesse steered the boat north. Hall again asked to stay along the southern shore. He wanted to be able to go ashore whenever an interesting feature came into sight. But was it his tenth or twentieth demand for a course change?

Hall sensed the anger when Koojesse refused to alter direction. Stung first by the impertinence, Hall then began to be afraid, as if Koojesse were aiming a gun at him.

> He acts the *devil* with me . . . I must submit, hard as it is. Why did not the fellow tell me this morning what he was intending to do? A few of the Innuits concert and act without saying one word to me. I will try and settle accounts with them when I get to the ship, especially with Koojesse. . . . Really I never took such insolence from any white man, nor will I while I have a right arm to defend my honor. . . . I must say that I believe my life is in danger; but God is with me here and every where. If I die at the hands of this treacherous people, I die in faith that I am in the performance of my duty. . . . There may be a time when I can again enter this bay to do the work for which I engaged my present company, but it will have to be with *civilized* men.

Yet Koojesse looked after the American's interests by guiding him back to Countess of Warwick Sound. Hall never fully acknowledged the importance of Koojesse's steady hand; the American regarded their return to the sound and, once there, to Newland Island as matter-of-factly as if he had piloted the course himself a dozen times. His spirits greatly improved, and he complained about nothing more serious than the pains in his shoulder, the dropping temperatures, and his guides' maddening determination to give chase to every caribou. That, and the winds and the fatigue from six weeks' travel. "Had a terrible time this morn loading Boat & getting aboard from the heavy Sea prevailing," he wrote on September 22.

It was the morning Koojesse rowed him north from Newland toward another island.

Inuit called it Kodlunarn, White Man's Island. It was, they said, where whites had lived a long time ago and built a house and a ship. "We are approaching the same—sailing over summer forests of sea vegetation—the bottom apparently of fine white sand."

On Kodlunarn, Charles Francis Hall became the person he hoped to be. He was commander in chief, detective, and clear-sighted Arctic explorer all in one. Ailments forgotten, he converted his excitement into efficient work—pacing off distances, dictating findings to himself, listening to the opinions of his guides but reaching conclusions independently.

First, he examined a trench cut like a deep wound in bedrock. Eighty-eight feet long, he recorded; an average of seven feet deep. Every feature was measured. Hall identified the trench as a mine dug by Martin Frobisher's men. Since the Inuit thought it was a water reservoir, he called it the Reservoir Trench. On the island's northern shore was a deeper cut that sloped into the waters of the sound. Frobisher's miners, in 1577, had started their diggings at that place and mined enough rock to fill the *Ayde,* the *Michael,* and the *Gabriel.* According to the Inuit, whites had built a ship there. Hall found wood at the bottom of the cut and named it the Ship's Trench.

By the time he hiked to the highest point of the island, he was sure of his findings. Just the stone foundations of Edward Fenton's cottage had survived there. Its elm walls and roof had long ago disappeared. "Gathered stone with cement at the Stone House— remains in the top of the Island. Tried hard to dig at the foundations that I might get several stones cemented together." Small rocks covered most of the island, as if paved with cobblestone.

Kodlunarn was Frobisher's Countess of Warwick Island. For Hall, it was Cathay, his own vein of gold. All of his hardships seemed justified, every annoyance unimportant. Scattered everywhere on the ground were fragments of glass, tile, and pottery. He collected as many shards as he could carry to the whaleboat. "We had been upon the Island 1 hour or about that time I should think tho I was really unconscious of time," he wrote. Rowing back to Newland

Island for the night, he found everything—the stars, the moon, the water—more glorious than ever before.

The next day his guides reached the place they called Tikkoon, the "point." It was the small spit extending from the mainland toward Kodlunarn and served as a noisy rookery for gulls. He found there one of the "heavy stones" the elders among the Inuit had described—a flattened ball of iron like a child's misshapen cap. Hall concluded that Martin Frobisher's assayers had made the twenty-pound iron loaf. He carried it into the whaleboat.

In the afternoon, rowing into a narrow canyon, he found another cache of coal—five tons of moss-covered coal on the shore of what became known as Victoria Bay. From the water, even in bright sunlight, the canyon walls remained a deep blue-gray. The water was the color of polished metal. At the head of Victoria Bay he reached a smooth curtain of rock and a deafening quiet.

A snowstorm kept everyone on Newland Island the next day. Then his guides were impatient to leave for the *George Henry*. "The weather not good on rising this morning—but Innuits were anxious to go. . . . My mind fully occupied in planning how I could get Innuits to go with me after starting to Kodlunarn & then stop awhile," Hall wrote. He struck a bargain with them: in exchange for nine boxes of percussion caps, his guides would revisit Kodlunarn.

He methodically examined the ground, measured, and sketched. From the Ship's Trench to the stone house was fifty paces. He interpreted a dense litter of charcoal, tiles, and flints laying on bare ground as the footprint of another structure, which he tentatively identified as the remains of a blacksmith shop. His drawings showed the Ship's Trench and Reservoir Trench extending along the same straight line, a played-out stratum of black rock. Koojesse meanwhile found another iron loaf half-buried at the bottom of the Ship's Trench. Hall bundled artifacts into his hat, mittens, cape, and old stockings, stuffing them full. Each item was labeled as to where it was found and what it seemed to be—wood from the bottom of the Ship's Trench, fragments of tile from the blacksmith shop, stones encrusted with cement from Edward Fenton's fort.

"O, that I could have remained instead of 2 hours—two days— or 2 weeks on Kodlunarn!" He was writing as his guides rowed, the scrawl of his handwriting betraying the motion of the boat. He wanted to record his experiences before reaching the next camp, to keep the freshness. Who in Cincinnati could imagine such success? The whaleboat was like home, the north was heaven. The two hours ashore traded for boxes of percussion caps seemed as great a bargain as the purchase of Manhattan for beads. He sat so as to protect the notebook from spray in the boat and filled twenty-one pages with details about his discoveries: "Now it will be known throughout all the enlightened nations of the Earth where Frobisher did attempt to establish the colony wh. Queen Elizabeth sent here in 1578."

His good fortune staggered him. "Why had not this been done before? Thought I also, why this poor, inexperienced, humble soul of mine to be *the one* to untomb the works of men [of] ten generations ago, by wh. the unknown becomes revealed as bright as truth?" He was on his way to the *George Henry,* where he could share the news. "All this, about like lightening, swept through my soul. . . . It was not only a strange—but almost a *spiritual* moment of my life."

Newland Island was the site of the mine Martin Frobisher knew as Winter's Furnace. In the early 1990s, archaeologists found the trench—a rough-edged gully, barely even that—where the miners had excavated five tons of black ore. One of Frobisher's ships had unloaded coal there for use in an assay furnace or for cooking the miners' meals—the coal later examined by Hall. Over the years, the Inuit had learned that the small black pebbles could make smoky fires.

Frobisher's headquarters on Kodlunarn were less than a mile from Newland. On Kodlunarn the Reservoir Trench was a long vent in the ground, as unadorned as Stonehenge. Frobisher's miners had applied their pickaxes until the trench was as deep as they

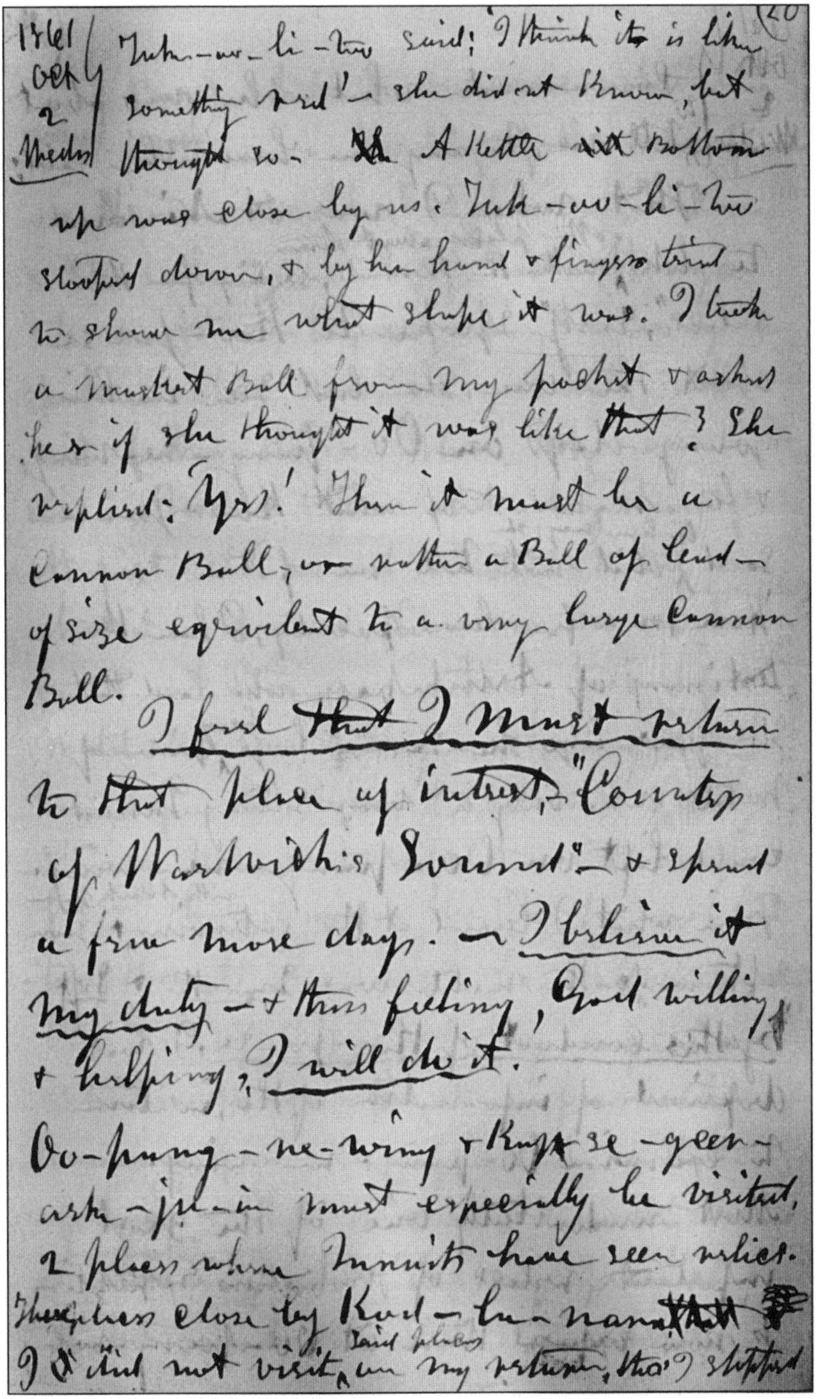

1861 Oct 2 Wednes

Tuk-oo-li-too said: 'I think it is like something red'—she did not know, but thought so.— A Kettle with bottom up was close by us. Tuk-oo-li-too stooped down, & by her hand & fingers tried to show me what shape it was. I took a Musket Ball from my pocket & asked her if she thought it was like that? She replied: 'Yes!' Then it must be a Cannon Ball, or rather a Ball of lead— of size equivalent to a very large Cannon Ball.

I feel ~~that~~ I must return to that place of interest,—"Countess of Warwick's Sound"—& spend a few more days.—I believe it my duty—& this feeling, God willing & helping, I will do it.

Oo-pung-ne-wing & Kup-se-geen-ark-je-in must especially be visited, 2 places where Innuits have seen relics. These places close by Kod-lu-narn ~~that~~ I did not visit, said places on my return, tho' I stopped

Charles Francis Hall's journal entry for October 2, 1861. "I feel that I must return to that place of interest,—'Countess of Warwick's Sound' . . . *I believe it my duty."* (Smithsonian Institution)

were tall. They had flung the cobbles and sand onto the outer edges of the cut, and the mounds of cobbles remain there, as if piled up by animals digging an outsized burrow.

Hall's several visits of a few hours each set the pattern for the small number of outsiders who followed him. In 1927 an expedition sponsored by the Field Museum of Natural History in Chicago rather casually examined the ruins of Edward Fenton's stone house during a stop lasting less than a day. During a return visit, in 1929, the team took photographs and conducted more diggings but without much effort to make sense of them. Walter Kenyon, of the Royal Ontario Museum in Toronto, made a more detailed survey in 1974. Somewhat relaxed about details, Kenyon devoted nearly as much attention in his report to the problems he had encountered traveling there—bad weather, crowded conditions aboard the boat that ferried him to Countess of Warwick Sound—as to his slender finds on the island. An entertaining story appealed to him as much as the dull, close work of sorting flints.

The first expert, detailed excavation was undertaken in 1981 by a team led by William Fitzhugh. He is archaeologist, circumpolar anthropologist, and curator of anthropology at the Smithsonian Institution in Washington, D.C., and director of its Arctic Studies Center. His knowledge extends from Vikings to Inuit to the Yup'ik of Alaska, and across the Bering Strait into Siberia. His platoon of Americans and Canadians spent a week on Kodlunarn mapping every feature. Where the ground seemed altered from the natural, they dug small square pits. The artifacts found during the digging hinted at what had occurred in and around each square. A metal detector led to the discovery of three additional iron loaves: two were found in the Ship's Trench and the third a short distance inland from the trench. The proper term for such a loaf is *bloom*—an incompletely smelted mass of wrought iron. But the blooms' function seemed a mystery.

In the early 1990s the platoon returned as a full regiment. A Canadian team took over the work on Kodlunarn, and Fitzhugh oversaw a survey of Inuit sites. A bureaucracy as formidable as Queen Elizabeth's Privy Council oversaw the joint effort. Judged by the results of the diggings, Kodlunarn Island had served Martin Frobisher as both a mine and a large assay shop. The finds—four hundred years after Frobisher's departure—included iron nails, slag, charcoal and coal, and more than a thousand fragments of the crucibles used by his assayers. Part of Edward Fenton's cache of food, buried for the next party of colonists, was discovered four and a half feet beneath the surface of the Ship's Trench. Fenton had left the food in barrels; the archaeologists unearthed wooden staves plus a bung. Fenton's store of sea biscuits had devolved into an unappetizing assortment of fuzzy-edged brown shapes, like bear dung. Several bushels' worth of small gray pellets were identified as long-frozen English peas. The excavators found debris from woodworking near the food cache, in company with rocks cracked by fire—evidence that the Ship's Trench had served as a hearth, and perhaps as a dry dock. In repairing one or another vessel, shipwrights would have sawed planks and, perhaps, forged nails in a fire there.

On the island, you see a few bare, trampled-looking plots scattered over a half acre near the Reservoir Trench. At those sites Frobisher had had an assay office, a workshop that may have served as a smithy, possibly a kiln for making charcoal, and possibly another workshop. William Fitzhugh called the area Elizabethan Alley. Frobisher's carpenters had built the assay office while miners swung their pickaxes in the trench nearby and sailors carried ashore barrels of food, the half acre of ground becoming fine-grained sand. After four hundred years, the tundra is still repairing itself.

Some of the cobbles on the ground near the Ship's Trench form a pattern, or a hint of one—the faint outline of a rectangle. Fitzhugh identified it as the remains of a building he called the "longhouse." With the power of this suggestion you can just see the long rectangle that is defined by the cobbles, then cobbles dividing it internally into a line of four squares. Each square is open on one side—perhaps four rooms opening onto a corridor, like a railroad flat. Digging there, Fitzhugh found bits of roof tiles and bricks. It was perhaps a storehouse or a barracks, a structure conveniently close to the trench, which served as a ramp down to the water. Sailors had hauled supplies from the pinnaces up the Ship's Trench and carried down the ore.

In August, the time of year Frobisher arrived, Kodlunarn was without a sound except for the wind. If they had chosen to stay, Frobisher's colonists would have quickly felt the weight of solitude. They had sea biscuits, salted beef, barrels of peas, and beer, but the Englishmen understood nothing of the environment. They would have stood no chance of survival. With cannibalism always on their minds, they had feared the worst from the natives and were slow to learn from them. The Inuit knew the limits of the land and would not have befriended such a large group of strangers. The niche was too narrow. Both groups were also influenced by the poisonous fear left from previous kidnappings and fighting. If against all odds the two peoples had established friendly relations, the Englishmen still would have starved. Their numbers were too large for this place; the same would be true today. On all three of his expeditions, Frobisher had failed to understand that the land was as demanding as the ocean. Maybe the colonists would have had the patience and luck to learn how to capture seals on the ice, from watching polar bears, or learned from Inuit how to clothe themselves properly in caribou fur. But probably not: outsiders did not begin learning those lessons until the 1850s and '60s, the era of Charles Francis Hall. On their own, the colonists might have lived into winter. After the first deaths, the survivors would have faced the temptation posed by the corpses of those already dead from starvation or scurvy.

What remains of Edward Fenton's house sits at the highest point of the island, covered by a blue tarp put in place by the archaeologists to protect the foundations from the elements. What remained was less "house" or "fort" than a faded mark of intentions, an X marking Queen Elizabeth's first claim to North America.

Her would-be first colony, under the blue tarp, consists of cool, mossy earth and low stone walls. Two of the building's corners alone remain visible; they are not quite a foot high. Crumbly bits of the mortar that the masons made from lime and sand litter the ground outside the tarp. On the east side of the house is a row of boulders standing on end like an outcrop of incisors. The house was the one place offering a sense of command over the island, a clear view in every direction. Tikkoon lay straight ahead, and Newland Island was at your back, as was the route from Countess of Warwick Sound into the main channel of Frobisher Bay. You could see the blue-white mountains on the bay's southern shore.

You could imagine the commotion and the hurry of Frobisher's men. From the house, in the evening light, the remains of Frobisher's assay shop and the smithy were like small handprints in the ground; the Reservoir Trench, a small fold in the island's flesh. On this August evening, both the moon and sun were shining brightly. The wind was rising; an ice floe tinged pale blue drifted into the sound.

After fifty days travel in the bay, Hall returned to the *George Henry* to discover that most of the whalers had long since given him up for dead. In fifty days, they had failed to catch even one whale. His own pleasure hardly fit with their mood. Hall radiated confidence just when the whalers felt nearly hopeless.

He looked for Tookoolito and Ebierbing—Hannah and Joe— but their tent contained a surprise. Hannah proudly showed him her newborn son, Tukerliktu, nicknamed Johny. In their previous months of work together, Hall either never noticed or neglected to record a word about her pregnancy.

He resumed his research by showing the Inuit camped near the *George Henry* his collection of objects from Kodlunarn. Examining one of the iron blooms, an old man remembered having seen a much larger "heavy stone" many years ago; the iron had been almost too heavy for people to lift it. Other people remembered using it as a seat, and recalled that one man had been strong enough to lift it chest-high. The hunter Ugarng sketched its shape for Hall and carved a model of it in wood; Suzhi carved the shape in a chaw of tobacco. They both made a flat-topped block with hourglass sides. Ugarng recalled from his visit to the United States seeing such an object used by blacksmiths. "This minute," wrote Hall, "10:15 A.M., have found out just what this relic is. *It is an anvil!*"

Hannah (Tookoolito): guide, teacher, and interpreter of Inuit stories.

Joe (Ebierbing), who pushed himself to exhaustion for both Hannah and Charles Francis Hall.

Hannah rejoined him as an interpreter. In his methodical approach to interviews, he was far ahead of his time as a collector of oral history. His prepared list of questions extended to thirty-six items. Each person was asked more or less the same questions, beginning with whether he had seen or visited Kodlunarn. The questions and corresponding answers were efficiently organized by number in the notebooks. He neither badgered people nor overtly led them toward giving a particular reply. The responses differed from person to person, and stories would change on a second telling, but Hall diligently continued taking notes.

Question two: "Why do Innuits call that island Kod-lu-narn?" Because *qallunaat*—which Hall rendered as *Kodlunarns*—had been there, his informants said.

Question three: "How many Kod-lu-narns lived there?" Five, he was told.

Question fifteen: "Are there any Innuits living who ever saw the Kod-lu-narns who built the ship?"

"It was a great while ago," said the hunter Shevekoo and his wife, Ooshoolanping. "Innuits all dead who saw them."

Question twenty-three: "Could the Kod-lu-narns talk *Innuit* [Inuktitut] with the Innuits?"

"Never heard," said Shevekoo and Ooshoolanping. "Do not know anything about it."

Question twenty-six: "When the Kod-lu-narns went away, where did they say they were going?"

"Did not tell the Innuits—but Innuits thought they wanted to go home."

People risked responding "never heard" and "do not know" because they trusted the interviewer. Rather than invent a tale designed merely to please, they faithfully retold the history of Kodlunarn as learned from their elders, the story of events that had occurred "a great while ago." Hall was not greatly alarmed by the accounts contradicting one another in many details: stories told about the summer just past would surely differ too. He was exploring along a poorly marked trail; the stories went in unexpected directions. *"One is often baffled,"* he confessed in the course of a second interview with Ookijoxy Ninoo, the mother of Ugarng. "A most difficult work, to get what I do relative to old Frobisher's visit here."

An outsider could not easily know if stories tangled several events. And newer stories had a way of overwhelming older ones. The whaling era, when contacts with outsiders occurred regularly, had drowned out most of the tales about people from distant times, or conflated them into a garble. But the elders recalled a few distinct threads about Kodlunarn; a culture perhaps never forgot its first contact with strangers.

What Hall's informants knew about Kodlunarn was this: whites had come a long, long time ago and spent a winter on the island. The whites had either built or repaired a vessel in the Ship's Trench. They had taken ship to Tikkoon, where they raised the masts by sliding them over a bluff and tilting them upright onto the deck. Then the whites had sailed away. That was the heart of the story. Depending on who told it, the whites were either never seen again or they suffered terribly from frostbite and were forced back by ice to Kodlunarn, where the Inuit cared for them. The whites again sailed away, or they died on Kodlunarn.

Hall went ashore in October 1861 for a last glimpse of the landscape. Captain Budington intended to sail home within days. Hall's telescope offered fine views of Cyrus Field Bay, where the *George Henry* lay at anchor, and of the Davis Strait. But instead of black water, everything through the telescope was white—"naught but *pack, pack*," blocking the route south. Within a week, ice four inches thick surrounded the ship; a few days later, seven inches. The *George Henry* was trapped for another winter.

Whalers could accept spending one winter in the north as necessary, ultimately profitable labor. But a second winter could only be torture. All the coming deprivations were too fresh in the whalers' minds, like barely healed wounds, and the cold loomed like a terrible beating everyone was doomed to suffer a second time. Diseases of the spirit—suspiciousness, self-pity, an exhausting boredom—would inevitably return, and the sailors could not help but dread the darkness. You craved the company of anyone except the people trapped with you for another year.

Budington did no better than the crew at hiding his anxiety, and foresaw a shortage of food. He reduced the number of meals from three a day to two; the men might survive the winter if they also relied on the hunting prowess of the Inuit. To feed the stoves, the sailors sawed the jawbones of a whale into logs; one cord of oil-rich whalebone could generate as much heat as four cords of fresh-cut oak. At Thanksgiving the crew dined on whale meat and arctic fox pie.

In that long dark season, Hall wished he were home organizing a search for Franklin's men. The only comfort came from his discoveries the previous summer on Kodlunarn. They seemed to bode well for finding word of the Franklin crew. "How *easy* to go back a score of years or so and get truthful history from among the Innuits, compared with what it is to plunge into the history of near three centuries, and draw out the truth!" he said, looking forward to the task. He was already mulling the need to raise money for a second expedition, and anticipating a speaking tour in the United States once the *George Henry* reached home.

In December 1861 he organized a sledge trip with an Inuit guide and one of the sailors. On the morning of their departure, his thermometer registered twenty degrees below zero Fahrenheit. His party stopped for an hour at Willows Island in a fruitless search for the anvil, then spent the night crowded together with a welcoming family in an igloo. Breakfast consisted of two ounces of whale skin; Hall remarked that he could have eaten two pounds. Hummocks in the ice were by then as ordinary to him as rocks in a wheat field. The sledge and the dog team served as his landau.

He reached another cluster of igloos on the second day, and everyone was immediately welcomed inside. He was struggling to take off his caribou stockings when a gray-haired woman entered the igloo. She was familiar to him from her visits to the *George Henry*. Her name momentarily escaped him.

"Are you well?" he said by way by greeting.

"Very well," replied Petato.

She warmed his feet, as he recorded in his notebook, by offering her torso as a radiator. His traveling companions crowded into the igloo; he kept his feet on her chest, draped by a caribou skin. "My feet must have been like lumps of ice," he said, "and yet she quailed not at their contact with her calorific body." The interview proved one of the most rewarding, now that he knew the questions by heart and was attuned to every detail of the answers. To emphasize how very long ago the events being described had occurred, Petato pulled at her gray hair and raised her voice loud enough to summon the dead. Whites had come a long, long, *long, long* time ago to the island that Inuit called Kodlunarn, Petato said. Some of the visitors' ships were wrecked during a storm. The whites then built a vessel in a place scooped out from the island's rock. They had built a house that used cement, as she demonstrated by stacking several rocks and putting snow between them. Petato used her few words of English, and Hall relied on his limited Inukitut. "When the ice broke up, went away in the ship," she said. "After a while came back again. Ice brought them back. Could not get out. Very cold—great storm." Then the whites had died on Kodlunarn.

Over the months, Hall had attuned himself to hearing a single, simple story that neatly fit his knowledge of Martin Frobisher. What he heard was that five whites had come to an island where a house stood and where a ship was built, and the whites had tried to sail away. He showed less interest in separating the several parts of the story and sorting out the chronology. Whether the people who built the ship had also built the house and how they were connected to the other man-made features on the island were subjects he left largely unexplored. He concluded that the tale explained the fate of the five sailors who had disappeared during Frobisher's first expedition aboard the *Gabriel,* in 1576. It didn't. Frobisher did not reach Kodlunarn until 1577, during his second expedition. Until then, neither Frobisher nor any of his sailors knew of Kodlunarn. If the five missing sailors had come there in 1576, they would have neither seen the house nor found wood for building a ship.

Hall's informants wove details from all three of Frobisher's voyages into a single story. Beginning in the 1980s, the anthropologists William Fitzhugh and Susan Rowley painstakingly untangled many of the threads. Whites had indeed come to the island; Inuit examining the miners' trenches could see the evidence for themselves. Frobisher's ships had almost surely left men behind in Frobisher Bay. They were left in 1578, and were in addition to the five sailors who went missing in 1576. In 1578, in the confusion whipped up by the gale during the fleet's last days in the bay, several dozen small boats had disappeared. They were swamped by waves or were last sighted struggling to return to the ships. One or another of the boats may have failed to rejoin the fleet yet survived the storm. It cannot be proved, but it is possible. Edward Fenton, Frobisher's second in command, had kept his ship near the mouth of the bay for an extra day despite the gale, in expectation of sighting at least one of the missing boats.

Any sailors or miners left behind would have known that their best chance for survival lay in sailing back to Kodlunarn, the land they knew as Countess of Warwick Island. Frobisher's just-abandoned headquarters was the one site prepared for habitation.

The remains of Edward Fenton's fort on Kodlunarn Island.

The men could live in the newly built stone cottage and rely for a time on the food that Fenton had buried for use by a future expedition. They could make use of the scattered wood, coal, and metal.

What happened next can by guessed at from the stories told by the Inuit. Before the onset of winter, the sailors overhauled their boat or built a new vessel with the timbers left by Fenton. On this matter Hall's informants should be taken at their word. All the other major events described in the Inuit stories—every element, that is, that can be checked against physical evidence on the island, or against the chronicles by Frobisher's officers—has proved true. So the sailors built a ship: the Inuit said the whites had done so, and in the Ship's Trench were splinters of wood and rocks cracked by fire. The detritus does not say who produced it, but it speaks of hard labor. At least some of the men survived the winter. They stood a better a chance than would have a colony of forty; in their stories, the Inuit said they had given food to the whites. When the ice pack began to melt, the whites tried to leave.

William Fitzhugh found the sailors' travails a possible explanation for the iron blooms, the smelted loaves of metal found on Kodlunarn and the Baffin mainland. There is no shortage of theories about the blooms' origin and purpose. Hall eventually presented one of the blooms to the Smithsonian, where for most of the next century the staff knew neither where the bloom had been placed nor what it was, beyond the fact that the donor had associated it with Martin Frobisher.

A Smithsonian chemist answered a first question by determining that the somewhat flattened metal ball was not a meteorite. The bloom was terrestrial iron that contained a high proportion of slag, along with carbon from the charcoal used during its smelting. The Brookhaven National Laboratory determined through carbon-14 dating that the iron loaf presented by Hall had been made between the years 1240 and 1400—long before Frobisher's expeditions. The dates were even earlier for the blooms that Fitzhugh's team found. Researchers sought to explain the puzzling dates by suggesting that the Norse, not sixteenth-century Englishmen, had brought the blooms to the area. They suggested as an alternative that the carbon-14 analysis had been skewed by a quirk in the smelting. This was the argument: if Frobisher's men smelted the iron on Kodlunarn, they might have burned centuries-old drift-wood to make charcoal for the smelting. The centuries-old carbon would have left a misleading signature in the blooms; hence the early date from the laboratory work.

Each of these possible solutions brought its own problems. Crediting the Norse for delivering the blooms ignored the lack of any other evidence of a Norse presence in Frobisher Bay. And Frobisher's men almost certainly could not have performed the smelting with old driftwood. Researchers calculated that the smelt-ing would have required 2,700 pounds of charcoal; making that quantity of charcoal would have required ten tons of wood. No one could find ten tons of driftwood in Countess of Warwick Sound.

Michael Lok, the treasurer of the Cathay Company, has in his ledger a likely solution to the bloom mystery. In 1576, in outfitting Frobisher's first expedition to the northwest, he recorded the pur-chase of six tons of Russian iron as ballast for the *Gabriel*. The ledger entry is for "ironstones of Russia." They cost eight pounds, six shillings, eight pence. Ballast could be iron, rock, or barrels filled with water. It might stay in the hold for the life of a ship. Usually, it stayed on board until the captain needed to make room for an especially valuable cargo, or if the accumulation of vomit and rotted food had made the stink in the hold unendurable and the captain wanted to wash the ballast clean in the surf. Ballast was necessarily sized to be manageable in the hold of the ship. Within the cramped confines of the *Gabriel,* bloom-sized would do. Whether the iron was new or several hundred years old made no difference to a captain. When the *Gabriel* reached Kodlunarn, in 1577 and 1578, the sailors had reason to empty the hold, to make room for more black ore. They could leave iron ballast on the island. Hall in the nineteenth century, and Fitzhugh in the twenti-eth century, found blooms in and near the Ship's Trench, where the cargo loading took place.

In their desperation, the sailors and miners left behind by the fleet would have treasured every scrap of metal. In building a hull, shipwrights needed drills, hammers, and dollies. A dolly was the counterweight placed against a plank when it was being worked on from the opposite side. The discarded blooms could serve as dollies; they were ballast or dollies or both. The archaeological evidence hints too that someone on the island attempted to rework some iron in a fire fed by coal instead of charcoal, an effort doomed to failure. Sulfur from a coal fire embrittles iron. Sailors ignorant of the basic practices of blacksmithing could have made such a mistake. The blooms—odd heavy loaves—do not speak clearly. But they hint of a vessel taking shape in the deep trench where most of them were found, at the hands of Englishmen anxious to escape Meta Incognita.

Hall fared better than most of the sailors during the *George Henry*'s second winter in the ice. He felt cloaked with the sense of specialness that came from firmly believing he had a higher calling. Like Hannah and Joe, he dressed in caribou skins. What could be better preparation for one day renewing the search for traces of John Franklin's men? Inuit ways seemed the answer to every problem. Their diet of meat—whether raw or cooked—was his prescription against scurvy. Caribou, he decided after some months, tasted better rancid than when it was fresh. Fresh meat seemed bland; so did any other style of life.

Compared to him, the sailors might as well have been helpless children. The seaman William Ellard returned to the *George Henry* after eight days on the ice without fully realizing that the numbness in his feet was frostbite. Captain Budington amputated all of Ellard's toes. Everyone stayed alive thanks to Budington's giving the Inuit tobacco in exchange for whale meat that they had buried during the autumn for just such an emergency.

In July 1862, still waiting for the ice to release the ship, Hall returned to Kodlunarn island. He kept the women busy for four days searching for bits of wood and glass, while the menfolk hunted on the mainland for their meals. The list of finds—flints, fragments of pottery, fragments of tile—extended to 136 items.

He felt more alive than he ever would in the United States. Facing an enraged polar bear, as he did during the spring, or being pursued by wolves seemed now just ordinary dangers, like high water harmlessly flowing past in a river. You simply needed to watch your step. When ice drifted back into the bay, his party spent hours portaging the leaky whaleboat over tightly packed floes, a task that now seemed a normal day's labor. All summer he confidently navigated past problems. Most of his meals consisted of walrus—after one day's hunt, the men came back with three tons of meat. Nothing fazed him except delay.

Finally, the ice freed the *George Henry*. On August 9, 1862, two years plus one day after it arrived at Baffin island, the ship set sail for home. Hannah and Joe and their baby, Johny, accompanied Hall on the voyage to the United States. Nothing could have pleased him more than their presence. He had tried to mold their sense of loyalty into a tool for himself, a project he had begun at their first meeting, when Hannah had demurely offered him a cup of tea. He was Father Hall, as he described himself; they were his children and he wished them to obey him. They had fed, clothed, and housed him, yet he considered them the dependents. He desperately wanted their services for a second trip to the north, in which he hoped to search for word of Franklin's men. What he needed most were companions willing to put his interests first.

Hannah and Joe proved their devotion to him a thousand times over. In Hall, they apparently saw a white man who seemed all-powerful, as was true of all *qallunaat,* yet who also clearly needed every kind of help. Unlike the whalers, he stood alone, and he showed flattering interest in the Inuit as a people. He gave his guides new purpose. He told Hannah and Joe he loved them, and they could not resist aiding him. Competent in so many ways, they helped Father in every way he wanted. They would keep him warm and ease his hunger, if Father would let them.

The first newspaper stories about Hall's exploits appeared on August 23, 1862, the day after the *George Henry* reached St. John's,

Newfoundland. Hall and Captain Budington heard the first mention of the American Civil War, then in its sixteenth month, from the harbor pilot. Hall was loquacious enough for the St. John's *Daily News* to publish an admiring account of the crew's tribulations and describe his finds on Kodlunarn Island. Captain Budington was congratulated in print for having returned with six hundred barrels of whale oil.

Hall telegraphed greetings to Henry Grinnell, his patron. "I am bound for the States, to renew my voyage," he said, as if organizing a second trip were a foregone conclusion. His message implied that the last two years had been just a warm-up for the real work; the trip home was presented as just a resupply mission. If he kept talking about a second trip north and sounded confident, then he might actually find the backing necessary for it. In St. John's he laid the groundwork. At first the stimulation of town nearly overwhelmed him; the sunlight itself seemed different, and the noise more intense, as if he were awakening from a life spent underground. Meanwhile, his telegrams began working their magic. The *New York Herald* found his arrival in St. John's worthy of a dispatch on August 23, sandwiched between a story on Union casualties and a report from Cincinnati describing the loss of two railroad bridges to the Southern rebels.

Then editors hailed him as a hero. On August 24, the *Herald* devoted a full page to his exploits and illustrated the story with a map of the Arctic printed across the width of the page: "NEWS FROM THE ARCTIC REGIONS—THE RETURN OF THE EXPLORER HALL— HIS WONDERFUL DISCOVERIES—RELICS OF FROBISHER FOUND—THE OUTLINE OF FROBISHER BAY."

It served, perhaps, as a relief from the drumbeat of war news. The papers published another round of stories after the *George Henry* reached New London, on September 13. They presented Hall to the public as a gentleman of tact and energy whose efforts, it was said, had put to shame expeditions organized by the British Admiralty. Readers also learned of Hannah, Joe, and Johny, deemed "excellent specimens of their race." Two dogs—Ratty and

Barbekark—completed the exotic party. However, a gentleman's return from the Arctic seemed no more than an entertainment in wartime. Union general George McClellan was leading an army through Maryland in hope of stopping a Confederate force led by General Robert E. Lee. By mid-September, the newspapers had focused their attention on the armies' clash at Antietam Creek. Nearly five thousand soldiers died and another twenty thousand were wounded in one day of fighting.

Hall planned a series of lectures to publicize his cause. The first was scheduled for a meeting of the American Geographical and Statistical Society in New York. Founding member Henry Grinnell helped make the arrangements. Hall wanted to establish beyond doubt the links between his finds on Kodlunarn island and the expedition of Martin Frobisher, and he prepared for the talk as if it were a long trek across thin ice. While he busied himself conducting research in New York, Hannah and Joe stayed at the Budington family home in Groton, Connecticut. Hall kept Captain Budington informed about his activities and made several requests.

> I am now anxious to use every moment of my time in preparing the paper I have referred to.—I wish to consult several old works that are only to be found in the libraries here. To do this probably I must keep myself busily engaged the next fifteen (15) days. . . . I wish Capt. B. you would have Hannah go to work as fast as she can & make up fine Esquimaux clothes of the rein-deer skins which I brought to New London—Let her make a complete suit & one for Joe & one for the baby. Of course have them made *Esquimaux style.* Have Joe make a seal-spear & such other instruments the Esquimaux use. Let him make 2 dog-harnesses. Whatever expense is incurred I will settle with you on my arrival there.

As a last thought, squeezed upside down into the top margin of the paper, he made a warmer acknowledgement of his guides:

Perhaps Joe & Hannah do not like it on account of my long absence—Friend B. Do not fail to try & keep them friendly to me. I think much of them as you know.

In his lecture to the society, in November 1862, Hall described his adventures on Kodlunarn Island. He touched on Inuit culture, including the importance of oral history. Members of the audience found him more impressive for his enthusiasm than his polish, but he sounded as if he had studied every book ever written about the Arctic. His survey proved that the waterway known as Frobisher Strait was in fact a bay. He talked about the artifacts discovered from Frobisher's expeditions of nearly three centuries ago. A sampling of the finds lay on a table for the audience's inspection, and maps of Baffin Island and Frobisher Bay were displayed behind him.

He knew he would need money for a second trip to the north. An audience would be more excited, of course, by artifacts than words. He was laboring as both explorer and publicist: he had learned from the painful work of raising money in Cincinnati the importance of garnering publicity and of employing every possible tool to ensure success. An explorer needed headlines, money, and trustworthy guides.

When he finished speaking, Hannah, Joe, and young Johny came into the lecture hall. Dressed in caribou fur and sealskins, the family served as his best exhibit. Who could fail to be impressed by Hannah as she answered questions from the audience? Who could not sense the explorer's devotion to his cause? Members of the American Geographical and Statistical Society certainly found it a fine, lively program—as memorable as Hall had hoped. He wanted only to be taken as seriously as he took himself.

CHAPTER SEVEN

Battles

In 1578, Martin Frobisher was hoping for a knighthood. Michael Lok heard him say it or heard the rumor at court, but the two men barely spoke to each other except to argue about money. Frobisher's homecoming had proved as nerve-racking as traveling through the ice, because the Cathay Company's investors now expected a full accounting. There was less talk about Frobisher's being a second Magellan. If the ore proved as valuable as the investors hoped, he would be welcome to pretend to be a second anyone. Frobisher, the Privy Council, and all the other investors were impatient for a reward—either money or honor.

The ships unloaded most of the ore at the wharf in Dartford. From the wharf it was carted to a royal manor house that King Henry VIII had built during the 1540s. Henry had thought little enough of the Dartford house to give Anne of Cleves, his fourth wife, the run of it after their marriage was annulled. Queen Elizabeth showed no special affection for the house either: in twenty years as monarch, she so far had spent exactly one night there. The manor house chapel was the one empty building within two miles of the company's new bank of furnaces deemed secure for storing the ore. It served as a storage room and vault; for convenience's sake, the keys were entrusted to the innkeeper at the Bull and George Inn on Dartford High Street.

Jonas Shutz, the chief assayer, tried several additives during the first Dartford assays. Two years earlier, in 1576, he had calculated that a ton of black ore would be worth £240 in gold. After Frobisher's second expedition, in 1577, he had determined the ore was worth £40 a ton. Then £23 a ton. The value had declined from the exhilarating to the satisfying to the merely profitable. Each series of assays had found less gold, as if a ship were slowly foundering. Now, in the first assays at Dartford, Shutz found the ore to be worth only £10 a ton. From the profitable to the unprofitable, as if the vessel had settled on the sea bottom.

Martin Frobisher responded by demanding the keys from the innkeeper at the Bull and George and beating him over the head with them. At about this time, he also stormed Michael Lok's house in the company of about forty men and accused his partner of fraud. "He entered into great storms and rages with me," said Lok, "like a mad beast." Each man believed himself betrayed by the other and went on the attack.

Frobisher accused Lok of embezzlement. Lok claimed the captain general had pocketed the wages of sailors who had died and, out of fear of having to share his glory, refused to help the would-be colonists—"would not help them one jot." Frobisher called his partner "a bankrupt knave." Lok said the captain general constantly lied— ". . . is so full of lying talk that no man may credit anything that he doth speak."

Frobisher could point to the black ore as proof of his own hard work. Lok possessed only the ledger, which reflected badly on him by documenting the debts of the company. The Cathay Company owed Harry Pyntell, baker, about £24 for sea biscuits long since eaten. Anthony Duffield, brewer, was due £130 for beer. The creditors included purveyors of beef, rope, ballast, nails, and canvas. Michael Lok had purchased all the supplies in his own name, as his fellow commissioners suggested, and he remained personally responsible for the debts. The Cathay Company—Lok, that is—owed an additional £1,300 in wages to the sailors, plus £4,000 in freight charges payable to shipowners. There was Lok, sitting amid the pile of invoices as messengers arrived with threatening letters signed by the creditors. William Borough, an eminent navigator and sometime associate of the learned John Dee, had sold the *Judith* to the company for a bargain price, but Lok still owed him most of the money—"which rest I could by no means get of him," Borough said.

Lok's fellow investors, meanwhile, ignored letters from the Privy Council demanding payment of the many surcharges. In a subsequent assay at Dartford, Jonas Shutz found that the ore was worth only £5 a ton. It would not be enough to pay the cost of the assays, much less the back wages or the freight bill. Most of the ore remained untouched, piled up in the royal manor house near Dartford High Street, or near the furnaces on the River Darent. Since 1576, Lok had spent at least £24,000 on the expeditions and the assays. The unpaid bills totaled more than £5,000. But any talk of depriving investors of their shares as a way of forcing payment of the balance now was an empty threat. The stock was worth only as much as the ore. The ore, now valued at £5 a ton, had changed back into just black rock.

In December 1578, the Privy Council removed Lok as treasurer of the company and ordered an audit. This helped create the paper trail that lets us peer over Lok's shoulder, as the auditors had. If not for the financial loss and the investors' anger, the expeditions to Meta Incognita would have generated fewer records; a smaller, less costly failure could have been ignored. But so many powerful people had lost money, someone had to be blamed.

Lok had made mistakes common to any executive with an expense account. The auditors found he had billed the Cathay Company for too many of the meals his household served to his fellow commissioners and investors. He had overspent on boat rentals when commuting to Her Majesty's palace at Greenwich. He had paid too much for the horses he rode to Dartford—£60 instead of the £40 that the auditors deemed reasonable. After reading the auditors' report, the Privy Council judged these to be insignificant slips.

"Mony paid the 13 of marche Anno 1578 for the Ayde yet more," from Michael Lok's account book. The paylist's fifth entry from the bottom is "To Jonas Shutes [Shutz]— [£]005-00-00." (Public Record Office E 164/35 f.128)

In important ways, though, Lok had indeed favored his own interests over the company's. On the rare occasions when the company had income, he used the money first to repay himself, for his own loans to the venture, and to pay interest on money he borrowed in his own name. Whatever little money was left then went to pay other creditors. His actions were no shadier than those of the great lords of the Privy Council, in their securing special privileges from Elizabeth or their outfitting their own vessels at the Royal Navy's expense. Privy Council members were among the largest stockholders in the company and, despite the financial losses, seemed to consider Lok an unlucky friend. These men were hardly disinterested: government, exploration, and trade were nearly a single enterprise, an affair of a small circle overseen by the queen. Having considered the auditors' findings, the Privy Council judged that Lok "hath dealt justly and truly with all." He was the one figure formally absolved from blame. Yet he would still suffer the most from the company's collapse.

A London merchant who had invested in the venture, Thomas Allen, replaced Lok as the Cathay Company's treasurer. After a month on the job, Allen asked for an audit of monies spent by Martin Frobisher. The auditors found that Frobisher had double-billed the company for food; had hired more than the authorized number of miners, charging their salaries to the company; and had charged the company for supplies, such as ballast, obtained at no cost. He was held responsible too for the disappearance of weapons valued at £120, a loss he blamed for no real reason on Christopher Hall, the chief pilot. Frobisher said that most of the weapons had disappeared aboard the pinnaces and skiffs lost during the last gale near the mouth of the bay: "And he that has put in such objections against me, I would he had been in my place."

The venture that had begun as a search for a new route to Cathay was reduced to a squabble among investors. Arguments over how best to pay the outstanding bills took the place of speculations about colonies and trade. To raise the needed money, the Privy Council ordered the company to sell its ships and other properties. The company's leading men responded by writing a letter to the Privy Council, asking it to order investors to pay the surcharges owed the enterprise. This was a difficult letter to write. Lord Burghley, the queen's treasurer, owed the Cathay Company £65; Secretary of State Francis Walsingham, £20; the Earl of

Warwick, previously Frobisher's most enthusiastic supporter on the council, £75.

Michael Lok met with his colleagues to sign the letter, and the session could not have been pleasant. These strong-minded figures had grown to distrust one another, and they apparently were all in one room. Lok signed the letter, as did Thomas Allen. Both Martin Frobisher and his rival Edward Fenton signed it. John Dee retained faith in the existence of a shortcut to Cathay, and he too signed.

Some of Frobisher's officers took equipment in lieu of back wages. In that way Christopher Hall acquired two anchors and an assortment of guns. Picking through leftover clothing, he also purchased a pair of gray trousers for four shillings. George Best acquired a kettle. It's a mystery why Frobisher paid two shillings for "a gray felt hat, rotten" but the ledger records the purchase. Charles Jackman, the discoverer of Jackman Sound, accepted payment in the form of six artillery pieces from the *Ayde*. William Borough, the previous owner of the *Judith,* took delivery of, among other items, pots, pickaxes, and a pair of bellows in partial payment.

After the creditors finished with the carcass of the company, Thomas Allen tried to sell what remained. Leftover food—"biscuit bread, moldy"—was sold barrel by barrel. The *Michael* changed hands for a modest £48. Allen was unsure what constituted a fair price for the little *Gabriel,* the one vessel that had reached Meta Incognita on all three expeditions. The asking price dropped from £150 to £100, then to £80. "I do hear that Mr. Frobisher has bid for her," Allen wrote, "but I think ready money is out of the way with him." Frobisher, who had expected to eclipse Magellan, had no cash. Someone else bought the ship for £60.

Despite the auditors' favorable report, Michael Lok went to prison. The courts ruled against him when creditors began to sue for credit. Lok's name was on all the bills, and he was held responsible. He was imprisoned at least seven times. The authorities would hold him at Fleet Prison and release him after reaching a settlement in one or another case; then the next suit would be filed and the humiliations would be repeated. William Borough sued for payment for the *Judith;* outfitters sought money for rope and tents; shipowners demanded payment of the long overdue freight charges. As an extra indignity, debtors sent to Fleet had to pay for their food and for the privilege of a place to sleep, unless they wished to sleep on the floor. During this time of troubles, Lok wrote of his wife and fifteen children being "left to beg their bread." His family, he wrote, was in "an extreme, foul, evil state."

He never lost interest in long-distance trade. In 1593, at age sixty-one, he accepted the position of consul in Aleppo, Syria, on behalf of the Levant Company, another consortium of fractious English merchants. He lost the post after criticizing the merchants for some of their practices, and moved to Venice. However improbably, a pilot there rekindled Lok's interest in searching for a northwest passage to Cathay. Lok learned after writing to eminent men in England, however, that his countrymen failed to share his enthusiasm for organizing a new expedition.

His contemporaries found him witty, notably honest, famously unlucky. In his ardor for expanding English trade, he proved more adventuresome than Queen Elizabeth, always unhappy about spending money. He helped the kingdom raise its ambitions. Unfortunately, when Martin Frobisher returned with a black stone, Lok placed his trust in assayers who were at best incompetent and at worst frauds. But Lok's fellow investors shared his cupidity and his mistakes. The eminent John Dee had watched the assays without finding fault with them. Prospects of a land of gold clouded everyone's judgment.

By financing the search for trade routes, Lok helped make the world seem a roomier place. George Best named as one of the venture's untarnished accomplishments the discovery of "great countries, and whole worlds." A new, northern continent seemed to await possession by Englishmen, as eagerly as a port would await merchant ships. That the black stone was nearly worthless proved less important than how it helped motivate English courtiers and the London merchants to take a greater interest in North America and to see the possible benefits of colonies. In Meta Incognita,

Frobisher tried to take gold from the ground. A few years later, Walter Raleigh envisioned his colony at Roanoke, well to the south, as a base for privateers seizing gold from Spanish ships. From the start, both projects were dedicated to making quick profits. The idea of a colony as a self-supporting community, something more than a staging ground for privateering, still lay in the future.

The Cathay Company gave the kingdom a taste of entrepreneurial adventure. Michael Lok understood the risks of long-distance trade, and he can be excused for wondering, after the Cathay Company collapsed, why he alone suffered the consequences of failure. In 1615, nearly forty years after the last of the expeditions to Meta Incognita, at least one of the company's creditors was still pursuing him in court. Lok lived at least into his eighties, but nothing is known of his death.

John Dee reversed direction, in a sense. In 1580, after the Cathay Company's demise, he trained navigators for an expedition sent northeast in search of a passage to Cathay. Charles Jackman, who had sailed with Martin Frobisher to Meta Incognita, captained one of the vessels and reached the waters above Russia before the ice stopped him. Jackman's ship disappeared with all hands during the voyage home.

Dee advised Humphrey Gilbert too, when Gilbert made plans to build a colony in North America. Gilbert's interest grew from rumors of a city called Norumbega, which maps placed in what would become New England; it was said that people in Norumbega wore clothes spun from gold. In payment for Dee's advice, Gilbert promised him ownership of all the lands above latitude 50 degrees north—most of Canada. Gilbert intended to establish the colony at what he called John Dee Bay—Narragansett Bay, in Rhode Island. But Gilbert died at sea.

As if to complement the terrestrial expeditions, Dee interested himself in angels. His first recorded session with them took place in 1581, when a willing laboratory assistant peered into one of Dee's crystal balls at Mortlake and claimed to see a spirit dressed in yellow with beams of light emanating from his eyes. Dee began keeping a diary of "conversations" with an enormous cast of angels, contacts that were nurtured by a succession of mediums.

Dee was an almost modern scholar until these conversations began. Much of his earlier work had relied on the empirical and the mechanistic, such as his appreciation of mathematics as a useful tool for society. However, he began to regard books and laboratory experiments as too slow a route to higher knowledge. There was the Earth and then there were the heavens, which being closer to God would necessarily be more nearly perfect. Angels residing there, he decided, could provide him with special knowledge. He prayed for God to send angels to instruct him.

A man named Edward Kelley arrived instead. He came uninvited, and anyone other than Dee would have found him sinister from the first day. The authorities had cropped Kelley's ears after convicting him of counterfeiting money or on some similar charge, and it was gossiped that he had dug up a corpse that was then heard to speak. Dee enthusiastically welcomed him as a scryer, his medium to the spirit world. Through Kelley, he sought every kind of advice from the spirits: where to live, whom to serve, how to discover a northwest passage to Cathay. Dee wanted angels to provide practical advice—the best route, the chances of success.

The angelic conversations were something other than hallucinations on Dee's part. He did not claim to see the angels himself; he believed in what Kelley told him. The séances continued for the better part of a decade, first in England and then on the Continent. Dee would ask questions, and Kelley maintained that angels visible only to him heard the queries. Kelley claimed to receive the angels' responses through voices that only he could hear, or through images seen in the crystal. Kelley expertly acted the part of scryer; his learned patron John Dee was the believing audience.

Dee believed in the angels as strongly as in shortcuts to Cathay or the reality of his library at Mortlake. Supremely confident of his own intelligence, he regarded these "conversations" with angels as evidence of his specialness. He believed the spirits had chosen him to receive their higher knowledge. To serve as the earthly vessel for God's wisdom was no more than the role Dee felt he deserved. He surrendered his judgment to that delusion, to voices he couldn't hear himself, emanating from spirits he couldn't see.

He traveled with Kelley to Cracow, then to Prague, from patron to patron. In Prague, Emperor Rudolf II granted Dee an audience. They should have been a natural pairing: Rudolf generously supported practitioners of the occult and took magic seriously enough to have arranged for a spell to be cast on his younger brother, and here was an Englishman who conversed with spirits. Dee introduced himself as God's prophet, since that was what he believed the angels told him.

Kelley's efforts to maintain the deception must have been exhausting, and in 1587 he tried to withdraw from the séances. Dee's son, eight-year-old Arthur, attempted to take Kelley's place as scryer. Young Arthur dutifully described shapes he glimpsed in the crystal, but he received no messages from spirits. Then Kelley resumed his services; he announced that an angel wanted the two men to exchange wives. This was in part another attempt to end the séances, and he surely counted on Dee being too outraged to comply. But Dee preferred to obey. He could either do as the angels supposedly ordered or accept that the angelic conversations had been a fraud all along. His wife, Jane, wept when informed of the angel's wish. *"Pactum factum,"* Dee wrote in his diary. "Agreement put into practice." Jane Dee, nine months after her intimacies with Kelley, gave birth to another son.

Queen Elizabeth sent an envoy to the Continent in 1588 to ask both men to return home. Hearing rumors that Kelley was able to make gold, her counselors wanted the two to put their alchemical skills to use for England. Kelley declined the invitation; Dee accepted.

His years back in England gave him little satisfaction. The gap between his position and his aspirations tormented him. He pawned his wife's jewelry and borrowed money at usurious rates, though the household employed eight servants. When Queen

Elizabeth promised him £100 in recognition of his difficult circumstances, he was tormented all the more because only half the promised amount arrived. For years, he lobbied to be appointed to some remunerative position as a reward for his past services, and sought special commissioners to study his case "to help me upon foot again, who have had so great a fall."

He obtained, finally, a dreadfully ordinary post at Manchester College. Poverty forced him to sell even some of his books. He suffered the early death of his wife and most of his children. Wanting to clear his name of rumors about casting spells, he unsuccessfully sought to be tried for witchcraft. It turned out to be easier to advise others how to find their way across oceans than for him to navigate life in England.

He tried to reestablish contact with the angels after returning to Mortlake. Eighty years old, Dee asked them questions appropriate to his situation. What would be his destination after death? Who would accompany him? What would be the fate of his two surviving children? What would happen to his books?

Right to the end, he insisted on his specialness. His unchanging goal was to acquire complete, perfect knowledge of the universe. Thus his lifelong interest in alchemy and his earnest attempts to converse with spirits. Those efforts failed, but he helped transmute English sailors into explorers, through his lessons on mathematics and navigation, and he helped change England into an empire, by insisting that empire was the kingdom's rightful inheritance from a mythical, glorious past.

Shakespeare offers us at least a glimpse of John Dee in *The Tempest,* through the character of Prospero. The playwright may have visited Mortlake before writing the play; he had almost certainly heard stories about the scholar who communicated with spirits and dearly loved his library. Prospero was a shipwrecked magician-scholar who valued his books over being Duke of Milan: "Me, poor man, my library / Was dukedome large enough." Shakespeare's Prospero is learned, attempts to control the spirits of the natural world, and employs magic only to do good.

John Dee died in 1609 at age eighty-one and was buried at Mortlake.

Martin Frobisher saw himself become overshadowed by rivals after the Cathay Company's collapse. In 1577, while the assayers were still squabbling about furnaces, Francis Drake had sailed from Plymouth. In 1580, he returned from circumnavigating the globe with booty worth at least £600,000, during which time Frobisher saw the ore from Meta Incognita change from gold to dross. Drake had sailed down the west coast of Africa, taken Spanish and Portuguese ships as prizes, crossed the Atlantic Ocean to South America, become the second European to pass through the Strait of Magellan, sailed north along the coast of California, crossed the Pacific, and rounded the Cape of Good Hope. His venture had cost £5,000, compared to the £24,000 spent by the Cathay Company for no profit. After the court calculated its earnings, Queen Elizabeth knighted him. England gained a hero, and the queen pocketed £300,000, enough to pay off the kingdom's foreign debt.

Frobisher helped organize a new expedition in 1582, but it did his reputation little good. The Earl of Leicester and a group of London merchants wanted a fleet to travel around the Cape of Good Hope to the Moluccas, in the Pacific. Frobisher was initially considered for commander but either withdrew or, more likely, was rejected out of concern that he would divert the ships to the northwest. Edward Fenton, his rival, took his place. The chief pilot was Christopher Hall. Frobisher retained responsibility for supplying some of the victuals, and stayed ashore when the ships sailed.

Once under way, the officers discovered that Frobisher had shortchanged the fleet. Twenty tons of beer were missing, as were other supplies. Christopher Hall surmised what had happened, as recorded in the diary kept by the expedition's chaplain, Richard Madox. Of the £1,600 earmarked for supplies, Hall said that Frobisher had pocketed £1,100. "He told me how Frobisher dealt with him, very headily sure," the Reverend Madox wrote, "and how Frobisher was not the mariner he was taken to be, as I easily believe."

Whatever Frobisher's flaws, Edward Fenton's proved worse. He behaved like a dictator, demanding at one point that Christopher Hall kneel before him in apology for some imagined offense, and distrusted almost everyone. He ignored his orders by sailing west to Brazil, and talked of staying there as king. "He doth not trust any one friend in the ship," said Madox, "nor any him." When Fenton returned to England, the Admiralty imprisoned him for at least a short time.

Frobisher served as Francis Drake's second in command in a fleet that sailed in 1585. As its vice admiral, Frobisher shelled the harbor forts at Cartagena, the Spanish outpost in Colombia, while a column of English soldiers fought on land. "We had the rudder of our pinnace shot away and the men's hats from their heads," reported the log from Frobisher's ship, the *Primrose,* "and the top of our mainmast beaten in pieces, the oars stricken out of men's hands as they rowed and our captain like to have been slain." Drake and Frobisher captured the city but relinquished control after six weeks, and the fleet sailed north to St. Augustine, Florida. ("There was about 250 houses in this town," the *Primrose* log recorded, "but we left not one of them standing.") From St. Augustine, the ships continued onward to Walter Raleigh's colony at Roanoke Island.

After the failures in Meta Incognita, Raleigh had sent an expedition to explore warmer waters. Two ships reached the North Carolina coast in 1584 and returned to England with willing natives as an advertisement of the territory's goodness. A year later a second expedition brought 107 colonists to Roanoke Island. Their colony was a year old by the time Frobisher arrived.

Frobisher has left no clue as to whether he recognized the colony as the offspring of his efforts in Meta Incognita. In any case, little existed at Roanoke to make him envious. The colonists' relations with the Algonquian tribes seemed as poor as his had been with the Inuit, and the settlement desperately needed food. Drake had planned to resupply it with food and weapons, until his fleet was scattered by a storm with hailstones the size of chicken eggs. The colonists decided to sail home with him rather than risk another season in the New World. In the haste of leave-taking, sailors threw the colonists' books and charts into the sea.

A second, even less fortunate group of colonists would arrive in 1578. They would wait there in vain for two years for supply ships from England. By the time the ships arrived, the colonists—the members of Raleigh's "Lost Colony"—had vanished.

In terms of his reputation, Frobisher's finest hour came in 1588 in battle against the Spanish Armada. He was the commander of the thousand-ton *Triumph,* the navy's largest ship. Whatever she lacked in speed or maneuverability, the *Triumph* gained in the terror induced by her size—twenty-eight guns to each side, six aft, four at the stern, plus a crew of about five hundred sailors.

Frobisher, through his own mistakes, was cut off at least twice from the bulk of the English fleet. But the *Triumph* successfully defended herself each time against superior Spanish forces, Frobisher keeping the ship at close range to concentrate his fire. A few days after the worst of the fighting, Lord High Admiral Charles Howard knighted him at sea on behalf of the queen.

Becoming Sir Martin Frobisher was no less than he felt he deserved. No one in the English fleet had fought harder or seemed more at home amid the noise of guns in action. He had been peculiarly well suited to the *Triumph,* a bulky platform that projected brute force. That was his style of command among his fellow officers, the Inuit of Meta Incognita, and the Spanish. Insist on your own way, create a straight path whatever the obstacles. Easier, clever routes might exist, but Frobisher always preferred the straight-ahead. Battle at close quarters became him. One never needed fear he would surrender. Finer points of strategy born of a defter style of leadership were the province of a different kind of mariner—someone like Drake.

Thanks to the spoils of the fighting, Frobisher became a landed gentleman with estates in Yorkshire and Nottingham. Queen Elizabeth restored him to her list of favorites. Frobisher Hall, as the family seat was known, was in little Altofts; Frobisher could ride from Altofts to the Manor of Whitwood, another of his properties, in less than a half hour. After his first wife died, he married a well-to-do widow, Dorothy Wentworth. From time to time he patrolled the English Channel in search of vessels carrying Spanish cargoes, and returned to piracy.

In 1594, the Privy Council chose Frobisher to help lead a hurriedly organized fleet and army. Their target was a fort that Spain had built in Brittany, thanks to the weakness of France. Spanish troops had erected El Leon, as they called it, at the tip of a peninsula pointing north toward Brest, which would be an ideal base for any force targeting England. John Norris, an experienced army man, took charge of the four thousand English soldiers. Frobisher commanded the fleet that carried them to France.

Norris's army began marching through Brittany in August. Frobisher blockaded El Leon from the sea. Pointe des Espagnoles, where El Leon stood, blooms with purple heather and golden broom in summer. The peninsula, sharp as ship's bow, rises four hundred feet from the water in granite and schist. A gravel bar at the water's edge offers just enough room for a foothold but disappears at high tide; at low tide, ships risk drifting from the point onto shoals on either side of it. Frobisher agreed with Norris that only a land assault could succeed.

It rained for much of the autumn. Supplies from England arrived late or not at all, and the army's carts had to navigate the muddy roads. The first English attack began October 23 with cannon fire aimed at El Leon's ramparts. Sixty soldiers chosen by lot then advanced in two waves, but the officers leading them were killed, as was the captain who led the retreat. Worse, a gunner accidentally set a barrel of gunpowder on fire; at least forty soldiers were burned by the flames. The offensive had failed.

On November 7, Norris's French allies exploded a mine that

breached the fort's ramparts. French and English troops then resumed their assault, "which was maintained exceedingly hotly without intermission from 11 of the clock until half-an-hour past four," Norris said. Frobisher joined an English contingent fighting near the fort's western tower. A Spanish soldier shot him in the hip, but Frobisher kept fighting. Some of the 350 Spanish defenders jumped into the sea, where they either drowned or were killed by the English fleet. Almost all the others were killed at the fort. "They defended it very resolutely. And never asked for mercy," Frobisher reported. "So they were all put to the sword saving five or six that hid themselves in the rocks."

He dictated that report a day after the fighting. His letter, addressed to the Lord High Admiral, noted that his fleet would soon be forced to sail home, for lack of victuals. He then mentioned his wound. "I was shot in with a bullet at the battery along the hucklebone. So I was driven to have an incision made to take out the bullet." Due to the surgeon's work, he could neither walk nor ride a horse.

Queen Elizabeth responded with a letter written in her own hand, "to our trusted and well beloved Sir Martin Frobisher, Knight." She warned him to beware of various hazards aboard the fleet, as if she were the admiral and he the amateur, but the queen also generously praised him: he had "won yourself reputation."

The French commander, in his own report, informed her that Frobisher had been only slightly wounded. *"Il y fut un peu blessé. Mais ce ne sera rien."* It will be nothing.

The surgeon had botched the operation, however, by failing to clean the wound. By the time the fleet reached Plymouth, an infection had set in. Martin Frobisher died in Plymouth on November 22, 1594.

CHAPTER EIGHT

Destinations

C harles Francis Hall tried to raise money for a new expedition by putting Hannah, Joe, and young Johny on exhibit. Barnum's Museum engaged them for two weeks in New York in November 1862, and they went next for a hundred dollars a week to Cotting and Guay's Aquarial Gardens in Boston. Unfortunately, Hall never managed to collect what was owed them. Then he lectured in a half dozen cities, with an appearance by the Inuit as the climax of each program. "Mr. Hall exhibited and described many implements of the Natives," the *Rhode Island Press* reported after a performance in Providence, where the audience was "immense." The *Elmira Daily Gazette,* in New York, found his talk "peculiarly novel and interesting; his contribution to science important and beneficial."

The Inuit family took ill in Elmira. Sidney Budington, the captain who had sailed the *George Henry* to Baffin Island, sent a letter from his home in Groton, Connecticut, urging Hall to let them rest from the constant travel. The suggestion greatly irritated Hall, for he considered the Inuit akin to his children, and his property. He did ask the Budington family if the Inuit could temporarily move to Groton because of the press of his own work in New

York. Hall confessed to being "overwhelmed with trouble. The infant & 'Hannah' are quite sick—the former dangerously so."

Johny, eighteen months old, died while under Hall's care. "I deeply regret to inform you that the mother is in a very precarious state of health," Hall wrote his patron Henry Grinnell, after accompanying the stricken parents to Connecticut. "On Monday we all thought her dying; but she finally revived. One of the best physicians in New London attended her & the succeeding day (Tuesday) she seemed better. In the P.M. she again became worse. The loss of her child is overwhelming her—she often calls: 'Where's my "Johny"?'—'Where's my "Johny"?'"

It was a terrible time for Hall. Over the next year he was reduced even to selling some of his clothes to support himself. Budington dared to argue that Hannah and Joe would be better off returning to Baffin Island without waiting for Hall to organize another expedition. The suggestion only widened the rift between the explorer and the captain. Hall's letters to Hannah and Joe assured them of his love for them in a cooing baby talk, and promised to make them happy.

Eventually a consortium of businessmen contributed enough cash and supplies for a second expedition. Hall intended to reach King William Island in the Canadian Arctic and search there for the logs and journals of John Franklin's men. By then, the Franklin expedition had not been seen by whites for nearly twenty years. "I have now a work before me that might make some shudder to undertake," he wrote in July 1864, two weeks after sailing north from New London aboard a whaling ship. "It is a great undertaking for one man, I will confess, but, having once put myself in the course, I must and will persevere." The undertaking was not strictly his alone, but his, Hannah's, and Joe's.

Hall predicted that the expedition to King William Island would require three years. The journey lasted five, and involved almost unspeakable hardship. A whole year was lost due to a lack of dogs; the party suffered too from a chronic shortage of able-bodied men. Hall added five whalers to the expedition, but suspected them of plotting mutiny against him. In July 1868, angered

Barnum's Museum advertised Hannah and Joe as having arrived from Greenland. (Smithsonian Institution)

by his demands and criticisms, the whalers loudly argued with him. When the argument was about to escalate into a fistfight, Hall shot and killed one of the men.

He reached King William Island in 1869. Inuit in the region told him of having seen many years ago a drifting vessel that was deserted except for corpses, plus a ship's boat that contained skeletons, papers, and books, and a tent littered with more skeletons. Some of the men who were found in the tent had sawed flesh off the limbs of their comrades or put each other out of their misery with a gunshot aimed at the head, the evidence being clearly visible in the limbs and skulls. Hall's informants said the tent had also contained more papers. Since the Inuit had no use for anything written, children had made a game of tearing the papers into shreds. Hall was so close to the logs and journals, yet clearly too late.

He found part of a human thigh bone, and some of his guides dug through snow and uncovered a complete skeleton. The findings were much worse than anything he had foreseen, discoveries offering not the smallest comfort. Everything spoke of suffering. He could not rescue Franklin's men.

Even worse was the story two Inuit told. They were among a group of Inuit who had been seal hunting when a large party of whites had walked into sight on the ice. Listening to the story, Hannah and Joe deduced that the events had occurred in 1848, shortly after Franklin's men had abandoned the *Erebus* and the *Terror*. The leader of the whites had signaled their hunger by pointing to his mouth. The Inuit had given them seal meat, and the two groups had camped within each other's sight during the night. But in the morning the Inuit had left. They had walked past the sailors, despite their leader again pointing to his mouth and saying the word for *seal,* and had not stopped. Hall made the two eyewitnesses repeat the story many times.

He had proved his suppositions right. The Inuit had known the fate of Franklin's men. What he considered his calling was finally fulfilled, at the cost of losing his idealized image of the north. In his journals the "noble children" of the north became "savages." All these years, his energy had come from believing that Franklin's men remained alive somewhere in the north through the kindness of natives, a faith that had burned in him like fire. He had cared more about giving comfort than in gaining rewards for himself, and he had wanted to be a savior. Writing Lady Jane Franklin, the widow of the lost commander, he confessed that after hearing the story the two Inuit told of abandoning the sailors, "my faith, till then so strong, was shaken, and ultimately was extinguished."

Hall's last enthusiasm was for reaching the North Pole. In 1870 President Ulysses S. Grant received him in Washington, D.C., along with Hannah and Joe, to hear his proposal for an expedition. Congress appropriated $50,000, and formally appointed him commander of the venture. On the streets of Washington, he was greatly pleased by hearing President Grant address him as *Captain*. The navy provided Hall with a steam-powered tug that he christened *Polaris*.

In recruiting a second in command, he overcame past disputes by enlisting Sidney Budington. A panel of science advisers appointed a young German physician, Emil Bessels, as the expedition's surgeon and the head of its three-member scientific staff. Hannah and Joe came aboard as Hall's guides to everything northern and, one imagines, as a salve against loneliness.

Dissension plagued the voyage from the beginning. Budington chafed under Hall's strict ways and turned to the comfort of alcohol, while Bessels considered Hall an annoying meddler in all things scientific. Yet in August 1871 the *Polaris* set a record for northern exploration, reaching latitude 82° 11' north, far up Greenland's western coast.

Hall was forty-nine and displayed no less energy than eleven years earlier, when he had reached Meta Incognita. For the ship's winter quarters, he chose a cove in Greenland that he named Thank God Harbor. After the *Polaris* was solidly iced in, in October 1871, he journeyed north by sledge for two weeks with four other men and glimpsed the northern extremity of Ellesmere Island. He returned to the *Polaris* in excellent spirits. Back aboard, he remarked that the coffee he was being served tasted strangely sweet. And then he vomited. A few minutes later, he suffered a seizure that left him partially paralyzed. Over the next few days he drifted in and out of delirium, accused Budington of trying to poison him, accused Bessels of a similar plot, talked of seeing blue vapors, and complained that Bessels had placed strange machinery in his berth. He complained that even his socks had been poisoned.

He died November 8, 1871, aboard the *Polaris.* Members of the crew labored for two days with crowbars and pickaxes to dig a grave in the frozen ground.

Over the next year, the other members of the expedition experienced almost unbearable adversity. Nineteen people, including Hannah and Joe, were accidentally marooned on an ice floe during a storm that sent the *Polaris,* with fourteen others aboard, drifting away from them. Joe then almost single-handedly kept everyone on the ice alive for the next six months, thanks to his prowess as a hunter. He led them from floe to floe as the temperatures rose, the little colony drifting fifteen hundred miles but rarely in sight of land. Finally, a whaling ship rescued them off southern Newfoundland. Meanwhile, the men left aboard the leaky *Polaris* ran her aground in northern Greenland, built boats from the wreckage for their escape, and were rescued by a whaling ship as they sailed south.

In Washington, a navy board of inquiry accepted Emil Bessels's diagnosis that his patient, Charles Francis Hall, had died from a stroke. If Hall had indeed suffered a stroke, it was not his only ailment. In 1968 his well-preserved body was exhumed from the Greenland ice and autopsied. The physician who performed the work took samples of Hall's hair and fingernails. A laboratory analysis found high enough concentrations of arsenic in the samples to suggest that in his last weeks Hall had suffered arsenic poisoning. Arsenic, among its other properties, lends things an intensely sweet taste. He may have overmedicated himself with potions from his own medicine kit, in an effort to ward off the lethargy that befell even the hardiest visitors marooned in an Arctic winter. Or he may have been poisoned by one of the men he accused in his delirium of wishing him harm.

• • •

You can still find on Kodlunarn island outcrops of the black ore that so enthralled Martin Frobisher and, much later, Charles Francis Hall. Glossy with silver sparkles, the black rock scattered on the island's surface has a satisfying heft and does not easily shatter or flake.

The rock is hornblende; mica accounts for the sparkles. In the sixteenth century, as now, hornblende had no special value. Mount Vesuvius is rich in hornblende, and so is New York City. Donald Hogarth, a Canadian geologist who has devoted many years to the subject, determined that the black rock contained less gold than one might find in formations chosen elsewhere at random. The earth's crust has (on average) three and a half parts gold for every billion parts of other crustal constituents; the black ore from Kodlunarn Island contains two to two and a half parts gold. In Hogarth's words (and emphasis) after his laboratory work: "Gold was *extremely* low."

Of the first four assayers who studied the original black stone, three had concluded it was just rock. They were right. Due to the mistaken findings of others, Martin Frobisher sailed twice more to Baffin Island to fill his ships with hornblende.

A historian from the Dartford Borough Museum showed me the way to the site of the Cathay Company's "great works." We walked down a brambly hill along a busy road, skirted the back of a truck terminal, and entered a copse of maple trees. The River Darent was twenty feet wide between low banks, carrying leaves past us at less than walking pace. A man-made island barely large enough for a picnic was in the middle of the waterway. A young couple was smooching on one of the riverbanks. All the furnaces and machinery and smoke and expectations had been right there, on the man-made island and the banks. Except for the island, every trace of the great works has disappeared.

We walked along Dartford High Street to see the site of the royal manor house where the black ore had been stored. We passed a dry cleaner's, a fish-and-chips establishment, and another restaurant, and came to a shopping strip where every parking space was filled. Behind it was a construction company with a clutter of steel tubing piled in an asphalt lot closed off on one side by a high stone wall. King Henry VIII's manor house had stood roughly there—at the shopping center and the asphalt lot. The house had boasted at least forty chimneys and sprouted battlements worthy of a castle. But it has disappeared. What remains is its brick gatehouse and the stone wall.

Workmen had slapped together the wall in the 1400s, long before the manor house. They piled together local ragstone and flint and slathered mortar into the gaps. It was the method that cost least in time and materials—very ropey work. A century later, in the early 1500s, the builders of the manor house extended the wall. They inelegantly cut an entrance through to the royal gardens. In one of the many cycles of repair and rebuilding, workmen extended the wall another 130 feet sometime after 1578. Every time, only the cheapest materials were used.

Nothing was cheaper than the black stone stored in the manor

Dartford wall where black ore was transmuted into just rock. (Courtesy of Dartford Borough Museum)

house. Martin Frobisher's cargo of black stone went into the wall, his gold-rich ore transmuted back into just rock. Some of the rock was used as paving stones. Some was tossed into the Darent and into cesspools. Over the years, people in Dartford half forgot the story of how the stones came to be present. They had been brought to town a long, long time ago. The high stone wall was just a checkerboard of gray and black. The gray ragstone had come from farmers' fields. The black stones had come—at the price of ocean crossings, kidnappings, and personal ruin—from some unknown shore.

Notes

Records gathered by other researchers helped guide my exploration of Meta Incognita. I relied heavily on the two-volume documentary history compiled by Vilhjalmur Stefansson and Eloise McCaskill, *The Three Voyages of Martin Frobisher* (London: Argonaut Press, 1938). Their work added to the materials gathered by Richard Collinson, *The Three Voyages of Martin Frobisher in Search of a Passage to Cathaia and India by the North-west, A.D. 1576–8* (London: Hakluyt Society, 1867).

Another essential source was the ledger of Michael Lok. His account books are divided between the Public Record Office (cataloged there as E164/35, E164/36) and the Huntington Library (HM 715) and have a challenging orthography. I owe a great debt to the unpublished transcription made by James McDermott, "The Account Books of Michael Lok, Relating to the Northwest Voyages of Martin Frobisher, 1576–1578," prepared as a thesis for a master of philosophy degree at the University of Hull, 1984. McDermott's work includes an enlightening biographical sketch of Lok.

The key sources of information about Charles Francis Hall are his notebooks, in the archives of the Smithsonian Institution, National Museum of American History. Full runs of Hall's two newspapers, the *Cincinnati Occasional* and the *Daily Penny Press,* are in the archives of the Cincinnati Historical Society. To prepare for a visit to Kodlunarn Island, I relied on the archaeological report prepared by William W. Fitzhugh and colleagues, *Archeology of the Frobisher Voyages* (Washington: Smithsonian Institution Press, 1993).

For the sake of consistency, I have used modern place-names whenever possible. (So King William Island, for example, is the name given for where Charles Francis Hall found remains of John Franklin's men, territory Hall knew as King William's Land.) For the sake of clarity, I have adoped modern spellings when quoting sixteenth-century documents (So Christopher Hall, aboard the *Gabriel* in 1576, sights "ice" rather than "yce.")

Some Elizabethan documents used "Old Style" dating: the calendar year changed on each March 25. I have altered dates to reflect the "New Style": calendar years begin January 1. Elizabethan England also relied on the Julian calendar, whose dates are ten days behind our own Gregorian system (George Best's June 1, for example, is our June 11.) But this book leaves the Julian calendar untouched.

Abbreviations

BL   British Library
CSP   *Calendar of State Papers*
CLSP   *Calendar of Letters and State Papers*
PRO   Public Record Office
SM   Vilhjalmur Stefansson and Eloise McCaskill, *The Three Voyages of Martin Frobisher* (London: Argonaut Press, 1938)

Prologue: North

1   *Listening in 1861, Charles Francis Hall:* Beginning in the late 1850s, Hall kept diaries chronicling his enthusiasm for all things Arctic and, later, his travels. He used the journals as the basis of a book—prepared with the help of a ghostwriter—published in Great Britain in two volumes as *Life with the Esquimaux* (London: Samson Low, Son, and Martson, 1864) and in the United States as *Arctic Researches and Life Among the Esquimaux* (New York: Harper & Brothers, 1865). Another key source of information about Hall is Chauncey C. Loomis's biography of the explorer, *Weird and Tragic Shores* (New York: Alfred A. Knopf, 1971; rpt. Lincoln: University of Nebraska Press, 1991).

2   *"Everything relating to the arctic zone":* Quotations from Hall are from his notebooks, his book *Arctic Researches,* and from Loomis's *Weird and Tragic Shores.* His first impression of the Arctic is part of his diary entry for June 20, 1860, and appears in *Arctic Researches,* p. 35.

3   *the* Gabriel *was a modest-sized vessel:* About 80 percent of the English merchant fleet was smaller than one hundred tons, but those vessels usually limited themselves to short trips to the Continent. Ian Friel, "The Three-Masted Ship and Atlantic Voyages," in *Raleigh in Exeter, 1985: Privateering and Colonisation in the Reign of Elizabeth I,* ed. Joyce Youings (Exeter: University of Exeter, 1985), p. 30.

3   *A naval ton measured volume:* One ton was two butts, each butt containing 126 gallons. Kenneth R. Andrews, *Elizabethan Privateering* (Cambridge: Cambridge University Press, 1964), p. 35; William Salisbury, "Early Tonnage Measurement in England," *Mariner's Mirror* 52, no. 1 (February 1966): pp. 41–42.

7   *Canadian government labeled the area the "E" district:* Alan Rudolph Marcus. *Relocating Eden: The Image and Politics of Inuit Exile in the Canadian Arctic* (Hanover, N.H.: University Press of New England, 1995), pp. 32–33.

10 *In Inuit tradition the northern lights are spirits:* John MacDonald, *The Arctic Sky: Inuit Astronomy, Star Lore, and Legend* (Toronto: Royal Ontario Museum, 1998), pp. 194–55.

1. Different Directions

13 *The one portrait:* The painting came to the Bodleian in 1674 as the gift of Dr. Walter Charleton, a physician to the royal court. William C. Sturtevant and David B. Quinn, "This New Prey: Eskimos in Europe in 1567, 1576, and 1577," in *Indians and Europe: An Interdisciplinary Collection of Essays,* ed. Christian F. Feest (Aachen: Rader Verlag, 1987), p. 73.
    Ketel became a favorite: Roy Strong, *Gloriana: The Portraits of Queen Elizabeth I* (New York: Thames and Hudson, 1987), pp. 100–03.

14 *recent discovery of starch:* Anne Somerset, *Elizabeth I* (New York: Knopf, 1991), p. 358.
    called his spellings "terrifying": William McFee, *The Life of Sir Martin Frobisher* (New York: Harper & Brothers, 1928), p. 243.

15 *"Since my comynge fourthe":* McFee, *The Life of Sir Martin Frobisher,* pp. 181–82.
    One of his descendants: Keith Frobisher, interview.

17 *A big farm would have ten acres:* Yorkshire's sixteenth-century textile industry and agriculture is discussed in David Hey, *Yorkshire from A.D. 1000* (London: Longman, 1986), pp. 139–58.

18 *A senior government minister:* The classic example of the blurring between public service and private gain occurred in the 1590s. Sir Robert Cecil, then principal secretary of state, owned the *Truelove* with Charles Howard, the Lord High Admiral, and outfitted it at the Royal Navy's expense for a profitable privateering voyage. N. A. M. Rodger, *The Safeguard of the Sea: A Naval History of Britain, 660–1649* (New York: W. W. Norton, 1998), pp. 226–27, 332, 338.
    In 1553 the Royal Navy: Rodger, *The Safeguard,* pp. 176–77; Tom Glascow, Jr., "Maturing of Naval Administration, 1556–1564," *Mariner's Mirror* 56, no. 1 (January 1970), pp. 4–5.

19 *Bristol ships had reached Iceland:* A stimulating, sometimes speculative examination of England's early contacts with Iceland and Greenland is Kirsten A. Seaver, *The Frozen Echo: Greenland and the Exploration of North America,*

ca. A.D. 1000–1500 (Stanford: Stanford University Press, 1996), esp. pp. 181–82, 252–53, 281–311.

19 *Giovanni Caboto:* David Beers Quinn, *England and the Discovery of America, 1481–1620,* (New York: Knopf, 1974), pp. 15–16, 93–101; Kenneth R. Andrews, *Trade, Plunder and Settlement: Maritime Enterprise and the Genesis of the British Empire, 1480–1630* (Cambridge: Cambridge University Press, 1984), pp. 45–52.

20 *"He is called Great Admiral":* Letter of Lorenzo Pasqualigo, quoted in Peter Firstbrook, *The Voyage of the Mathew: John Cabot and the Discovery of North America* (London: BBC Books, 1997), p. 169.

   "as your Lordship knows": The letter writer was John Day, a member of a merchant family well established in Bristol and Spain. Quinn, *England and the Discovery of America,* pp. 5–6, 13–14, 109–10.

   Their new **Mathew***:* Firstbrook, *The Voyage,* pp. 80–81, 84–85.

21 *Captain Thomas Wyndham:* Wyndham's story, and that of early English trade in West Africa, is told in John William Blake, *Europeans in West Africa, 1450–1560,* 2 vols. (London: Hakluyt Society, 1942), especially vol. 2, pp. 309–25, 382–88. Additional details are in P. E. H. Hair and J. D. Alsop, *English Seamen and Traders in Guinea, 1553–1565: The New Evidence of Their Wills* (Lewiston, N.Y.: Edwin Mellen Press, 1992), especially pp. 8–11. Also, P. E. H. Hair, "The Experience of the Sixteenth-Century English Voyages to Guinea," *Mariner's Mirror* 83, no. 1 (February 1997), pp. 6–7.

   Since the 1470s, Portuguese traders: Robin Blackburn, *The Making of New World Slavery: From the Baroque to the Modern, 1492–1800* (London: Verso, 1997), pp. 103, 106. For the story of Mina, see P. E. H. Hair, *The Founding of the Castelo de São Jorge da Mina: An Analysis of the Sources* (Madison: University of Wisconsin Press, 1994), p. 14, and A. J. R. Russell-Wood, *The Portuguese Empire, 1415–1808* (Baltimore: Johns Hopkins, 1998), pp. 60, 85, 132. The value of Mina's annual gold trade is in Pierre Vilar, *A History of Gold and Money, 1450–1920* (London: Verso, 1991), pp. 55–56.

22 *The Admiralty court in London issued letters of reprisal:* Kenneth R. Andrews, *Elizabethan Privateering,* pp. 4–5, 229–34; Kenneth R. Andrews, "Elizabethan Privateering," in *Raleigh in Exeter, 1985: Privateering and Colonisation in the Reign of Elizabeth I,* ed. Joyce Youings (Exeter: University of Exeter, 1985), pp. 3–4, 22–24; Rodger, 182, 199–200.

24 *They saw an endless green swamp:* Description of the West African coast is drawn from P. E. H. Hair, ed., *Travails in Guinea: Robert Baker's 'Brefe Dyscourse' (?1568)* (Liverpool: Liverpool University Press, 1990); and Hair, *The Founding,* pp. 20–21.

25 *yellow fever:* J. J. Keevil, *Medicine and the Navy, 1200–1900,* vol. 1 (Edinburgh and London: E. & S. Livingstone, 1957), p. 88.

26 *John Lok possessed an impeccable lineage:* James McDermott, "The Account Books of Michael Lok, Relating to the Northwest Voyages of Martin Frobisher, 1576–1578" (M. Phil. thesis, University of Hull, Quebec, 1984), pp. 1–3, 6.

By the end of 1554, he was aboard one of John Lok's ships: Blake, *Europeans in West Africa,* pp. 326–46. Richard Eden's account also appears in Richard Hakluyt, *The Principal Navigations Voyages Traffiques & Discoveries of the English Nation,* vol. 6 (Glasgow: James MacLehose and Sons, 1903), pp. 154–77.

27 *"Martin, by his own desire":* Richard Eden, in Blake, *Europeans in West Africa,* pp. 289, 332–34.

"whereof some were tall": Richard Eden, in Blake, *Europeans in West Africa,* p. 346.

Frobisher said the Portuguese: PRO SP70/37, item 72, cited in Blake, *Europeans in West Africa,* pp. 359–60.

28 *Sebastian Cabot:* David Loades, *The Reign of King Edward VI* (Gwynedd, Wales: Headstart History, 1994), pp. 139–40; Andrews, *Trade,* pp. 50–51, 66–68.

a papal bull: Pope Alexander VI in 1493 divided everything south of the latitudes of Madrid and Lisbon between Spain and Portugal. All territories west of a line near the Cape Verde Islands was assigned to Spain, everything to the east of it to Portugal. A 1494 treaty adjusted the dividing line, and in 1529 Spain and Portugal tried without much success to resolve overlapping claims in the Pacific. D. W. Waters, *The Art of Navigation in England in Elizabethan and Early Stuart Times* (New Haven: Yale University Press, 1958), p. 81.

29 *a man named Dr. John Dee:* Dee has inspired a vast literature about his career. His biographers use as their starting point Dee's own account of his accomplishments, "The Compendious Rehearsall," published in *The Autobiographical Tracts of Dr. John Dee,* ed. James Crossley (Manchester: Chetham Society, 1851). Recent works relied on here are William H. Sherman, *John Dee: The Politics of Reading and Writing in the English Renaissance* (Amherst: University of Massachusetts Press, 1995); Nicholas H. Clulee, *John Dee's Natural Philosophy: Between Science and Religion* (London: Routledge, 1988); and Julian Roberts and Andrew G. Watson, eds., *John Dee's Library Catalogue* (London: Bibliographical Society, 1990). Also, Peter J. French, *John Dee: The World of an Elizabethan Magus* (London: Routledge, 1972), and Wayne Shumaker, *Renaissance Curiosa,* Medieval and Renaissance Texts and Studies, vol. 8 (Binghamton: Center for Medieval and Early Renaissance Studies, 1982).

30 *Reading explorers' accounts:* William H. Sherman, "John Dee's Columbian Encounter: A Marginal Discovery" (paper presented at Queen Mary and Westfield College, University of London, 1995).

Dee kept a diary: His diary began as entries scattered in the margins of manuscripts. Only long after his death were some of his entries collected in book form. For many years, the best available version was *The Private Diary of Dr. John Dee,* ed. James Orchard Halliwell (London: Camden Society, 1842). This has been superseded by *The Diaries of John Dee,* ed. Edward Fenton (Charlbury, England: Day Books, 1998). "All the night very strange knocking" is part of Dee's entry for August 3, 1581. "I dreamed that I was dead" is part of his entry for November 24, 1582.

30   *His library was the largest scholarly collection:* Roberts and Watson, *John Dee's Library Catalogue,* pp. 10–11, 23–24, 196. Roberts and Watson take their description of the library's physical arrangement from Dee, "Compendious Rehearsall," pp. 28–29.

32   *His laboratory apparatus:* The mirror is cataloged at the British Museum as MLA 1966 10-1-1. Dee's crystal ball is MLA 0A.232. They are discussed in Hugh Tait, "'The Devil's Looking Glass': The Magical Speculum of Dr. John Dee," in *Horace Walpole, Writer, Politician, and Connoisseur,* ed. Warren Hunting Smith (New Haven: Yale University Press, 1967), pp. 195–212, 337–38.

On May 10, 1553, Willoughby's three ships: Willoughby's fate, and Richard Chancellor's experiences in Moscow, are chronicled in Richard Hakluyt, *The Principal Navigations,* vol. 2, pp. 216–70. For a summary of early English-Russian relations, see E. Delmar Morgan and C. H. Coote, eds. *Early Voyages and Travels to Russia and Persia* (London: Hakluyt Society, 1886), pp. i–clxii.

35   *"The sputum which he brings up":* quoted in David Loades, *John Dudley, Duke of Northumberland, 1504–1553* (Oxford: Clarendon Press, 1996), p. 239.
"calculating and conjuring": Clulee, *John Dee's Natural Philosophy,* p. 34.
"who was burnt": Dee, "Compendious Rehearsall," p. 20.

36   *"singularis amicus":* Roberts and Watson, *John Dee's Library Catalogue,* pp. 4–5.
"The realm exhausted": Remarks of Armigal Waad, former Privy Council secretary, in Penry Williams, *The Later Tudors: England, 1547–1603* (Oxford: Clarendon Press, 1995), p. 229.
At age thirteen, in a letter to her half brother: Elizabeth's letter was dated May 15, 1547, and apparently was accompanied by a portrait of herself. Karen Hearn, ed., *Dynasties: Painting in Tudor and Jacobean England, 1530–1630* (New York: Rizzoli, 1996), p. 78.
She and Cecil that day were seen: Alison Weir, *The Life of Elizabeth I* (New York: Ballantine, 1998), pp. 20–22.

37   *"She is a woman of extreme vanity":* Spanish ambassador Count de Feria, in Williams, *The Later Tudors,* p. 230.
"Her face is comely": Dispatch of Giovanni Michiel to the Venetian doge, in Strong, *Gloriana,* p. 19.

37 *"She desired to know of me"*: Report of Sir James Melville, minister to England from Mary, Queen of Scots after an audience with Elizabeth in 1564, in Elizabeth W. Pomeroy, *Reading the Portraits of Queen Elizabeth I* (Hamden: Archon Books, 1989), p. 39.

38 *In one of his recent works*: This is John Dee's *Propaedeumata Aphoristica (An Aphoristic Introduction)*. Clulee, *John Dee's Natural Philosophy*, pp. 21–22 et passim.
    "My careful and faithful endeavors": Dee, "Compendious Rehearsall," p. 21.
    Her courtiers sought in every sense: For a portrait of court life, see Weir, *The Life of Elizabeth I*, pp. 248–52. A list prepared in 1580 of Elizabeth's loans included one of £10,000 to the Earl of Leicester. Ralph M. Sargent, *At the Court of Queen Elizabeth: The Life of Lyrics of Sir Edward Dyer* (London: Oxford University Press, 1935), pp. 14, 53. Also, Loades, *The Tudor Court*, p. 185.

39 *"To fawn, to crouch, to wait, to ride, to run"*: Edmund Spenser, *Mother Hubberds Tale*, cited in Katherine Duncan-Jones, *Sir Philip Sidney, Courtier Poet* (New Haven: Yale University Press, 1991), p. 86.

42 *In 1559, witnesses testifying at the Admiralty Court:* For details of Frobisher's career as a pirate, the two touchstone sources are R. G. Marsden, "The Early Career of Sir Martin Frobisher," in *English Historical Review* 21 (1906), pp. 538–44; and K. M. Eliot, "The First Voyages of Martin Frobisher," in *English Historical Review* 32 (1917), pp. 89–92.

43 *"true and faithful service heretofore done"*: PRO SP40/1 f.119, cited in D. D. Hogarth, P. W. Boreham, and J. G. Mitchell, *Martin Frobisher's Northwest Venture, 1576–1581: Mines, Minerals and Metallurgy* (Hull, Quebec: Canadian Museum of Civilization, 1994), p. 149.

44 *Gilbert served as one of the great dashing men:* The most complete source on Humphrey Gilbert is David Beer Quinn, *The Voyages and Colonising Enterprises of Sir Humphrey Gilbert*, 2 vols. (London: Hakluyt Society, 1940).
    Jenkinson had already attempted to reach Cathay: Jenkinson's little known expeditions to Uzbekistan and Persia are described in Hakluyt, *Principal Navigations*, vol. 2, pp. 449–79.

45 *Sailing for France, in 1523, Giovanni da Verrazzano:* W. F. Ganong, *Crucial Maps in the Early Cartography and Place-Nomenclature of the Atlantic Coast of Canada* (Toronto: University of Toronto, 1964), p. 151; Samuel Eliot Morison, *The European Discovery of America: The Northern Voyages, A.D. 500–1600* (1971; rpt. New York: Oxford University Press, 1993), pp. 288–89.

46 *His supporters told the story for him:* Many of the key documents are in the two documentary histories of Frobisher's expeditions: SM, and Richard Collinson, *The Three Voyages of Martin Frobisher: In Search of a Passage to Cathaia and India by the North-west, A.D. 1576–8* (London: Hakluyt Society,

1867). George Best did not accompany Frobisher in 1576 but described the preparations and the subsequent voyage in his pamphlet *A true discourse of the late voyages of discoverie, for the finding of a passage to Cathaya, by the northwest, under the conduct of Martin Frobisher generall* (London, 1578), reprinted in SM, vol. 1, esp. pp. 47–51. Michael Lok tells his version of events in letters addressed to the queen and the Privy Council (in SM), and in his caustic overview of the venture, written c. 1581, *The Doyings of Captayne Furbisher*, BL Lansdowne 100/1.

48 *"chief friend":* Quotations from Lok are, as noted above, from reports and correspondence collected in SM, and from his *The Doyings of Captayne Furbisher.* His description of the first months of planning are in SM, vol. 2, pp. 183–84.

49 *The ledgers he maintained:* Lok's account books are transcribed in McDermott, "The Account Books."

50 *at just this time the clerk of the Privy Council:* CSP Foreign, Elizabeth 1575–77, pp. 316–17.
    An Irish earl being held in England: This was Gerald Fitzgerald, Earl of Desmond. Frank Jones, *The Life of Sir Martin Frobisher* (London: Longman, 1878), p. 13.
    "He is the best seaman": The writer was Antonio de Guaras, a banker who for a time also served as his country's de facto ambassador to England. Francis Walsingham later imprisoned him for espionage. CLSP Simancas, vol. 2, p. 520.
    The "someone" in charge of secrets: Charles Nicholl, *The Reckoning: The Murder of Christopher Marlowe* (Chicago: University of Chicago Press, 1995), pp. 103–04.

51 *"Mr. Frobisher had very little credit":* Collinson, *The Three Voyages,* pp. 335–36.
    Lord Burghley . . . invested £50: Details about investments, wages, and the outfitting of Frobisher's ships are taken from Lok's account books, transcribed in McDermott, "The Account Books."

53 *Those are large sums:* Henry Phelps Brown and Sheila V. Hopkins, *Perspective of Wages and Prices* (London: Methuen, 1981), and Steve Rappaport, *Worlds Within Worlds: Structures of Life in Sixteenth-Century London* (Cambridge: Cambridge University Press, 1989), pp. 159–60.
    The **Gabriel** *and the* **Michael***:* Andrews, *Elizabethan Privateering,* p. 35; and Friel, "The Three-Masted Ship," p. 30.

54 *Hugh Morgan, an apothecary:* A full list of the drugs is in McDermott, "The Account Books," pp. 170–71. Also, Keevil, *Medicine and the Navy,* pp. 198–99.

55 *"a virtuous Gentleman":* John Dee, *General and Rare Memorials Pertayning to the Perfect Arte of Navigation* (London, 1577; rpt. New York: Da Capo Press, 1968), p. 2.

"learned man" . . . *"a great good opinion"*: SM, vol. 2., p. 82.

"Mathematicall Praeface": Dee's essay was published in London in 1570 as the preface of *The Elements of Geometry of Euclid in Megara,* trans. Henry Billingsley (London).

56 *Seething Lane:* Ben Weinreb and Christopher Hibbert, *The London Encyclopaedia,* rev. ed. (London: Macmillan, 1995), pp. 773, 799–800.

The books Frobisher was supposed to read: His tutors purchased Robert Record's *Castle of Knowledge,* published in 1556, and William Cunningham's *Cosmographical Glasse,* 1559. André Thevet's chronicle, originally published in 1557, was translated into English in 1568 as *The New found World or Antarctike.* James McDermott, *The Navigation of the Frobisher Voyages,* Hakluyt Society Annual Talk 1997 (London: Hakluyt Society, 1998), pp. 4–5.

57 *The lessons on Seething Lane:* Dee, *General and Rare Memorials,* pp. 2–3.

"deep to the knees": Dee, *General and Rare Memorials,* pp. 49–50.

2. "A Land of Ice"

59 *They left with the tide:* The most useful record of Frobisher's 1576 voyage is Christopher Hall's log, which survives in what is probably an edited version, in SM, vol. 1, pp. 149–54. George Best describes some of the events, in SM, vol. 1, pp. 47–51. A third source is Michael Lok's record of the expenses, transcribed in McDermott, "The Account Books."

60 *"Worshipful Sir"*: His letter is in Richard Hakluyt, *Principal Navigations,* vol. 6, pp. 136–37.

61 *wrote a letter to the learned John Dee:* Dee, *General and Rare Memorials,* p. 3.

62 *The latest edition of* **Sailing Directions**: *Sailing Directions (Enroute): Greenland and Iceland,* publication 181, 5th ed. (Defense Mapping Agency, Hydrographic/Topographic Center, 1994), pp. 4–5.

63 *The Canadian Department of Fisheries:* Its list of typical damage from ice includes "strained or broken shaft, broken blades or loss of propellers, strained or broken rudder-head and rudder, damage to steering gear, damage to stern and plating, crushing of the hull and breaking of frames, buckling of plating and tearing out of rivets." *Sailing Directions, Arctic Canada,* 4th ed., vol. 1, (Ottawa: Department of Fisheries and Oceans, 1994), pp. 96–97.

Frisland was brought into existence: Richard Henry Major, ed., *The Voyages of the Venetian Brothers, Nicolo and Antonio Zeno* (London: Hakluyt Society, 1873). For the Zeno brothers' probable route, see Donald S. Johnson, *Phantom Islands of the Atlantic* (New York: Walker and Company, 1994), pp. 44–48, 58–62.

64 *So Frisland appeared on a vellum sailing chart:* One of John Dee's most eminent students, the pilot William Borough, prepared the chart two

weeks before Frobisher's departure. Waters, *The Art of Navigation,* pp. 528–29.

Hall had equipped himself with twenty compasses: Most of the instruments were supplied by Humfrey Cole, an engraver at the Royal Mint. McDermott, "The Account Books," p. 84; E. G. R. Taylor, *Tudor Geography 1485–1583* (London: Methuen, 1930), pp. 106, 121.

ancestor of the theodolite: Waters, *The Art of Navigation,* p. 531, identifies the instrument as a "horizontal plane sphere."

69   *A captain in familiar waters could see:* Sixteenth-century navigation methods are described in Waters, *The Art of Navigation,* pp. 10–11, 496, and Andrews, *Trade, Plunder and Settlement,* pp. 29–30.

The modern, scientific vocabulary for Arctic ice: Sailing Directions, Arctic Canada, pp. 88–93.

70   *"By the signs they made":* Christopher Columbus, *The Log of Christopher Columbus,* trans. Robert H. Fuson (Camden, Maine: International Marine, 1987), p. 79.

71   *"Of anything they have":* Columbus included the observation in his formal report to King Ferdinand and Queen Isabella. Samuel Eliot Morison, *Christopher Columbus, Mariner* (1942. rept. New York: Meridian, 1983), p. 207.

A Spanish official, after more than thirty years: The official was Gonzalo Fernández de Oviedo y Valdes. Anthony Pagden, *European Encounters with the New World* (New Haven: Yale University Press, 1993), p. 57.

In the Caribbean, Spanish soldiers took bets: Bartolomé de Las Casas, *The Devastation of the Indies: A Brief Account,* trans. Herma Briffault (Baltimore: Johns Hopkins University Press, 1992), pp. 33–34.

Would-be colonists from France: Roger Schlesinger and Arthur P. Stabler, eds., *André Thevet's North America* (Kingston: McGill–Queen's University Press, 1986), p. 15.

72   *Inuit had encountered other strangers:* Robert McGhee, "Contact Between Native North Americans and the Medieval Norse: A Review of the Evidence," *American Antiquity* 49, no. 1 (1984), pp. 15–22.

73   *He touched or pointed:* Kenn Harper drew my attention to Hall's head-to-toe progression, in a paper presented at the Meta Incognita Project Symposium, Trent University, Peterborough, Canada, 1997. The word list appears in SM, vol. 1, p. 154.

74   *Whatever their motivation, the five sailors:* Michael Lok provides the most detailed account, in SM, vol. 1, p. 162.

75   *sketched the waterway:* Waters, *The Art of Navigation,* pp. 528–29.

76   *"one Captayne Furbusher":* Letter written October 18, 1576, by Thomas Wood to Richard Bagot. Sturtevant, "This New Prey," p. 114.

77 *In the 1560s, French sailors:* Sturtevant, "This New Prey," pp. 61–62, 130–31. *A small watercolor:* The drawing is by Lucas de Heere, who was a costume artist and tapestry designer. Sturtevant, "This New Prey," pp. 74–75, 88–89. *"I have thought good":* Transcribed from BL Cotton Otho EVIII f.53v., in Sturtevant, "This New Prey," pp. 69–80.

78 *wanted a grand name:* Lok's draft character is in SM, vol. 2, pp. 103–07. *Frobisher secretly proposed a different scheme:* McDermott, "The Account Books," p. 64. Frobisher's petition is in SM, vol. 2, p. 94.

80 *ship she proffered:* The *Ayde* still had a long life ahead of it and remained afloat until at least 1599. Tom Glascow, Jr., and W. Salisbury, "Elizabethan Ships Pictured on Smerwick Map, 1580," *Mariner's Mirror* 52, no. 2 (May 1966), pp. 157–65; Hogarth, *Mines,* p. 53. *"vouched to them absolutely":* McDermott, "The Account Books," p. 46. *Richard Willes:* Willes's treatise, *The History of Travayle,* included translations of a Portuguese merchant's report on China, a Jesuit's description of Japan, and chronicles of India and Arabia. Waters, *The Art of Navigation,* pp. 148, 176–77; McDermott, "The Account Books," p. 45. *"M. Furbishers prosperous voyage":* SM, vol. 1, p. 144.

81 *Anyone in Lok's position:* Lok described his actions along with the comments of the assayers and others in a letter dated April 22, 1577, addressed to the queen. SM, vol. 2, pp. 84–90.

86 *Gold is, in a sense, everywhere:* Robert R. Brooks, ed., *Noble Metals and Biological Systems* (Boca Raton: CRC Press, 1992), pp. 50–61; and Robert W. Boyle, *Gold, History and Genesis of Deposits* (New York: Van Nostrand Reinhold, 1987), p. 11.

87 *"a certain Frobisher":* Steuart A. Pears, *The Correspondence of Sir Philip Sidney and Hubert Languet* (London: William Pickering, 1845; rpt. Westmead, England: Gregg International Publishers, 1971), pp. 118–19. *Another story making the rounds:* SM, vol. 1, p. 51. *Everyone's confidence was writ large:* A list of investors is in McDermott, "The Account Books," p. 197. On John Dee's investment, see p. 50.

88 *now akin to an employee:* Carole Jeanette Shammas, "The Elizabethan Gentlemen Adventurers and Western Planting" (Ph.D. diss., Johns Hopkins University, 1971), esp. p. 193; also McDermott, "The Account Books," p. 66. *"no small raging":* E. G. R. Taylor, ed., *The Troublesome Voyage of Captain Edward Fenton* (Cambridge: Hakluyt Society, 1959), p. 3. *In their formal instructions:* Collison, *The Three Voyages,* pp. 117–20.

3. A Cold Addiction

92 *During the 1850s he and his wife:* Details about Hall's life in Cincinnati are drawn from issues of the newspapers he published, the *Occasional* and the *Daily Press,* and from Loomis, *Weird and Tragic Shores,* pp. 27–50.

95 *John Barrow had the power:* Pierre Berton, *The Arctic Grail: The Quest for the North West Passage and the North Pole, 1818–1909* (New York: Viking, 1988), pp. 19–21.

   "peculiarly British" . . . "interesting discovery": John Barrow, *A Chronological History of Voyages into the Arctic Regions* (London: John Murray, 1818; rpt. Devon: David & Charles, 1971), pp. 364–65.

96 *On Greenland's northwest coast:* Berton, *The Arctic Grail,* pp. 15–16; Kenn Harper, *Give Me My Father's Body* (Iqaluit: Blacklead Books, 1986), pp. 4–5.

97 *The last of the three expeditions led by John Franklin:* Of the many books devoted to Franklin's last expedition, I relied mainly on Patricia D. Sutherland, ed., *The Franklin Era in Canadian Arctic History, 1845–1859* (Ottawa: National Museums of Canada, 1985); William Barr, ed., *Searching for Franklin: The Land Arctic Searching Expedition* (London: Hakluyt Society, 1999); and David C. Woodman, *Unraveling the Franklin Mystery: Inuit Testimony* (Montreal: McGill–Queen's University Press, 1991). For capsule biographies of Arctic explorers, see Richard C. Davis, ed., *Lobsticks and Stone Cairns: Human Landmarks in the Arctic* (Calgary, Alta.: University of Calgary Press, 1996).

100 *"Some of the bodies":* Rae's letter of July 29, 1854, in Barr, *Searching for Franklin,* p. 20.

   "We believe every savage": "The Lost Arctic Voyages," *Household Words* 245 (December 2, 1854), quoted in Sutherland, *The Franklin Era,* p. 3.

101 *"The decks are cleaned." . . . "We have cards sometimes":* Elisha Kent Kane, *Arctic Explorations: The Second Grinnell Expedition,* vol. 1 (Philadelphia: Childs & Peterson, 1856), pp. 169–73.

103 *"Does Sir John Franklin Still Live":* *Daily Press,* May 25, 1859. Cited in Loomis, *Weird and Tragic Shores,* p. 43.

   "All men must feel a lively interest": *Daily Press,* June 2, 1859.

104 *In its weather reports:* *Daily Press,* June 9, 1859.

   "The **Daily Press** *is about to pass":* *Daily Press,* July 15, 1859.

   "In one word, then": Hall, *Arctic Researches,* p. xix.

106 *"O Lord of life and death":* Sutherland, *The Franklin Era,* p. 134.

   "There will be no more Arctic expeditions": *Daily Press,* October 12, 1859.

107 *"Why should not attempts be made":* Hall, *Arctic Researches,* p. xix.

   Merchants either donated: Hall's list of donors is in *Arctic Researches,* pp. 585–88.

110   *"painted black and sold":* A whaler named Jestin Martin made the remark in a letter to his brother Charles in 1844. Robert Owen Decker, *The New London Merchants: The Rise and Decline of a Connecticut Port* (New York: Garland Publishing, 1986), pp. 183–84.

111   *The senior men would take charge of the flensing:* W. Gillies Ross, *Arctic Whalers, Icy Seas: Narratives of the Davis Strait Whale Fishery* (Toronto: Irwin Publishing, 1985), p. 85; Basil Lubbock, *The Arctic Whalers* (Glasgow: Brown, Son & Ferguson, 1937), pp. 22–23.
      Of the eight whaling ships that had left New London: Decker, *The New London Merchants,* pp. 317–18a.
      "A miserable time": Comments by Hall, unless otherwise noted, are from *Arctic Researches,* which quotes his journals. His complaint about his first days at sea appears on p. 31.

112   *he had voluntarily spent a winter:* Ross, *Arctic Whalers,* p. 151.

113   *William Penny . . . Eenoolooapik:* Ross, *Arctic Whalers,* pp. 112, 119, 120–25; and Marc Stevenson, *Inuit, Whalers, and Cultural Persistence: Structure in Cumberland Sound and Central Inuit Social Organization* (Toronto: Oxford University Press Canada, 1997), pp. 59–61. Relations between the Inuit and whalers are also among the subjects of Dorothy Harley Eber, *When the Whalers Were up North: Inuit Memories from the Eastern Arctic* (Norman: University of Oklahoma Press, 1996).
      In 1847 . . . Captain John Parker: W. Gillies Ross, *This Distant and Unsurveyed Country: A Woman's Winter at Baffin Island, 1857–58* (Montreal: McGill–Queen's University Press, 1997), pp. 50–52; and Ross, *Arctic Whalers,* p. 110.

114   *"gentle, docile, grateful":* quoted in Ross, *Arctic Whalers,* p. 110.

121   *they had met Captain Budington:* Ross, *This Distant and Unsurveyed Country,* pp. 55–56.

122   *"Had seen before luncheon":* Queen Victoria's journal entry of February 3, 1854, quoted in Ross, *This Distant and Unsurveyed Country,* p. 55.
      found the queen "very kind": Ross, *This Distant and Unsurveyed Country,* p. 55; and J. E. Nourse, *Narrative of the Second Arctic Expedition Made by Charles F. Hall* (Washington, D.C.: Government Printing Office, 1879), p. 443.

126   *You cannot depend on the stars:* Macdonald, *Arctic Sky,* pp. 177–82.

130   *remarkable step-by-step analysis:* Richard K. Nelson, *Hunters of the Northern Ice* (Chicago: University of Chicago Press, 1969), pp. 334–40, 394–95.

131   *A hunter-gatherer could load everything:* Robert McGhee, *Ancient People of the Arctic* (Vancouver: University of British Columbia Press, 1996), p. 143.
      Inuktitut was especially rich: Rosemarie Kuptana, "Ilira, or Why It Was Unthinkable for Inuit to Challenge Qallunaat Authority," in *Inuit Art*

Quarterly," 8, no. 3 (1993), p. 6. Also, Julie Cruikshank, "Oral Tradition and Oral History: Reviewing Some Issues," *Canadian Historical Review* 75, no. 3 (1994), pp. 403–18.

133 *"We had twelve bottles":* The celebrations were described by boatsteerer Albert Johnson Whitehouse, in Ross, *Arctic Whalers,* p. 160.
     suffering horribly from scurvy: Cartier's description of scurvy is in Hakluyt, *Principal Navigations,* vol. 8, pp. 246–47.

136 *"No longer have I doubts!":* Journal, May 11, 1861.

4. Treasure Island

138 *Michael Lok . . . had supplied them:* Details about the outfitting are from Lok's ledger, transcribed in McDermott, "The Account Books."

139 *When the ships stopped at Harwich:* Frobisher's second expedition is chronicled by George Best, in SM, vol. 1, pp. 52–79, and Dionites Settle, *A true reporte of the laste voyage into the west and northwest regions, etc. 1577, worthily achieved by Capteine Frobisher of the sayde voyage, the finder and generall,* in SM, vol. 2, pp. 3–25. Other details are from Lok's correspondence, and McDermott, "The Account Books."

140 *"so big as a walnut":* SM, vol. 1, p. 57.
     an oddly subdued ceremony: The differing styles of taking possession of new territories are described by Patricia Seed, *Ceremonies of Possession in Europe's Conquest of the New World, 1492–1640* (Cambridge: Cambridge University Press, 1995), esp. pp. 69–99.

141 *At each first encounter with a new people:* Stephen Greenblatt, *Marvelous Possessions: The Wonder of the New World* (Chicago: University of Chicago Press, 1991), pp. 97–98.

142 *Arthur Barlowe:* David Beers Quinn, ed., *The Roanoke Voyages, 1584–1590,* vol. 1 (London: Hakluyt Society, 1955), pp. 97–98, 105–06.

143 *"We were entertained with all love":* Quinn, *Roanoke Voyages,* p. 108.

144 *Two seagulls a long, long time ago:* James Houston, *Confessions of an Igloo Dweller* (Boston: Houghton Mifflin, 1995), pp. 215–16.

145 *Christopher Hall failed to take off his cap:* Michael Lok describes the argument in *The Doynges of Captain Furbisher,* quoted in Taylor, *The Troublesome Voyage,* pp. 3–4.

146 *plug and feather:* Hogarth, *Mines,* pp. 10–12.

147 *George Best, examining the interiors:* Reginald Auger et al., *Material Evidence from the Frobisher Voyages: Anglo-Inuit Contact in the North American Arctic in the Late Sixteenth Century,* British Museum Occasional Paper 109 (London: British Museum, 1995), p. 15.

149 *A painting of the battle:* Sturtevant and Quinn, "This New Prey," pp. 106, 108; Paul Hulton and David Beers Quinn, *The American Drawings of John*

White, 1577–1590 (Chapel Hill: University of North Carolina Press, 1964), p. 144; William W. Fitzhugh and Dosia Laeyendecker, "A Brief Narrative of the Frobisher Voyages," in William W. Fitzhugh and Jacqueline S. Olin, eds., *Archeology of the Frobisher Voyages* (Washington: Smithsonian Institution Press, 1993), pp. 12–13.

151   *The earliest ancestors of the Inuit:* My summary of the Independence, Dorset, and Thule cultures is drawn from McGhee, *Ancient People,* and Robert McGhee, "Disease and the Development of Inuit Culture," *Current Anthropology* 35, no. 5 (December 1994), pp. 567–77.

153   *In even the coldest winters, a polynya:* Anne Henshaw, *Central Inuit Household Economies: Zooarchaeological, Environmental, and Historical Evidence from Outer Frobisher Bay, Baffin Island, Canada* (Ann Arbor: UMI Dissertation Services, 1996), pp. 43, 273, 290.

155   *Kamaiyuk, as the Inuit called it:* The Kamaiyuk excavations are described in Henshaw, *Central Inuit,* esp. pp. 179–248, 380–90.

157   *The Nugumiut . . . numbered about 80:* The population figure from 1883–84 was the estimate of Franz Boas. The Reverend A. L. Fleming made the 1913–14 census. Henshaw, *Central Inuit,* p. 140, and Kenn Harper, "Iqaluit," *Above and Beyond* 1, no. 4 (Autumn 1989), p. 9. Also, Franz Boas, *The Central Eskimo* (Lincoln: University of Nebraska Press, 1964), pp. 14–15.

160   *the name of God, in whom we all believe":* Best included the letter in his pamphlet. SM, vol. 1, p. 72.

163   *The seas were rough enough that William Smith:* Best told William Smith's story. SM, vol. 1, pp. 76–77.

164   *The queen bestowed a name:* SM, vol. 1, p. 80.
      The map is gray with age: BL Augustus I.i.1.

165   *"most certain" . . . "great riches of lead":* Dee, *General and Rare Memorials,* pp. 27–29.
      A woodcut used on the book's title page: Strong, *Gloriana,* pp. 91–93; Clulee, *John Dee's Natural Philosophy,* pp. 184–85.

166   *The book . . . informed its readers:* Dee, *General and Rare Memorials,* p. Δ iii–ε ii.
      "18 June. Borrowed £40": Fenton, *Diaries of John Dee,* pp. 2–3.

167   *Meriwether Lewis:* Stephen E. Ambrose, *Undaunted Courage* (New York: Simon & Schuster, 1996), p. 285.
      Kalicho entertained the townspeople: SM, vol. 2, pp. 237–38; Neil Cheshire et al., "Frobisher's Eskimos in England," *Archivaria* 10 (Summer 1980), pp. 30–31; and Sturtevant, "This New Prey," pp. 80–81.

169   *Dr. Edward Dodding examined him:* The autopsy report appears in Cheshire, "Frobisher's Eskimos," pp. 38–42.
      Arnaq's baby boy survived long enough: McDermott, "The Account Books," p. 236.

the French ambassador in London: Conyers Read, "The Despatches of Castelnau de la Mauvissière (on Frobisher, Gilbert, de la Roche and Drake), 1577–1581," *American Historical Review* 31 (1925–26), pp. 286–87.

170   *"As the business is managed with great secrecy":* Dispatch of March 31, 1578, in CLSP Simancas, vol. 2, pp. 567–69.

Ambassador de Mendoza recruited at least one spy: Bernard Allaire and Donald Hogarth, "Martin Frobisher, the Spaniards and a Sixteenth-Century Northern Spy," *Terrae Incognitae* 28 (1996), pp. 46–57.

"I shall never find another so intelligent": CLSP Simancas, vol. 2, pp. 653–54.

"I send them herewith": CLSP Simancas, vol. 2, p. 576.

171   *Philip Sidney . . . wrote a friend:* Sidney wrote his letter on October 1, 1577. Pears, *The Correspondence of Sir Philip Sidney,* pp. 119–20, 124–28.

5. Colonizing Dreams

173   *An assay of metal usually involved:* Hogarth, *Mines,* pp. 74, 80–81, 170–71; Bernard Allaire, "Methods of Assaying Ore and Their Application in the Frobisher Adventures," in *Meta Incognita: A Discourse of Discovery,* vol. 2, ed. Thomas H. B. Symons (Hull, Quebec: Canadian Museum of Civilization, 1999), pp. 481–82.

174   *"And albeit the ore in report":* William Winter's letter, dated November 25, 1578, was probably sent to Walsingham. SM, vol. 2, p. 138.

175   *Burchard Kranich:* M. B. Donald, "Burchard Kranich (c. 1515–1578), Miner and Queen's Physician, Cornish Mining Stamps, Antimony, and Frobisher's Gold," in *Annals of Science* 6 (1950), p. 316.

The town of Dartford: [P. W. Boreham], *The Choice of Dartford as a Centre for Frobisher's Smelting Works* (Dartford: N.p., n.d.) pp. 5–6.

177   *A sketch drawn for him:* PRO MP 304, reproduced in Hogarth, *Mines,* p. 89.

Burghley wrote some figures: PRO SP 12/130/95.

181   *"the richness of that earth" . . . "is well pleased":* Letter of March 11, 1578, from Walsingham to Burghley and the Earl of Sussex. SM, vol. 2, p. 131.

182   *Frobisher retained the title:* PRO SP 12/25/f. 146 contains a draft of the commissioners' instructions; also SM, vol. 2, pp. 155–61.

183   *"And now Captain Frobisher":* BL Lansdowne 100/1, quoted in James McDermott, "'A Right Heroicall Heart': Sir Martin Frobisher," in Symons, *Meta Incognita: A Discourse of Discovery,* vol. 1, p. 113.

Francis Walsingham wrote to some: Letter of March 11, 1578. SM, vol. 2, p. 131.

184   *Burghley . . . complained of having to write:* He mentioned the burden of letter writing in June 1565, and by the 1570s his workload had probably increased. Stephen Alford, *The Early Elizabethan Polity: William Cecil and*

the British Succession Crisis, 1558–1569 (Cambridge: Cambridge University Press, 1998), p. 13.

185   *"We think it most convenient"*: McDermott, "The Account Books," p. 73; for details about Lok's mingling of personal and company finances, see pp. 57–58.

Sea biscuits were made from: Conrad Heidenreich and Nancy Heidenreich, "A Nutritional Analysis of the Food Rations for Frobisher's Second Expedition," paper delivered at Meta Incognita Symposium, Trent University, Peterborough, Canada, 1997.

186   *"our little king"*: These are the comments of Richard Madox, who sailed with Fenton in 1582. Elizabeth Story Donno, *An Elizabethan in 1582: The Diary of Richard Madox, Fellow of All Souls* (London: Hakluyt Society, 1976), pp. 174, 194, 269.

187   *She was distracted . . . by a toothache:* Zillah Dovey, *An Elizabethan Progress: The Queen's Journey into East Anglia, 1578* (Phoenix Mill: Alan Sutton Publishing, 1996), p. 7.

188   *"She expressed herself very warmly"*: Dispatch of April 22, 1578. CLSP Simancas, vol. 2, p. 576.

He worked like a traffic policeman: James McDermott and David W. Waters, "Cathay and the Way Thither: the Navigation of the Frobisher Voyages," in Symons, ed., *Meta Incognita: A Discourse of Discovery*, vol. 2, p. 365.

In his orders to the captains: Frobisher's third voyage is chronicled by George Best, in SM, vol. 1, pp. 80–139; by Edward Fenton in his journal, transcribed as "The Canadian Arctic Journal of Capt. Edward Fenton, 1578," ed. W. A. Kenyon, in *Archivaria* 11 (Winter 1980–81), pp. 171–203; by the notary Edward Sellman, "Account of the Third Voyage," in SM, vol. 2, pp. 55–73; and by Christopher Hall's log, BL Harley 167/42 f.183 ff. Other details are from Michael Lok's ledger, in McDermott, "The Account Books."

Christopher Hall sketched part: BL Harley 167/42 f.187v.

192   *"I told him that it was not the Straits"*: BL Harley 167/42, f.191v; and James McDermott, "Frobisher's 1578 Voyage: Early Eyewitness Accounts of English Ships in Arctic Seas," *Polar Record* 32, no. 183 (1996), p. 331.

197   *One of the captains nearly drowned:* The captain was Thomas Courtney, commander of the one-hundred-ton *Armonell*. Kenyon, "The Canadian Arctic Journal," p. 191.

203   *When the royal party crossed:* Elizabeth's progress, and the extravagance of her hosts, are described in Dovey, *An Elizabethan Progress*, pp. 40–45, 116; and Susan Watkins, *The Public and Private Worlds of Elizabeth I* (New York: Thames and Hudson, 1998), pp. 114, 154.

Members of the Privy Council decided to dispatch: Dee, "Compendious Rehearsall," p. 22.

204 *Thomas Wiars . . . wrote of the ship:* Thomas Wiars, "The report of Thomas Wiars, passenger in the Emanuel, otherwise called the Buss of Bridgewater," SM, vol. 2, p. 253. Later sightings are detailed in Johnson, *Phantom Islands,* pp. 68–73; 85–87.

About forty of his four hundred men: Best, in SM, vol. 1, p. 122.

205 *The* Emanuel *lost her masts:* Hogarth, *Mines,* pp. 61–63.

"Her Majesty hath very great expectations": SM, vol. 2, p. 169.

6. Kodlunarn

208 *"Great God, Thou has rewarded me":* Journal for August 11, 1861.

210 *"I never saw in the States":* Journal for August 25, 1861, quoted in Hall, *Arctic Researches,* p. 393.

213 *"He acts the* devil *with me":* Hall, *Arctic Researches,* pp. 421–22.

"Had a terrible time" . . . "We are approaching the same": Journal, September 22, 1861.

214 *"Gathered stone with cement":* Journal, September 22, 1861.

"We had been upon the Island": Journal, September 22, 1861.

215 *"The weather not good":* Journal, September 25, 1861.

216 *"Now it will be known":* Journal, September 25, 1861.

In the early 1990s archaeologists found the trench: Hogarth, *Mines,* p. 118.

218 *In 1927 an expedition . . . Field Museum:* Findings of the twentieth-century expeditions are summarized by Fitzhugh, *Archeology of the Frobisher Voyages,* pp. 21–25.

Walter Kenyon, of the Royal Ontario Museum: Walter Kenyon, *Tokens of Possession: The Northern Voyages of Martin Frobisher* (Toronto: Royal Ontario Museum, 1975), pp. 121–54.

The first expert, detailed excavation: Fitzhugh, *Archeology of the Frobisher Voyages,* esp. pp. 59–151. Some of the findings were also published in Stephen Alsford, ed., *The Meta Incognita Project: Contributions to Field Studies* (Hull, Quebec: Canadian Museum of Civilization, 1993).

223 *His prepared list of questions:* Journal, October 12, 1861. The list is reproduced in Fitzhugh, *Archeology of the Frobisher Voyages,* p. 32.

"One is often baffled": Journal, June 10, 1862; also in Fitzhugh, *Archeology of the Frobisher Voyages,* p. 39.

224 *An outsider could not easily know:* Susan Rowley analzyed the notes Hall made during the interviews. Rowley also interviewed elders in Iqaluit in the early 1990s who remembered stories about Kodlunarn. Fitzhugh, *Archeology of the Frobisher Voyages,* pp. 37–38; and Alsford, *The Meta Incognita Project,* pp. 216–18.

225   *a gray-haired woman entered the igloo:* Hall, *Arctic Researches,* pp. 474–77.

227   *the anthropologists William Fitzhugh and Susan Rowley:* Fitzhugh, *Archeology of the Frobisher Voyages,* pp. 37–40, 231–36.

228   *There is no shortage of theories:* The theories are presented by Jacqueline S. Olin, Garmon Harbottle, Henry Unglik, and Robert M. Ehrenreich, in Fitzhugh, *Archeology of the Frobisher Voyages,* pp. 49–55, 175–80, 209–11, 222–26.

229   *Michael Lok . . . has in his ledger:* Fitzhugh, *Archeology of the Frobisher Voyages,* pp. 236–37.

231   *The first newspaper stories:* St. John's *Daily News,* August 23, 1862.

232   *"I am bound for the States":* New York Herald, August 24, 1862.
       "NEWS FROM THE ARCTIC REGIONS": New York Herald, September 24, 1862.
       a gentleman of tact and energy: New York Herald, September 15, 1862.
       "excellent specimens": St. John's *Daily News,* August 23, 1862.

233   *"I am now anxious":* Letter of October 22, 1862.

234   *In his lecture to the Society:* Loomis, *Weird and Tragic Shores,* pp. 149–52; and Nourse, *Narrative of the Second Arctic Expedition,* pp. 8–10.

7. Battles

235   *carted to a royal manor house:* Boreham, *Dartford's Royal Manor House* (Dartford, England: Dartford Borough Council, 1991), pp. 51, 55.

236   *Jonas Shutz . . . tried several additives:* His efforts at Dartford are summarized in Hogarth, *Mines,* pp. 74–75, 91–92.
       "He entered into great storms": Lok described Frobisher's actions in a report prepared in January 1579 for auditors and his fellow commissioners, "Michaell Lok saluteth the worshipfull Commissioners and Auditors . . . ," in SM, vol. 2, esp. p. 189. He described his tribulations again in "Abuses of Captayne Furbusher Agaynst the Companye," in SM, vol. 2, pp. 208–12.

237   *had spent at least £24,000:* McDermott, "The Account Books," p. 107.

238   *On the rare occasions when the company had income:* McDermott, "A right Heroicall heart," in Symons, *Meta Incognita,* p. 144, and Carole Shammas, "The 'Invisible Merchant' and Property Rights: The Misadventures of an Elizabethan Joint Stock Company," in *Business History* 17 (1975), pp. 95–108.

239   *"And he that has put in such objections":* In McDermott, "The Account Books," p. 323; for the auditors' findings, see pp. 333–34.
       Lord Burghley . . . owed the Cathay Company: McDermott, "The Account Books," pp. 498–99.

240   *Lok signed the letter, as did Thomas Allen:* PRO SP 12/130/f.40–40v.
       "I do hear that Mr. Frobisher": SM, vol. 1, p. 166.
       He was imprisoned at least seven times: Details about Lok's later years are

drawn from McDermott, "The Account Books," pp. 14, 17–22, 59. For Fleet Prison, see Ben Weinreb and Christopher Hibbert, *The London Encyclopaedia,* rev. ed. (London: Macmillan, 1995), pp. 291–92.

241 *His contemporaries found him witty:* The compliments are those of the Reverend Richard Madox, who also befriended Christopher Hall. Donno, *An Elizabethan in 1582,* p. 224.

242 *what he called John Dee Bay:* William B. Goodwin, "The Dee River of 1583 (Now Called Narragansett Bay) and Its Relation to Norumbega," in *Rhode Island Historical Society Collections* 27, no. 2 (1934), p. 40.

243 *Dee began keeping a diary of "conversations":* Though Dee never intended his records of the talks to become public, many of them were published by Meric Causaubon in 1659 as *A True and Faithful Relation of what passed for many years between Dr. John Dee and Some Spirits.* A selection of Dee's spiritual conversations also appear in Fenton, *Diaries of John Dee,* pp. 21ff.

A man named Edward Kelley: An account of Kelley's career as scryer and alchemist is in R. F. W. Evans, *Rudolf II and His World* (Oxford: Oxford University Press, 1973), pp. 224–28.

244 **"Pactum factum":** Fenton, *Diaries of John Dee,* p. 223.

His years back in England: Dee describes this period in "Compendious Rehearsall," written as part of his campaign for recognition; see esp. pp. 14, 43.

245 *Eighty years old, Dee asked them questions:* Roberts and Watson, *John Dee's Library,* p. 60.

The playwright may have visited Mortlake: Frank Kermode, ed., *The Arden Edition of the Works of William Shakespeare: The Tempest* (Cambridge: Harvard University Press, 1958), p. xli; and Sandra Clark, *William Shakespeare: The Tempest* (London: Penguin, 1986), pp. 33–34.

246 *Frobisher was initially considered for commander:* Taylor, *The Troublesome Voyage,* p. 16.

Christopher Hall surmised what had happened: Donno, *An Elizabethan in 1582,* pp. 185, 194.

247 *"We had the rudder of our pinnace":* Mary Frear Keeler, ed., *Sir Francis Drake's West Indian Voyage, 1585–86* (London: Hakluyt Society, 1981), pp. 198–99.

"There was about 250 houses": Quinn, *Roanoke Voyages,* pp. 304–05.

248 *Frobisher's finest hour:* Julian S. Corbett, *Drake and the Tudor Navy,* vol. 2 (London: Longman, 1898), pp. 243–44, 250–59.

249 *Spanish troops had erected El Leon:* A sketch of the fort by an anonymous artist with the English forces is PRO SP 78/34/f.278. The best modern

account of the English campaign is John S. Nolan's "English Operations Around Brest, 1594," *Mariner's Mirror* 81, no. 3 (August 1995), pp. 259–74.

250   *"which was maintained exceedingly hotly":* Norris to Lord Burghley, in List and Analysis of State Papers, Foreign Series, Elizabeth I, vol. 5, July 1593–December 1594 (London: 1989), p. 310.

"They defended it very resolutely": In McFee, *The Life of Sir Martin Frobisher,* pp. 266–67; and McDermott, "A right Heroicall heart," in Symons, *Meta Incognita,* p. 104.

"to our trusted and well beloved Martin Frobisher: McFee, *The Life of Sir Martin Frobisher,* pp. 268–69.

"Il y fut un peu blessé": The French commander was Jean d'Aumont. His letter is SP 78/34/f.254–5.

8. Destinations

251   *Barnum's Museum:* Some of Hall's correspondence with various promoters is in the Smithsonian's Hall collection, folder 45. Loomis, *Weird and Tragic Shores,* pp. 152–53, describes the Inuit family's work with Barnum.

"Mr. Hall exhibited": Rhode Island Press, January 10, 1863. The Smithsonian collection includes some of Hall's press clippings.

"peculiarly novel and interesting": Elmira Daily Gazette, January 23, 1863.

The Inuit family took ill in Elmira: Hall's correspondence documents the family's tribulations, as well as his own financial problems, as also described in Nourse, *Narrative of the Second Arctic Expedition,* pp. 27–42; and Loomis, *Weird and Tragic Shores,* pp. 155–77.

252   *"overwhelmed with trouble":* Letter of February 27, 1863, misdated 1862 by Hall.

I deeply regret to inform you": Letter of March 4, 1863.

Budington dared to argue: Reflected in Hall's June 21, 1863 letter to Budington; also Loomis, *Weird and Tragic Shores,* p. 169.

"I have now a work": Letter of July 13, 1864, in Nourse, *Narrative of the Second Arctic Expedition,* p. 43.

The journey lasted five: My account of Hall's second expedition is drawn from Nourse, *Narrative of the Second Arctic Expedition,* pp. 359–62, 400–07; Loomis, *Weird and Tragic Shores,* pp. 215–25; and Woodman, *Unraveling the Franklin Mystery,* pp. 124–27.

255   *"My faith, till then so strong":* Letter of January 10, 1871, in Nourse, *Narrative of the Second Arctic Expedition,* pp. xxii–xxiii.

Hall's last enthusiasm: Loomis, *Weird and Tragic Shores,* pp. 261–355, includes an insightful synthesis of the government reports and hearings on Hall's last expedition. Those reports include C. H. Davis, *Narrative of* the *North Polar Expedition, U.S. Ship* Polaris, *Captain Charles Francis Hall Commanding* (Washington: Government Printing Office, 1876); and *Annual Report of the Secretary of the Navy on the Operations of the Department for the Year 1873* (Washington, D.C., 1873).

256   *In 1968 his well-preserved body:* Chauncey Loomis arranged for the exhumation, was present when it took place, and describes the results in *Weird and Tragic Shores,* pp. 339–49.

257   *a Canadian geologist:* Hogarth, *Mines,* pp. 122, 127, 136–37.

Selected Bibliography

Books

Alford, Stephen. *The Early Elizabethan Polity: William Cecil and the British Succession Crisis, 1558–1569*. Cambridge: Cambridge University Press, 1998.

Alsford, Stephen, ed. *The Meta Incognita Project: Contributions to Field Studies*. Hull, Quebec: Canadian Museum of Civilization, 1993.

Ambrose, Stephen E. *Undaunted Courage*. New York: Simon & Schuster, 1996.

Andrews, Kenneth R. *Elizabethan Privateering*. Cambridge: Cambridge University Press, 1964.

———. "Elizabethan Privateering." In *Raleigh in Exeter, 1985: Privateering and Colonisation in the Reign of Elizabeth I*, edited by Joyce Youings. Exeter: University of Exeter, 1985.

———. *Trade, Plunder and Settlement: Maritime Enterprise and the Genesis of the British Empire, 1480–1630*. Cambridge: Cambridge University Press, 1984.

Auger, Reginald, et al. *Material Evidence from the Frobisher Voyages: Anglo-Inuit Contact in the North American Arctic in the Late Sixteenth Century*. British Museum Occasional Paper 109. London: British Museum, 1995.

Barr, William, ed. *Searching for Franklin: The Land Arctic Searching Expedition*. London: Hakluyt Society, 1999.

Barrow, John. *A Chronological History of Voyages into the Arctic Regions*. London: John Murray, 1818. Rpt. Devon: David & Charles, 1971.

Berton, Pierre. *The Arctic Grail: The Quest for the North West Passage and the North Pole, 1818–1909.* New York: Viking, 1988.

Blackburn, Robin. *The Making of New World Slavery: From the Baroque to the Modern, 1492–1800.* London: Verso, 1997.

Blake, John William. *Europeans in West Africa, 1450–1560.* 2 vols. London: Hakluyt Society, 1942.

Boas, Franz. *The Central Eskimo.* Lincoln: University of Nebraska Press, 1964. Originally in *Sixth Annual Report of the Bureau of Ethnology.* Washington: Smithsonian Institution, 1888.

Boreham, P. W. *Dartford's Royal Manor House Re-Discovered.* Dartford, England: Dartford Borough Council, 1991.

Boyle, Robert W. *Gold, History and Genesis of Deposits.* New York: Van Nostrand Reinhold, 1987.

Brooks, Robert R., ed. *Noble Metals and Biological Systems.* Boca Raton: CRC Press, 1992.

Brown, Henry Phelps, and Sheila V. Hopkins. *Perspective of Wages and Prices.* London: Methuen, 1981.

Calendar of State Papers, Foreign Series, Elizabeth 1575–77. London, 1880.

Calendar of Letters and State Papers Relating to English Affairs, Preserved Principally in the Archives of Simancas. Vol. 2. *Elizabeth, 1568–1579.* London, 1894.

Casas, Bartolomé de las. *The Devastation of the Indies: A Brief Account.* Trans. Herma Briffault. Baltimore: Johns Hopkins University Press, 1992.

Clark, Sandra. *William Shakespeare: The Tempest.* London: Penguin, 1986.

Clulee, Nicholas H. *John Dee's Natural Philosophy: Between Science and Religion.* London: Routledge, 1988.

Collinson, Richard. *The Three Voyages of Martin Frobisher: In Search of a Passage to Cathaia and India by the North-west, A.D. 1576–8.* London: Hakluyt Society, 1867.

Columbus, Christopher. *The Log of Christopher Columbus.* Trans. Robert H. Fuson. Camden, Maine: International Marine, 1987.

Corbett, Julian S. *Drake and the Tudor Navy.* 2 vols. London: Longman, 1898.

Davis, Richard C., ed. *Lobsticks and Stone Cairns: Human Landmarks in the Arctic.* Calgary, Alta.: University of Calgary Press, 1996.

Decker, Robert Owen. *The New London Merchants: The Rise and Decline of a Connecticut Port.* New York: Garland Publishing, 1986.

Dee, John. "The Compendious Rehearsall." In *The Autobiographical Tracts of Dr. John Dee,* edited by James Crossley. Manchester: Chetham Society, 1851.

———. *The Diaries of John Dee.* Ed. Edward Fenton. Charlbury, England: Day Books, 1998.

———. *General and Rare Memorials Pertayning to the Perfect Arte of Navigation.* London, 1577. Rpt. Amsterdam and New York: Da Capo Press, 1968.

————. *The Private Diary of Dr. John Dee.* Ed. James Orchard Halliwell. London: Camden Society, 1842.

Donno, Elizabeth Story. *An Elizabethan in 1582: The Diary of Richard Madox, Fellow of All Souls.* London: Hakluyt Society, 1976.

Dovey, Zillah. *An Elizabethan Progress: The Queen's Journey into East Anglia, 1578.* Phoenix Mill, England: Alan Sutton Publishing, 1996.

Duncan-Jones, Katherine. *Sir Philip Sidney, Courtier Poet.* New Haven: Yale University Press, 1991.

Eber, Dorothy Harley. *When the Whalers Were up North: Inuit Memories from the Eastern Arctic.* Norman: University of Oklahoma Press, 1996.

Evans, R. F. W. *Rudolf II and His World.* Oxford: Oxford University Press, 1973.

Firstbrook, Peter. *The Voyage of the Mathew: John Cabot and the Discovery of North America.* London: BBC Books, 1997.

Fitzhugh, William W., and Jacqueline S. Olin, eds. *Archeology of the Frobisher Voyages.* Washington: Smithsonian Institution Press, 1993.

French, Peter J. *John Dee: The World of an Elizabethan Magus.* London: Routledge, 1972.

Friel, Ian. "The Three-Masted Ship and Atlantic Voyages." In *Raleigh in Exeter, 1985: Privateering and Colonisation in the Reign of Elizabeth I,* edited by Joyce Youings, pp. 21–37. Exeter: University of Exeter, 1985.

Ganong, W. F. *Crucial Maps in the Early Cartography and Place-Nomenclature of the Atlantic Coast of Canada.* Toronto: University of Toronto, 1964.

Greenblatt, Stephen. *Marvelous Possessions: The Wonder of the New World.* Chicago: University of Chicago Press, 1991.

Hair, P. E. H. *The Founding of the Castelo de São Jorge da Mina: An Analysis of the Sources.* Madison: University of Wisconsin Press, 1994.

————. *Travails in Guinea: Robert Baker's "Brefe Dyscourse" (?1568).* Liverpool: Liverpool University Press, 1990.

Hair, P. E. H., and J. D. Alsop. *English Seamen and Traders in Guinea, 1553–1565: The New Evidence of Their Wills.* Lewiston, N.Y.: Edwin Mellen Press, 1992.

Hakluyt, Richard. *The Principal Navigations, Voyages, Traffiques and Discoveries of the English Nation.* Vols. 2, 6, 7. Glasgow: James MacLehose and Sons, 1903. (Rpt. from 2nd ed. of 1598–1600.)

Hall, Charles Francis. *Arctic Researches and Life Among the Esquimaux.* New York: Harper & Brothers, 1865. (Originally published as *Life with the Esquimaux.* 2 vols. London: Sampson Low, 1864.)

Harper, Kenn. *Give Me My Father's Body.* Iqaluit: Blacklead Books, 1986.

Hearn, Karen, ed. *Dynasties: Painting in Tudor and Jacobean England, 1530–1630.* New York: Rizzoli, 1996.

Henshaw, Anne. *Central Inuit Household Economies: Zooarchaeological, Environmental, and Historical Evidence from Outer Frobisher Bay, Baffin Island, Canada* (Ph.D. diss., Harvard University, 1995). Ann Arbor: UMI Dissertation Services, 1996.

Hey, David. *Yorkshire from A.D. 1000.* London: Longman, 1986.

Hogarth, D. D., P. W. Boreham, and J. G. Mitchell. *Martin Frobisher's Northwest Venture, 1576–1581: Mines, Minerals & Metallurgy.* Hull, Quebec: Canadian Museum of Civilization, 1994.

Houston, James. *Confessions of an Igloo Dweller.* Boston: Houghton Mifflin, 1995.

Hulton, Paul, and David Beers Quinn. *The American Drawings of John White 1577–1590.* Chapel Hill: University of North Carolina Press, 1964.

Johnson, Donald S. *Phantom Islands of the Atlantic.* New York: Walker and Company, 1994.

Jones, Frank. *The Life of Sir Martin Frobisher.* London: Longman, 1878.

Kane, Elisha Kent Kane. *Arctic Explorations: The Second Grinnell Expedition.* 2 vols. Philadelphia: Childs & Peterson, 1856.

———. *The U.S. Grinnell Expedition in Search of Sir John Franklin.* New York: Harper & Brothers, 1854.

Keeler, Mary Frear, ed. *Sir Francis Drake's West Indian Voyage, 1585–86.* London: Hakluyt Society, 1981.

Keevil, J. J. *Medicine and the Navy, 1200–1900.* Vol. 1. Edinburgh and London: Livingstone, 1957.

Kenyon, Walter. *Tokens of Possession: The Northern Voyages of Martin Frobisher.* Toronto: Royal Ontario Museum, 1975.

Kermode, Frank, ed. *The Arden Edition of the Works of William Shakespeare: The Tempest.* Cambridge: Harvard University Press, 1958.

List and Analysis of State Papers, Foreign Series, Elizabeth I. Vol. 5. *July 1593–December 1594.* London: 1989.

Loades, David. *John Dudley, Duke of Northumberland, 1504–1553.* Oxford: Clarendon Press, 1996.

———. *The Reign of King Edward VI.* Gwynedd, Wales: Headstart History, 1994.

———. *The Tudor Court.* Bangor, Wales: Headstart History, 1992.

Loomis, Chauncey C. *Weird and Tragic Shores.* New York: Alfred A. Knopf, 1971. Rpt. Lincoln: University of Nebraska Press, 1991.

Lubbock, Basil. *The Arctic Whalers.* Glasgow: Brown, Son & Ferguson, 1937.

MacDonald, John. *The Arctic Sky: Inuit Astronomy, Star Lore, and Legend.* Toronto: Royal Ontario Museum, 1998.

Major, Richard Henry, ed. *The Voyages of the Venetian Brothers, Nicolo and Antonio Zeno.* London: Hakluyt Society, 1873.

Marcus, Alan Rudolph. *Relocating Eden: The Image and Politics of Inuit Exile in the Canadian Arctic*. Hanover, N.H.: University Press of New England, 1995.

McDermott, James. "The Account Books of Michael Lok, Relating to the Northwest Voyages of Martin Frobisher, 1576–1578." M. Phil. thesis, University of Hull, Quebec, 1984.

———. *The Navigation of the Frobisher Voyages*. The Hakluyt Society Annual Talk 1997. London: Hakluyt Society, 1998.

McFee, William. *The Life of Sir Martin Frobisher*. New York: Harper & Brothers, 1928.

McGhee, Robert. *Ancient People of the Arctic*. Vancouver: University of British Columbia Press, 1996.

Morgan, E. Delmar, and C. H. Coote, eds. *Early Voyages and Travels to Russia and Persia*. London: Hakluyt Society, 1886.

Morison, Samuel Eliot. *Christopher Columbus, Mariner*. 1942. New York: Meridian, 1983.

———. *The European Discovery of America: The Northern Voyages, A.D. 500–1600*. New York: Oxford University Press, 1993.

Nelson, Richard K. *Hunters of the Northern Ice*. Chicago: University of Chicago Press, 1969.

Nicholl, Charles. *The Reckoning: The Murder of Christopher Marlowe*. Chicago: University of Chicago Press, 1995.

Nourse, J. E. *Narrative of the Second Arctic Expedition Made by Charles F. Hall*. Washington, D.C.: Government Printing Office, 1879.

Pagden, Anthony. *European Encounters with the New World*. New Haven: Yale University Press, 1993.

Pears, Steuart A. *The Correspondence of Sir Philip Sidney and Hubert Languet*. London: William Pickering, 1845. Rpt. Westmead, England: Gregg International, 1971.

Pomeroy, Elizabeth W. *Reading the Portraits of Queen Elizabeth I*. Hamden, Conn.: Archon Books, 1989.

Quinn, David Beers. *England and the Discovery of America, 1481–1620*. New York: Knopf, 1974.

———, ed. *The Roanoke Voyages, 1584–1590*. Vol. 1. London: Hakluyt Society, 1955.

———. *The Voyages and Colonising Enterprises of Sir Humphrey Gilbert*. 2 vols. London: Hakluyt Society, 1940.

Rappaport, Steve. *Worlds Within Worlds: Structures of Life in Sixteenth-Century London*. Cambridge: Cambridge University Press, 1989.

Roberts, Julian, and Andrew G. Watson, eds. *John Dee's Library Catalogue*. London: Bibliographical Society, 1990.

————. *John Dee's Library Catalogue, Additions and Corrections*. London: John Dee Colloquium, University of London, April 1995.

Rodger, N. A. M. *The Safeguard of the Sea: A Naval History of Britain, 660–1649*. New York: W. W. Norton, 1998.

Ross, W. Gillies. *Arctic Whalers, Icy Seas: Narratives of the Davis Strait Whale Fishery*. Toronto: Irwin Publishing, 1985.

————. *This Distant and Unsurveyed Country: A Woman's Winter at Baffin Island, 1857–58*. Montreal: McGill–Queen's University Press, 1997.

Russell-Wood, A. J. R. *The Portuguese Empire, 1415–1808*. Baltimore: Johns Hopkins University Press, 1998.

Sailing Directions, Arctic Canada. 4th ed. Vol. 1. Ottawa: Department of Fisheries and Oceans, 1994.

Sailing Directions (Enroute): Greenland and Iceland. Publication 181, 5th ed. Washington, D.C.: Defense Mapping Agency Hydrographic/Topographic Center, 1994.

Sargent, Ralph M. *At the Court of Queen Elizabeth: The Life and Lyrics of Sir Edward Dyer*. London: Oxford University Press, 1935.

Schlesinger, Roger, and Arthur P. Stabler, eds. *André Thevet's North America*. Kingston: McGill–Queen's University Press, 1986.

Seaver, Kirsten A. *The Frozen Echo: Greenland and the Exploration of North America, ca. A.D. 1000–1500*. Stanford: Stanford University Press, 1996.

Seed, Patricia. *Ceremonies of Possession in Europe's Conquest of the New World, 1492–1640*. Cambridge: Cambridge University Press, 1995.

Shammas, Carole Jeanette. "The Elizabethan Gentlemen Adventurers and Western Planting." Ph.D. diss., Johns Hopkins University, 1971.

Sherman, William H. *John Dee: The Politics of Reading and Writing in the English Renaissance*. Amherst: University of Massachusetts Press, 1995.

Shumaker, Wayne. *Renaissance Curiosa*. Medieval and Renaissance Texts and Studies. Vol. 8. Binghamton: Center for Medieval and Early Renaissance Studies, 1982.

Stefansson, Vilhjalmur, and Eloise McCaskill. *The Three Voyages of Martin Frobisher*. London: Argonaut Press, 1938.

Stevenson, Marc. *Inuit, Whalers, and Cultural Persistence: Structure in Cumberland Sound and Central Inuit Social Organization*. Toronto: Oxford University Press Canada, 1997.

Strong, Roy. *Gloriana: The Portraits of Queen Elizabeth I*. New York: Thames and Hudson, 1987.

Sturtevant, William C., and David B. Quinn. "This New Prey: Eskimos in Europe in 1567, 1576, and 1577." In *Indians and Europe: An Interdisciplinary Collection of Essays*, edited by Christian F. Feest, pp. 61–140. Aachen: Rader Verlag, 1987.

Sutherland, Patricia D., ed. *The Franklin Era in Canadian Arctic History, 1845–1859*. Ottawa: National Museums of Canada, 1985.

Symons, Thomas H. B., ed. *Meta Incognita: A Discourse of Discovery*. 2 vols. Hull, Quebec: Canadian Museum of Civilization, 1999.

Tait, Hugh. " 'The Devil's Looking Glass': The Magical Speculum of Dr. John Dee." In *Horace Walpole, Writer, Politician, and Connoisseur*, edited by Warren Hunting Smith. New Haven: Yale University Press, 1967.

Taylor, E. G. R., ed. *The Troublesome Voyage of Captain Edward Fenton*. Cambridge: Hakluyt Society, 1959.

———. *Tudor Geography, 1485–1583*. London: Methuen, 1930.

Vilar, Pierre. *A History of Gold and Money, 1450–1920*. London: Verso, 1991.

Watkins, Susan. *The Public and Private Worlds of Elizabeth I*. New York: Thames and Hudson, 1998.

Waters, D. W. *The Art of Navigation in England in Elizabethan and Early Stuart Times*. New Haven: Yale University Press, 1958.

Weinreb, Ben, and Christopher Hibbert. *The London Encyclopaedia*. Rev. ed. London: Macmillan, 1995.

Weir, Alison. *The Life of Elizabeth I*. New York: Ballantine, 1998.

Williams, Penry. *The Later Tudors: England, 1547–1603*. Oxford: Clarendon Press, 1995.

Woodman, David C. *Unraveling the Franklin Mystery: Inuit Testimony*. Montreal: McGill–Queen's University Press, 1991.

Periodicals and Other Texts

Allaire, Bernard, and Donald Hogarth. "Martin Frobisher, the Spaniards and a Sixteenth-Century Northern Spy." *Terrae Incognitae* 28 (1996): 46–57.

[Boreham, Peter]. *The Choice of Dartford as a Centre for Frobisher's Smelting Works*. Dartford, n.d.

Cheshire, Neil, et al. "Frobisher's Eskimos in England." *Archivaria* 10 (Summer 1980): 23–50.

Cruikshank, Julie. "Oral Tradition and Oral History: Reviewing Some Issues." *Canadian Historical Review* 75, no. 3 (1994): 403–18.

Donald, M. B. "Burchard Kranich (c. 1515–1578), Miner and Queen's Physician, Cornish Mining Stamps, Antimony, and Frobisher's Gold." *Annals of Science* 6 (1950): 308–22.

Eliot, K. M. "The First Voyages of Martin Frobisher." *English Historical Review* 32 (1917): 89–92.

Glascow, Tom, Jr. "Maturing of Naval Administration, 1556–1564." *Mariner's Mirror* 56, no. 1 (January 1970): 3–26.

Glascow, Tom, Jr., and W. Salisbury. "Elizabethan Ships Pictured on Smerwick Map, 1580." *Mariner's Mirror* 52, no. 2 (May 1996): 157–65.

Goodwin, William B. "The Dee River of 1583 (Now Called Narragansett Bay) and Its Relation to Norumbega." *Rhode Island Historical Society Collections* 27, no 2 (1934): 38–50.

Hair, P. E. H. "The Experience of the Sixteenth-Century English Voyages to Guinea." *Mariner's Mirror* 83, no. 1 (February 1997): 3–13.

Harper, Kenn. "The Frobisher Inuit Word List and Inuit Names." Paper presented at Meta Incognita Project Symposium. Trent University, Peterborough, Canada, 1997.

———. "Iqaluit." *Above and Beyond* 1, no. 4 (Autumn 1989): 6–17.

Heidenreich, Conrad, and Nancy Heidenreich. "A Nutritional Analysis of the Food Rations for Frobisher's Second Expedition." Paper presented at Meta Incognita Symposium, Trent University, Peterborough, Canada, 1997.

Kenyon, W. A., ed. "The Canadian Arctic Journal of Capt. Edward Fenton, 1578." *Archivaria* 11 (Winter 1980–81): 171–203.

Kuptana, Rosemarie. "Ilira, or Why It Was Unthinkable for Inuit to Challenge Qallunaat Authority." *Inuit Art Quarterly 8*, no. 3 (1993): 5–7.

Marsden, R. G. "The Early Career of Sir Martin Frobisher." *English Historical Review* 21 (1906): 538–44.

McDermott, James. "Frobisher's 1578 Voyage: Early Eyewitness Accounts of English Ships in Arctic Seas." *Polar Record* 32, no. 183 (1996): 325–54.

McGhee, Robert. "Contact Between Native North Americans and the Medieval Norse: A Review of the Evidence." *American Antiquity* 49, no. 1 (1984): 4–26.

———. "Disease and the Development of Inuit Culture." *Current Anthropology* 35, no. 5 (December 1994): 565–94.

Nolan, John S. "English Operations Around Brest, 1594." *Mariner's Mirror* 81, no. 3 (August 1995): 259–74.

Read, Conyers. "The Despatches of Castelnau de la Mauvissière (on Frobisher, Gilbert, de la Roche and Drake), 1577–1581." *American Historical Review* 31 (1925–26): 285–96.

Salisbury, William. "Early Tonnage Measurement in England." *Mariner's Mirror* 52, no. 1 (February 1966): 41–51.

Shammas, Carole. "The 'Invisible Merchant' and Property Rights: The Misadventures of an Elizabethan Joint Stock Company." *Business History* 17 (1975): 95–108.

Sherman, William H. "John Dee's Columbian Encounter: A Marginal Discovery." Paper presented at Queen Mary and Westfield College, University of London, 1995.

Acknowledgments

This book was a long voyage that I could not have navigated on my own. My wife, Holly Selby, helped keep the venture on course. She enthusiastically supported every trip, whether by snowmobile, freighter, or undersized boat.

Deborah Harris, my agent, once again provided vital support from beginning to end. David Mosser Brown offered inspiring examples of artful writing and clear thinking and pointed the way forward. Scott Shane read draft after draft, made generous gifts of his time, and helped keep the story in sight.

At Henry Holt, Marian Wood supplied all-important backing at the start after a quick look at one of Frobisher's maps. David Sobel took over the editing reins and, in company with Anne Geiger, adjusted the course in ways large and small.

In Iqaluit, Kenn Harper and Jack Hicks were generous, patient teachers of everything Arctic. I owe thanks to Colin Crosbie of C. A. Crosbie Shipping (and, again, to Kenn Harper) for a memorable trip aboard the *Lady Franklin*. Captains Ralph Templeman and Gordon Williams proved patient hosts while I was aboard. On an expedition of my own devising, Guy Vachon and Mark Erkidjuk showed me the way through icy waters to Countess of Warwick Sound and on to Kodlunarn Island.

My father-in-law, John E. Selby, helped me gain entrée to sixteenth-century English history through his own scholarship. Nancy Forgione put books that I needed right into my hands. Bill and Linda Glauber sheltered me in London and, at just the right time, talked of campfire stories. Support in many forms came from Michael Hill, Sheila Mooney, and Mark Reutter. I also owe thanks to William Fitzhugh for making large gifts of expertise and time, and to Keith Frobisher for a long conversation about the Frobisher family tree. Important help also came from Peter Boreham, Conrad Heidenreich, Donald Hogarth, Susan Rowley, and William H. Sherman. Early on, Thomas H. B. Symons introduced me to a roomful of experts by inviting me to a symposium at Trent University devoted to Martin Frobisher and Meta Incognita.

I am grateful too to the editors of the *Baltimore Sun,* especially William K. Marimow, for granting me the leave of absence that allowed me to do the work. No less important was their then welcoming me back.

Help came from staff members of the Bodleian Library, the British Library's manuscript division, the Cincinnati Historical Society, the Library of Congress, the Public Record Office, and the Smithsonian's National Museum of American History. Jennifer Jones and Kathleen Golden rescued me more than once from the tangles of Charles Francis Hall's handwriting.

In the course of the project, the only truly alarming moment occurred when I was about to be left alone on Kodlunarn Island by my guides. Before sailing away in search of freshwater, they handed me a shotgun with seven extra shells. "For polar bear," the guides said.

They asked if I could hit a target.

"Maybe a barn door."

"Then you could hit a polar bear."

Index

Entries in *italics* refer to illustrations.

About the Author

ROBERT RUBY has reported from Europe, Africa, and the Middle East for the *Baltimore Sun*. He is an editor at the newspaper and the author of *Jericho: Dreams, Ruins, Phantoms*.